RADIO
SOUND
EFFECTS

To the men and women of live broadcasting
who made this book such a joy to write

RADIO SOUND EFFECTS

*Who Did It, and How,
in the Era of
Live Broadcasting*

by ROBERT L. MOTT

McFarland & Company, Inc., Publishers
Jefferson, North Carolina, and London

Acknowledgments: My deep appreciation to the following people whose unselfish help and kind words made this book a lot easier to write. At the top of the list, of course, is my wife, Cinda, who for the past two years had to put up with a husband who only came out of the past for his meals.

Gus Bayz	Larry Gassman	Mel Morehouse
Sydney Bean	Robert J. Graham	Ross Murray
Barney Beck	Mrs. Walter Gustafson	Harry Nelson
William Brown	Ray Kemper	Walter Pierson
Bill Cole	Lenore Kingston-Jensen	Virgil Reimer
Keene Crockett	Durward Kirby	Raymond Sills
Ray Erlenborn	David Light	Paul Courtland Smith
Monty Fraser, Jr.	Frank Loughran	Doc Taylor
Opal Fraser	Tom McLoughlin	Bob Thaves
Jerrell Frederick	Gerard McCarty	Malachy Wienges
John Gassman		

British Library Cataloguing-in-Publication data are available

Library of Congress Cataloguing-in-Publication Data

Mott, Robert L.
    Radio sound effects : who did it, and how, in the era of live
broadcasting / by Robert L. Mott.
      p. cm.
    Includes index.
    ISBN 0-89950-747-6 (lib. bdg. : 50# alk. paper) ∞
    1. Radio broadcasting—Sound effects—Anecdotes. 2. Radio
broadcasting—United States—History. I. Title.
PN1991.8.S69M68 1993
791.44′024—dc20   92-50313
                                          CIP

Manufactured in the United States of America

McFarland & Company, Inc., Publishers
  Box 611, Jefferson, North Carolina 28640

CONTENTS

PREFACE

IN TRYING TO DOCUMENT any series of events, the passage of time is your enemy. Records get lost or destroyed and recollections become hazy. This is especially true when your subject matter is as unique as the men and women of sound effects.

Sound effects are to our ears what pulling rabbits out of a hat is to our eyes. It's the art of deception. It's the art of painting pictures for the imagination. It's taking an ordinary bowl of cooked spaghetti and convincing the listening audience they are hearing a giant worm hungrily devouring people in their sleep. It's eating an ear of corn in such a way as to conjure a picture in the audience's mind of a horde of terrified rats trying to escape from drowning by gnawing their way through the wooden walls of a lighthouse. Or using glass wind chimes for the sound of sunlight— or two moist rubber gloves twisted and stretched for the sound of a human body being turned inside out... or... or... The list of sounds is endless.

Despite how creative all those sounds were, what made this sleight of hand for the ears so convincing was the listeners' imagination. How frightening these scenes were depended on the listeners' involvement with the words and sounds that came out of their radio. Involvement—that's what made radio magic, the involvement of sound and imagination. Little wonder radio was called the theater of the mind.

As you might imagine, people who earned their living going around looking for things that sound like a terrified rat or a people-eating worm were members of a rather unusual occupation. An occupation that even during the heyday of radio probably had fewer members than the University of Michigan marching band.

You might also imagine that people who knew how to make things go bump in the night also knew how to dream up some rather bizarre pranks and practical jokes. And you'd be right. Have you ever tried to do the sound effect of opening a door and discover it's locked? Or push a button labeled DOORBELL and the *telephone* rings?

Although there was nothing new about mischief in the workplace, it was new when the workplace also happened to be live radio or television and the mischief was overheard by millions of people.

Today, in this world of computerized thinking, it's difficult to imagine some of the bizarre and outrageous stories and practical jokes that occurred during the early days of radio and television. But, as you are about to read, occur they most certainly did.

One explanation for these practical jokes held that they were a test to see how resourceful and quick-thinking we were under fire. The problem with that theory was, doing a show live for an audience of millions was enough of a test. Most of us didn't need any more excitement in our lives. This however didn't keep the pranksters from removing the phonograph needles from your pickup arms and replacing them with blunt pieces of paperclips—or fixing your door so that it would fall off its hinges the first time you opened it—or any number of other dirty deeds designed to keep you constantly on the alert for trouble—real or manufactured.

However, it's one thing to be prepared for a calamitous act. When it never happens, you begin to worry about that, too. It begins to create an atmosphere of paranoia. Waiting for the other shoe to drop will do that to a person.

To paraphrase Mark Twain, once a cat sits on a hot stove, it will never sit on a hot stove again. Then again, it will never sit on a cold one, either.

That was what it was like during the live days of radio and television. In addition to the pressures of doing programs that were live, we had to be constantly in a state of preparedness for the unpredictable because, like Twain's cat, we never knew when that seemingly cold stove was suddenly going to burn us.

Strangely enough, with the removal of the pressures that were inherent with live broadcasting, the pranks and practical jokes became less frequent. Today, with the increasing reliance on computers, they are all but nonexistent. It appears that Fred Allen, the radio comedic genius, was accurate when he prophesied those many years ago, "Broadcasting is rapidly becoming a triumph of technical equipment over people."

Perhaps that is true today, Fred. But back in the golden days of live radio and television, it most certainly was the people who mattered. And as important and serious as broadcasting was way back then, there were always a few, as this book shows, who refused to take it that seriously.

CHAPTER I

WALK LIKE A WOMAN

LISTENING TO THE RADIO today, it is difficult to imagine how important radio once was and what a tremendous influence it had. But back in 1942, at the height of its heyday, it was different. Radio, unlike films or newspapers or even a good book, could both inform and entertain with no more effort on your part than simply listening, all in the comfort of your easy chair or bed, or while doing the housework, or in the evening gathered in the living room with your family. In addition, it was free, unlike many things in the 1930s.

If the news of bread lines in America or war clouds over Europe got too depressing, by simply turning the dial listeners could always find something on one of the stations to cheer them up.

To start the day off, you got to march around the breakfast table with Don McNeill's "Breakfast Club" or perhaps have "Breakfast at Sardi's" or even "Breakfast in Hollywood." After that, you had your choice of news, religion, talk shows, or those perennial favorites, the daily soap operas, beginning at ten o'clock in the morning with "Life Can Be Beautiful," and with a different one every 15 minutes thereafter until 4:30 in the afternoon. Then, as mother wiped away a final sympathetic tear for the trials and tribulations of "The Second Mrs. Burton" and headed for the kitchen to prepare dinner, the children took over. And what a list of goodies they had to choose from! "Jack Armstrong, the All-American Boy," "Buck Rogers in the 25th Century," "Little Orphan Annie," "Dick Tracy," "Tom Mix," "Don Winslow," "The Lone Ranger," "Captain Midnight," "Terry and the Pirates," "Bobby Benson's Adventures". . . what red-blooded American child could ask for anything more? Well . . . perhaps a "Little Orphan Annie" decoding ring for only two box tops would be nice.

Next it was Dad's turn. All the world news was at his fingertips from such learned commentators as Gabriel Heater ("There's good news tonight"), Fulton Lewis, Jr. (". . . and that's the top of the news the way it

1

looks from here"), Edward R. Murrow ("...this is London"), and Lowell Thomas ("...and so long until tomorrow").

After dinner the family would huddle around the radio in the living room and decide which programs they were going to listen to that evening. Although selecting the one program that was agreeable to everyone was often a source of lively discussions, the evening always started out on a high note with "Amos 'n' Andy." So popular was this nightly program for chasing away the depression blues of the 1930s or the bleak war news of the early 1940s that America came to a standstill while it was cheered by these beloved characters. Their popularity was so enormous that movie theaters, in an effort to bolster falling attendances, offered to play the "Amos 'n' Andy" show over their loudspeakers so fans wouldn't miss any of the episodes!

To those of us who worked in radio between the early 1930s and 1950s, radio was neither old time nor golden; it was simply live. This meant that whatever we did, good or bad, it went out over the air and into the homes of millions of listeners. If it was good, it was simply what was expected of us and therefore went largely unnoticed. If we made a mistake, however, it most certainly didn't go unnoticed. Unlike the movies, with their countless takes and retakes, radio was immediate and final. We only got one chance. Do it right the first time or suffer the consequences. As one movie actress so indelicately, but accurately, put it, "My God, if you make a mistake on radio, everybody hears it. It's just like farting in church!"

You might argue with her choice of words but no one who has ever done live radio would dispute the acumen of her statement. Once a sound went into the mike, it was gone forever.

In the theater, the fear of forgetting lines, missing a cue, being late for an entrance, or simply looking foolish in front of an audience is called stage fright. In radio, it was called mike fright. In some victims, it made the throat so dry that they were unable to speak. For that reason, mike fright was also referred to as "drying up."

Interestingly enough, sufferers of this occupational hazard were always fine during rehearsals. But once the curtain went up, or the ON THE AIR light went on, something happened to their confidence, or focus, or whatever else it was, and these actors suddenly forgot their lines or became speechless.

Radio casting directors dealt with this problem in a number of ways. In the beginning, they hired the most competent actors they could find, crossed their fingers, and prayed that they had made the right choice. Through this process of elimination, actors who had on-air experience and had proven themselves under fire were given priority over actors without radio experience. Experienced actors were indeed the chosen few. They were all excellent actors, had good radio voices, could do several dialects, needed little if any rehearsal, were sober and reliable and impervious to that radio bugaboo, mike fright.

You would think that anyone possessing these talents could look forward to a bright and financially rewarding career in radio. Well, maybe, but only if they paid attention to some of radio's less obvious and rarely discussed requirements.

Radio was a very intimate medium. If the scene was busy, actors often pressed their bodies against one another as they delivered their lines. It was not a time for wandering romantic hands or overdoses of heavy, cloying perfumes. And if the luncheon or dinner special downstairs at ColBeeS had been liberally laced with garlic or preceded by dry martinis, experienced actors carried a generous supply of breath fresheners. Actors who ignored these and other good personal hygiene practices never understood why their radio calls became less and less frequent. Sen-Sen became so popular as a mask for boozy drinks that most actors were afraid to use it for fear of being guilty by association.

All in all, being an actor during the days of live radio was not easy. The few men and women who successfully met all these requirements were difficult to find. It therefore wasn't unusual for directors to put together their own little stock company of people they could rely on and with whom they felt comfortable working.

When I worked on "Mr. Chameleon," I asked the star, Karl Swenson, why he did just about every show that required a Scandinavian accent. He told me it wasn't because he was that extraordinarily good (he lied; he was), it was because of his reputation: Directors were notoriously insecure about taking a chance with someone new. Besides, Swenson added, North Country voices were probably the trickiest to do. And if the directors put an ad in *Daily Variety* asking for auditions, there would be 10,000 actors knocking down the door, while probably only 50 would be acceptable. Here he paused and smiled, "What director has the time or inclination to find that fifty out of ten thousand?"

That, in a nutshell, sums up why it was so difficult to break into radio: Insecurity on the part of the directors plus radio inexperience on the part of the actors. The lack or abundance of talent among untried actors never entered into it. There simply wasn't enough time or inclination to go looking for it.

In 1942, an actor working on a 15-minute commercial program received $6 an hour for rehearsals and $15 for the broadcast. Although this doesn't sound like much, some actors worked on as many as four soaps in a day. In order to do this, they hired rehearsal stand-ins who read the lines and took cuts and corrections. Very often the "real" actor didn't walk into the studio until the show was actually on the air! The stand-in would hand the script to the actor and perhaps whisper, "They changed the character you play from Irish to Italian and made him older." This practice of hiring stand-ins was so common that there were cases where even the stand-ins had to hire stand-ins.

So magical was this inner circle that many experienced theatrical actors spent years trying to break into radio. Even after they were accepted, they were given only minor parts until they could prove themselves. In this way, if they did come up with a bad case of mike fright, another member of the cast could step in and do the part.

At the very start of radio, this fear of the microphone was so devastating to some performers that engineers even tried putting a shade over the mike to disguise it as a lamp. They soon learned, however, that it wasn't the appearance of a microphone that was so frightening; it was the knowledge that your words—as you spoke them—were being listened to by an unseen audience numbering in the millions.

When mike fright struck, all the victim could do was stare in wordless terror at the mike (or lamp shade) and utter small gagging sounds. That was the cue for the nearest actor to unceremoniously push the comatose actor aside and do the part. In addition to the embarrassment, the far more serious consequence was that the victim's résumé could be given a black mark that might not be erased for an entire career. Being kicked off one show when there were so many other shows around doesn't seem that terrible unless the kickers were Frank and Anne Hummert. Not only would the victim not work that one show, he or she wouldn't work any of the other shows that came out of the Hummerts' production house: "Amanda of Honeymoon Hill," "Backstage Wife," "David Harum," "Evelyn Winters," "Front Page Farrell," "John's Other Wife," "Just Plain Bill," "Lora Lawton," "Lorenzo Jones," "Mr. Chameleon," "Mrs. Wiggs of the Cabbage Patch," "Nona from Nowhere," "Orphans of the Storm," "Our Gal Sunday," "Real Stories from Real Life," "The Romance of Helen Trent," "Second Husband," "Stella Dallas," or "Young Widder Brown."

Even if an actor got along just fine with the Hummerts, what if Irna Phillips, the prolific soap writer, didn't care for the portrayal of one of her characters? The poor actor or actress might not bother auditioning for any of *her* shows: "Brighter Day," "Woman in White," "The Guiding Light," "Lonely Women," "The Right to Happiness," and "The Road of Life."

It should be pointed out that unlike television today, where the cost of producing shows is so prohibitive that the successful ones go into syndication as soon as possible, radio shows and their production companies had a far greater staying power. "One Man's Family," for instance, went on the air on April 29, 1932, and didn't go off until May 8, 1959. Getting on the wrong side of the producer, director, or writer of that show could seriously limit the places an artist could work. In addition to not working their shows, the word would soon get out along the radio grapevine that the artist wasn't acceptable on "One Man's Family." And as you might suspect, being unacceptable on one show (for whatever reason) didn't make the artist attractive to other producers.

One of the reasons radio shows stayed on the air so long was the listeners' imagination. Unlike television, the audience didn't get tired of the same old faces. Nor did favorite characters outgrow their parts. On radio, Helen Trent remained just a shade over 35 for more than two decades.

And yet, in all those years, if the listening audience had the talent to draw a picture of Ms. Trent, no two pictures would be identical—not the clothes she wore, or the color of her hair, or even where she lived. It was all in the mind of the listener. All radio did was give you the voice, or the sound effects, and the audience at home did the rest.

In appreciation for the listener's unswerving loyalty to their favorite programs, radio made certain its programming schedule was suitable entertainment for the whole family. There was no such thing as an "adult" station or entertainment, no sly sexual innuendos or double entendres. What came out over the airwaves and into the American home was suitable for all ears. Any violation of this trust by a producer, director, writer, or actor could mean the end of a career.

The first scheduled radio program in the United States went on the air on November 2, 1920, over KDKA, Pittsburgh, and gave the results of the Harding-Cox election. Although this was an historic occasion, the program was only heard locally. It wasn't until New Year's Day, 1927, that a play-by-play report of the Rose Bowl football game was heard from coast to coast.

As the popularity of radio grew, so did the demand for new programming ideas. Radio tried to meet this demand with more news, music, sports, and talk shows—lots and lots of talking. Many critics began insisting that there was too much talking already. What was radio to do?

In vaudeville, there had been a very popular dancing chicken act. In the beginning, audiences were not so much interested in how well the chicken danced; they were just amazed that the chicken could dance at all.

But once audiences saw the act, they wanted to know what else the chicken could do. All of a sudden, radio began to feel like that dancing chicken.

Being a unique and revolutionary form of entertainment, radio was faced with some very serious problems, not the least of which was that of entertaining audiences who couldn't see who was doing the entertaining.

This concept was unique, there was nothing in the entertainment field to compare it with. As a result, radio was confused as to what to do next . . . or for that matter, what *could* be done next.

Despite all this indecisiveness, radio's success exceeded everyone's expectations. And to meet this demand for a more rounded programming schedule, radio needed not so much new faces as new voices.

For these, it turned to the actors and actresses of the theater and the performers of vaudeville. Although there was a wealth of talent in the theater available just for the asking, the majority of the actors and performers were unacceptable. In the theater, an actor's appearance counted a great deal. Hours were spent with wigs, makeup, and costumes. Having the actors look the part they played not only helped audiences accept the character more readily, it was a tremendous aid for the actor's portrayal of the part.

Years of studying the proper way to move on the stage, apply makeup, dance, project their voices, juggle, bring a rabbit out of a hat—none of these talents impressed radio. All it was interested in was, what do you sound like?

When radio turned to the stage for comedy, many of the comedians showed up in the studios wearing their outrageous clothes, funny makeup, and all their other familiar stage aids for getting laughs. Unfortunately this was before the studio audience was allowed to laugh or applaud. Not only did this lack of reaction throw the comedians' timing off in the studio, the listeners at home heard nothing funny in jokes that were dependent on mugging, baggy pants, and a red putty nose.

Radio quickly concluded that the techniques used by other mediums didn't lend themselves to the intimacy of the microphone. Although it was very indifferent about whether the actors were short, thin, fat, old, young, handsome, less than handsome, or even if they were male or female, what did matter was how the microphone made them sound. On "Fibber McGee and Molly," for instance, the part of the black maid Beulah, was played by a white man. In fact, the actor Marlin Hurt made a comfortable living impersonating both male and female Negro voices.

Writers were having an equally difficult time. Techniques used in writing for the stage were terribly confusing to an audience that was so dependent on listening alone. As a result, new techniques in writing as well as acting were needed. The theater's time-honored dramatic pause was nothing but dead air in radio. Therefore, no more long pauses, dramatic or otherwise, since they might cause the valued listeners to panic and turn to a competitive station for reassurance that their receivers were still working.

Prior to the use of sound effects on radio, some writers and directors had to resort to this type of confusing dialogue: "I wonder why that car is stopping in front of our house?" To which audiences throughout America would ask each other, "What car? I didn't hear a car. Did you hear a car?" It was obvious that this deceptive use of dialogue to describe sounds couldn't continue, that what was needed was for the audience to hear the actual sounds, or at least what they *imagined* were the actual sounds. Inexperienced as radio was, they knew that driving a car around in a studio just for its sound was not the answer. Again, radio turned to the theater for help (see Figure 1.1).

Although many of these primitive effects were adopted by the desperate soundmen of early radio, others, such as the theaters' sound for thunder—a cannon ball rolling down a trough and falling onto a huge drum head—were left for the theater.

This effect had been popular since Shakespearean days, but even in 1708, some people were not pleased with this cumbersome technique. In that year, John Dennis, an English theatrical critic, wrote a play, *Appius and Virginia*. In it was a scene involving a rain storm with a great deal of thunder. Rather than use the ball and drum effect, he invented something more realistic and controllable, a large piece of thin copper sheeting suspended from a frame by wires. By vibrating the metal, a very realistic thunder effect could be produced. Dennis called his effect a thunder sheet. The thunder sheet was a great success (more so than the play, in fact), and as a result, other stage productions began using his effect. This infuriated Dennis to the point where he would angrily confront the offending producer by charging, "You, sir, are stealing my thunder!"

The thunder sheet has long been forgotten, but as Figure 1.2 demonstrates, "stealing one's thunder" has become part of the English language.

Sound effects in the theater were never known for their subtlety, but because they were often combined with visual effects, they were accepted by the audience. For example, to create the illusion of waves, stagehands sometimes got on their hands and knees under a large green floor-cloth and undulated their backs in rhythmic wave-like fashion. (On one occasion

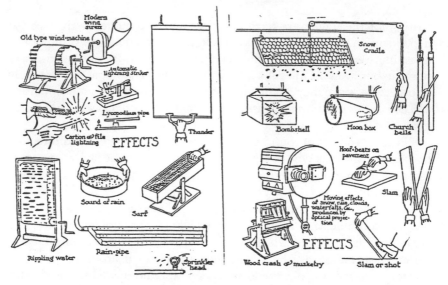

Figure 1.1. Some of the special effects and sound effects that have been in use in the theater since the days of Shakespeare. Not surprisingly, early radio, desperate for "new" ways of making sounds, adopted many of these effects. Krow, Equipment for Stage Production, D. Appleton and Co.; 1928. Reprinted by permission of the publisher.

Figure 1.2. Proof of John Dennis' impact. Cartoon reprinted courtesy of Bob Thaves and NEA Inc.

during a scene depicting a naval battle, one overly exuberant stagehand lifted up too hard against a half-rotted spot in the canvas and his startled head suddenly poked up out of the "ocean." Before the audience could realize what had happened, a quick-witted actor cried out, "Man overboard!" and hauled him up on the deck.)

In addition to the visual support that sounds gave in the theater, audiences had grown accustomed to a form of stylized sounds that were

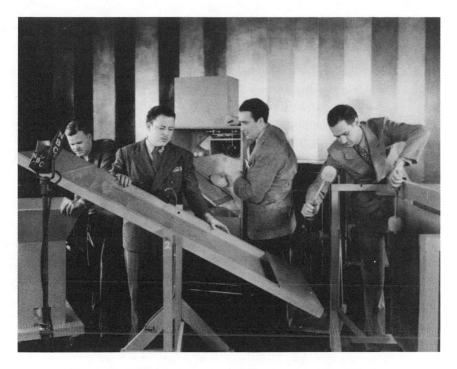

Figure 1.3. Creating a storm at sea. Photo courtesy of Virgil Reimer.

meant more to suggest rather than to imitate. Because of this, many of the sounds that had been used in the theater since Shakespeare's time were unsuitable for this young whipper-snapper, radio.

But radio sound-effects people through a process of selective elimination were creative in adapting old techniques to the new medium, as Figures 1.3 and 1.4 show.

Pictured on the left in Figure 1.3 is a wind machine. By cranking a wooden shaft that rubs lightly against a heavy piece of canvas, a very realistic wind effect can be produced. The sound of rain was created when the operator — in this case George Lehman — turned a hopper that dropped bird seed onto a piece of stretched wax paper. To the right, the artist creates the sound of thunder (see Figure 1.12 for a different version). In the center is Virgil Reimer see-sawing a shallow box filled with buck shot back and forth rhythmically to produce the sound of waves. As you might suspect, a storm at sea took a lot of hands to create. Unfortunately, the identity of the wind and thunder makers in Figure 1.3 has been lost.

Another method of creating the sound of waves is shown in Figure 1.4.

In 1935, the radio audience listening to "The March of Time" sat on the edges on their chairs as they listened to a ship's brave radio operator frantically tapping out a distress SOS signal, while in the background they could hear angry waves pounding against the sides of the unfortunate, foundering ship. Tapping out the SOS signal on her telegrapher's "bug" is Mrs. Ora Nichols, while Henry Rinaldi, also of CBS, has the somewhat more tedious job of manipulating some BB shot inside an open bass drum and fooling the tilted microphone into thinking they are angry ocean waves.

Radio sound effects received tremendous help from the more daring and risqué burlesque houses and vaudeville theaters, especially from the techniques and talents of the trap drummers. In addition to musical responsibilities, a trap drummer was expected to supply sound effects for the various acts. Such off-handed and succinct requests as "Give me the sound of a fight gong when I hit my wife in the ass" were common. To accommodate these performers, the drummers had a huge assortment of props and other trappings or "traps." It made no difference whether an act wanted a "whiz-bang" or a "temple block," a "ratchet" or a "klaxon horn," these versatile drummers had them. Figures 1.5 and 1.6 show the range of such traps that soundmen turned to for their sound effects during the early days of radio.

Figure 1.5 shows Charles Forsyth knee-deep in hundreds of manual sound effects in his Hollywood studio. In the background, next to a thunder drum, is Len Wright, a former vaudeville trap drummer. He and Forsyth teamed up to do "The Black and Blue Detectives" at KNX in Hollywood.

Figure 1.6 illustrates the number of drummers' traps used by the artists during the early days of radio.

Figure 1.7 shows another example of how much the early sound-effect artists depended on vaudeville's trap drummers to supply them with sounds. This particular trap or "manual effect" was called a scratch box. It consisted of a shallow wooden box and a piece of tin with rough holes punched in it. By rhythmically sweeping a stiff wire brush over the rough holes, a very realistic steam engine "chugging" out of a station could be imitated. All that was needed was an actor to bawl out, "Alllll Aboard." The main problem was that once the engine was out of the station, directors expected this chugging sound to accelerate rapidly and continue for as long as needed—or until the artist's arm fell off, whichever came first. Little wonder that sound-effects departments in those early days recruited drummers so heavily.

If you could rummage through these hundreds of effects you would

Figure 1.4. Creating a ship in distress. Photo courtesy of Walter Pierson.

come across something called a "nail-pulling" effect, shown in Figure 1.8. In order to create this elusive little sound, the thin piece of wood on the top was scraped against the lower box, creating the illusion of a nail being pulled out of a stubborn piece of wood.

Although these manual effects produced realistic sounds, they could never be relied on to produce the same sounds every time, or even every *other* time. But they were still better than taking a chance of pulling a real nail out of a real piece of wood, all done with your fingers crossed. But that's what made doing manual effects and live radio so exciting. You never knew when the parachute wasn't going to open.

Surprisingly, Len Wright (Figure 1.5) and Ora and Arthur Nichols (Figure 1.10) were part of only a handful of drummers lured into radio. No doubt there was a natural skepticism that something so new and untried as radio would ever last. After all, how could a lot of talk coming from a

piece of furniture ever compete with the excitement and glamour of seeing performers in person on the stage?

The first use of sound effects on a dramatic show was at WGY in Schenectady, New York, between 1922–23. Although there is no record of what the show was, it is a fair guess that the sound effects used were of the most basic type. From this awakening interest until the late 1920s, many sound-effect prospects came from curious radio-station employees looking for a job change. Although they were totally inexperienced (but then, who wasn't?), they were at least familiar with the day-to-day operation of a radio station.

As might be expected, many were called but only a handful were chosen. It seems that the orderly, nine to five world of their clerical jobs did not prepare them for the rigorous world of live radio. Most of these early applicants went back to their old jobs after they learned the true meaning of On the Air, since being virtual prisoners in a small, windowless studio was not their idea of show business. They also quickly learned they were not allowed to move about, talk, laugh (no matter how funny the script), cough (no matter how bad the tickle) . . . in short, no extraneous noise whatsoever. None.

This dread of making a noise by accidentally dropping a sound-effect prop while we were on the air was deeply embedded in my mind. Long after those early years I was at home in my workshop when I accidentally dropped a sledge hammer. The good news is that my reflexes were still good enough that I cushioned its fall so it didn't make any noise. The bad news is, I broke my foot.

By the late 1920s, radio decided it was time to take sound effects seriously. At CBS in New York, they were fortunate enough to hire two people with sound-effects experience from the Judson Radio Program Corporation, Arthur and Ora Nichols. The husband and wife team had started out in vaudeville where Arthur played the violin while Ora played the piano. Although the CBS job was only on a freelance basis, they jumped at the opportunity.

Following a number of successful years as performers on stage, after silent movies came along, Arthur and Ora suddenly found it more and more difficult to get work. Although these were difficult times for vaudeville performers, they were luckier than most. Unlike the fire eaters, dancers, jugglers, contortionists, comedians, balancing acts, gymnasts, knife throwers, quick change artists, and animal acts, they at least had their music. Many vaudeville performers found themselves without a job after

Opposite: *Figure 1.5. A drummer's traps. Photo courtesy of Pacific Pioneer Broadcasters.*

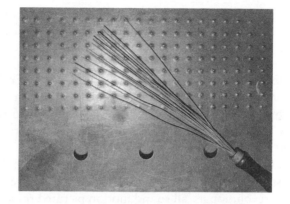

Figure 1.7. Scratch box. Photo by author.

Figure 1.8. "Nail-puller." Photo by author.

having careers spanning many years—two decades in the case of vaudeville headliner Maurice "Navarre" McLoughlin (see Figure 1.9). McLoughlin demonstrates why these talented performers were called Fire Eaters. An act such as this took years to master and was always in demand in vaudeville. However, once the movies and radio began luring away their audiences, performers with these specialty acts found themselves out of work.

Opposite: *Figure 1.6. More traps. Photo courtesy of Robert J. Graham.*

Making the transition from the live and rowdy stage of vaudeville to silent films was difficult for Arthur and Ora Nichols. For one thing, in addition to supplying the music that accompanied the film, they had to supply the sound effects as well. Not just the occasional sounds they were accustomed to doing for vaudeville, but *all* the sounds. As difficult as it was, both Ora and Arthur found the challenge of doing the sound effects even more interesting and exciting than their music, so much so that Arthur switched from the violin to drums so he could provide better and more realistic sound effects.

Just when Ora and Arthur were becoming comfortable doing sound effects for the silent films, Hollywood came out with *The Jazz Singer* starring Al Jolson. This revolutionary all-sound motion picture brought an end to silent films and to such old friends as Charlie Chaplin's Little Tramp.

This was not a happy time for Ora and Arthur, or for that matter, for the *benshis* over in Japan. A *benshi* was a man who stood on stage next to the silent-film screen and not only did all the dialogue for both men and women but all the film's sound effects as well. So popular were these versatile gentlemen that many people in the audience came to see the *benshis* no matter what film was playing. To these fans, watching the *benshis* do the ranting of an outraged emperor, the protestations of his suffering wife, and the growls of the royal pekingese—all in the same scene—were well worth the price of admission.

Although the *benshis* fought valiantly, they could not compete with the new sound-on-film motion picture. And so the *benshis* from the silent films and performers such as the fire eaters from vaudeville, had something in common: Each was a victim of technological progress.

In 1928, after a 23-year career of supplying sounds for vaudeville and the silent screen, Arthur and Ora began receiving offers to furnish sound effects for a new and challenging source—radio. The idea of creating sounds that took the place of scenery, rather than merely augmenting it, appealed to them both. Without a moment's hesitation, they eagerly accepted radio's invitation.

For several years they freelanced their sound-effects talents to CBS and NBC. Then as the demand for sound effects increased, CBS decided to put this unusual husband and wife on staff. Ora and Arthur, in turn, hired and trained Henry Gauthiere and a former dancer from vaudeville, George O'Donnell. These four people were the first network staff sound-effects artists in the country. In fact, Ora Daigle Nichols was the only woman in the entire universe who made a living doing sound effects at that time.

The media was so impressed with Ora's talents and accomplishments

Figure 1.9. Maurice "Navarre" McLoughlin. Photo courtesy of the McLoughlin family.

that they voted her one of the most influential women in radio. Other women so honored included Kate Smith, Amelia Earhart, and Mrs. Franklin Roosevelt.

Ora Nichols and her husband, Arthur, are generally regarded as the two people most responsible for bringing sound effects to radio. In addition to their many years of theatrical and silent film experience, they brought many much-needed sound-effects props to radio as well.

One effect took Arthur nine months to build, working 14 hours a day. It had nine ⅛-horsepower motors and one 1¼ horsepower motor. It even had

Figure 1.10. Ora and Arthur Nichols. Photo courtesy of Walter Pierson.

Figure 1.11. Michael Eisenmenger. Photo courtesy of Robert J. Graham.

tanks of compressed air, for operating all the whistles. The machine was five feet high and two feet deep and could reproduce sounds ranging from a small bird chirping to 500 gunshots a minute. And all this was back in the 1920s. As sophisticated as this machine was, Arthur had one fear – that sooner or later, he'd push the wrong button and instead of getting the whoosh of an ocean wave, he'd get the quacking of an outraged duck.

With the increase in popularity of sound effects on radio, Ora found herself needing a larger staff. The first people she contacted were her old friends, the trap drummers. Ora recalled, "When I told these gentlemen what their job was to be, they looked at me as if I were crazy. One remarked, 'Lady, I'm a musician. You couldn't pay me enough money to get up in front of a studio filled with people and walk like a woman!' When I tried to explain that it wasn't that awful and that I very often walked like a man, he gave me a strange look and left."

In Figure 1.11, Michael Eisenmenger proves conclusively that when it came to walking like a woman, some sound-effects artists would go to any extreme to avoid looking foolish. He's shown crossing from a "car," on the right side, to a "front door," on the left side, while still managing to escort his rather thin-legged lady friend.

Figure 1.12. CBS sound-effects department, 1935. Photo courtesy of Walter Pierson.

Fortunately for the radio listener, men were found who didn't mind doing footsteps for women. In addition, they learned that dropping flashlight bulbs into a glass sounded like ice cubes, that a cork dipped in turpentine and rubbed against a bottle sounded like a monkey chattering or a squealing rat, that a box of corn starch sounded like footsteps in the snow when it was squeezed in a rhythmic fashion, that hitting their elbows and arms on a prop table made an excellent body-fall sound. The list of effects that were suitable for the sensitive microphone began to grow. At long last, the business of breathing excitement and action into the spoken word was rapidly becoming an art.

Figure 1.12 shows the CBS, New York, sound-effects department in May, 1935. Walt Pierson had taken over the business of running the department and Ora Nichols went back to her first love, the creation of sound effects. As shown in the picture, Ora can be seen cueing up a record on the turntables.

Others in the picture are (left to right): Ora Nichols, Al Van Brackel, Walt Pierson, Max Uhlig, Vic Rubei, and Henry Gauthier. Some items of particular interest are the "marching feet" operated by Vic Rubei and the large tub in the center of the picture, one of the first "splash tanks." These tanks were used for everything from washing dishes on a soap opera to a storm at sea on "Jack Armstrong, the All-American Boy."

How popular was radio by then? A survey showed that 79 percent of Americans interviewed would stop going to the movies rather than give up their beloved radio. And this was after Orson Welles scared the nation half to death with his radio adaptation of H. G. Wells' *War of the Worlds*.

During the Depression, radio gave its audience everything—comedy, drama, sports, news . . . and just a little bit more. For example, during the Depression when President Roosevelt had to take drastic steps and declare a so-called Bank Holiday, he succeeded in stopping a potential banking disaster, but he had difficulty convincing the nation that it was only a temporary measure and that their money was safe in banks.

In an effort to quiet the growing fears of an already nervous America, the president appealed to an unusual source to explain to the country the reasons for the closures—the beloved "Amos 'n' Andy" radio show. The president knew that if anyone could ease the growing tensions, it would be these two beloved entertainers. The public might distrust whatever he or other politicians might say, but if Amos and Andy said everything was okay, then it must be okay. In addition to everything else radio offered, it was a good friend you could trust.

The bleak economic condition facing the country only made radio more popular. And to keep up with this demand for more and more dramatic programming, Pierson had to increase his staff from 8 to over 40 artists.

The men Pierson recruited came from all walks of life. Roland Fitzgerald was a recent engineering graduate and built such much-needed props as a sink with a recirculating water supply. Jack Armhein and Jimmy Rinaldi were recruited from the Paramount film studios, and Jimmy Rogan had been the music arranger for the Emory Deutch Orchestra and had coauthored the music standard, "When a Gypsy Makes His Violin Cry." As the department grew, four distinct but unofficial types of sound-effects artists began to emerge. I say unofficial because the networks, trying to make the job of scheduling easier, always tried to convince shows that one artist was as good as another. However, if the producer had a show with top ratings, he or she would just give a knowing smile and say fine, and then demand the person they wanted or they were calling the sales department!

At the top of these sound-effects groupings were the stars, followed by the artists, the button-pushers, and the technicians. This was the pecking order of the sound-effects department, and although it would be charitable to say that each category was afforded the same treatment, that wouldn't be quite the truth. Each artist filled a necessary demand, but it was the stars who got the spot light and those all-important fees.

The technicians were the people responsible for designing, building,

Figure 1.13. McQuade's thunder screen. Photo courtesy of Malachy Wienges.

and maintaining the sound-effect equipment, and in a pinch, they helped out on a busy show as the second or third set of hands or feet. They were also valuable for doing vacation relief on quiz shows and soaps. Although few of these creative geniuses have been given credit, their contributions to the art of sound effects were substantial.

Stuart McQuade of NBC, for instance, invented the rain machine, speed-controlled wagon wheels, and dozens of other smaller but equally valuable effects.

The thunder screen (Figure 1.13) is another example of the creative mind of Stuart McQuade. A contact microphone (one sensitive to vibrations) was placed against the screen so that by striking the copper screening with a mallet, you were rewarded with a very convincing clap of thunder.

The second group in the sound-effects hierarchy was the button pushers. Although this name doesn't sound too flattering, it was quite close to being accurate. These people were mostly assigned to shows that had a very limited need for sound effects. Even then, the effects they were required to produce usually had buttons attached to them. Playing the Beulah Buzzer on the quiz show "Truth or Consequences" is one example.

Others were the sounds for the soaps and included door bells, door chimes, door buzzes, phone bells, and oven timers to signal that the cookies were done. To go with the cookies came a tea kettle whistle in the winter, or the clinking of ice cubes for lemonade in the summer. Perhaps one of the most difficult sound-effects decisions the director of a soap had was whether it was too late in the year for lemonade or too early for hot tea.

Many sound-effects artists hated the button-pusher shows, even though the work was certainly easier, the hours were better, and the pay was the same. The big problem was boredom, especially if they didn't work the show regularly.

Another part of the problem was the actors. Because they were so good at what they did, rehearsals were minimal. Usually the cast did the first reading of the script while seated at a table having coffee and cigarettes. After that there was a sort of dress rehearsal using the microphone, for sound levels, and then the next time would be the on-air performance.

Between these rehearsals, the actors would either be on the phone with their answering service or talking among themselves. These conversations covered diverse subjects, such as the comings and goings of fellow actors or how to get started in poisonous herb gardening.

During these lively discussions, the sound-effects artists (certainly the relief artists) usually busied themselves with a crossword puzzle, far from the cast.

This separation was more by design than by snobbery. The networks discouraged their employees—the engineers and soundmen—from getting overly friendly with outside production people—the producers, directors, agency personnel, and actors.

It was this combination of few effects and little else to do (thank God for the puzzles) that made the schedule of a button pusher so unappealing. Furthermore, it was common knowledge that, except in a few rare cases, the talents of the top sound men in the department were too valuable to be squandered on shows requiring so few sounds. Therefore, being relegated to the role of a button pusher was not without a stigma. Considering that some of these shows were on the air five times a week, year after year, however, it's clear that the button pushers of sound effects served a very real need.

The third group were the people who made up the bulk of the sound-effects department. Although they weren't actually characterized by any labels, these were the artists who could be put on any show and do an excellent job. It was because of these talents, however, that they were used almost exclusively on the prime-time dramatic and comedy shows. These

Figure 1.14. George O'Donnell. Photo courtesy of Walter Pierson.

artists usually lacked the flamboyant personalities of the stars, but they were always in demand.

The final category consisted of a handful of people referred to as stars. They differed from the artists not so much in talent as in their uninhibited approach to doing effects. It might not come as a surprise, but most of these stars worked on the Hollywood comedy shows. Not only were these stars flamboyant and uninhibited, they often challenged the comedians they worked for in their ability to get laughs. Bob Hope, for instance, felt that Virgil Reimer was getting too many laughs doing sound effects on the stage in front of the audience so he requested that Reimer be positioned behind a curtain. When Reimer threatened to take his talents elsewhere, Hope changed his mind.

Figure 1.15. Ray Erlenborn. Photo from Ray Erlenborn file.

Even comedy writers respected the laugh-getting abilities of these star soundmen. When they wrote comedy sound cues, they always left room for the stars to improvise. A comedy-crash cue might be as basic as BIG FUNNY CRASH. Allowing the stars the freedom to come up with their own comedy effects was most often the surest way of getting laughs. As might be expected, these stars very often demanded and received fees as well as other considerations: Extra overtime to load in their effects, extra overtime to load out their effects, even a day away from the department to locate a much needed effect (at the show's expense, of course). Although these stars sound like a pretty crass bunch of individuals, the real question

Figure 1.16. Ray Nugent. Photo from author's collection.

is, were they worth it? How much of a price would you put on the sound effects that accompanied Jack Benny's visit to the vault? Or the Maxwell car? Or Fibber's closet?

Figures 1.14 and 1.15 show George O'Donnell (CBS, New York) and Ray Erlenborn (CBS, Hollywood) producing the sound of horses hooves. Each artist is equally skilled in this endeavor and yet one, Ray Erlenborn, specialized in doing comedy shows.

In Figure 1.16, Ray Nugent (NBC, Hollywood) makes certain that the Las Vegas slot machine is in good working order. It was technicians such as Ray who were depended upon to keep the sound-effects equipment in good shape. They also created new sound-effects props.

Figure 1.17. Harry Nelson and Jimmy Flynn. Photo courtesy of Harry Nelson.

Members of a sound-effects team worked together closely to make their magic. In Figure 1.17, Harry Nelson and Jimmy Flynn (ABC, New York) demonstrate how much a team depended on one another to create a convincing illusion. While Nelson sounds the steamship whistle and cranks up the anchor, Flynn uses his right hand to churn the water in the splash tank while his left hand hauls in the gangplank. To the listener at home, it added up to the perfect image of a tramp steamer about to leave an exotic South Seas port for another adventure on "Terry and the Pirates."

If a radio program as prestigious as "Lux Radio Theater" was doing an adaptation of *The Three Musketeers*, it would not be at all unusual to have four artists doing the various sounds. Figure 1.18 shows the team of (left to right) Lloyd Creekmore, Virgil Reimer, Wayne Kenworthy, and Tiny Lamb. All were loyal subjects of NBC, Hollywood.

Not only did a large team help with the work load, it also gave the newer artists experience doing some of the less critical effects. However, in the heat of the live broadcast, the real challenge was to keep from being stabbed in the rear by a fellow musketeer's errant épée.

Figure 1.18. The Four Musketeers at NBC (Hollywood). Photo courtesy of Virgil Reimer.

In sound effects, things were rarely what they seemed. Figure 1.19 shows Betty Boyle demonstrating the fine art of milking a cow, sound-effects style, while Monty Fraser (right) holds the bucket and Floyd Caton (left) for some reason holds a "boing box." On the table at Betty's right is a second "cow" in case the first one runs dry. Although seltzer bottles were the usual method of doing this milking effect, syringes filled with water and water pistols were two alternatives. While seltzer bottles were by far the most efficient, water pistols were better for squirting an actor in the back of the head during a long boring rehearsal.

In addition to superb timing and a fertile imagination, it helped if an artist knew how to fix things—in a special way, of course. Figure 1.20 shows Jack Amrhein (CBS, New York) painstakingly taking clocks apart in search of their tuned metal coils (Figure 1.21). These spring-like coils were actually the clock's chimes, and when struck by a small hammer, they tolled the witching hour of midnight on "Lights Out." Whether these clocks ever kept time correctly again was immaterial. What was important was that they chimed when they were supposed to chime. Although Amrhein's ability as a watchmaker might be doubted, Jack was considered by both

Figure 1.19. Milking a cow. Photo courtesy of Opal Fraser.

Figure 1.20. Jack Amrhein. Photo courtesy of Walter Pierson.

Figure 1.21. Chimes. Photo by author.

Figure 1.22. Al Van Brackels. Photo courtesy of Walter Pierson.

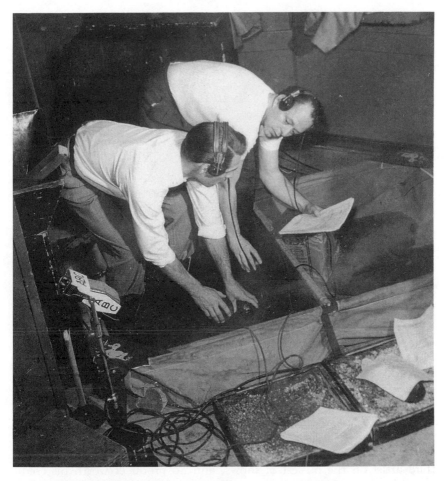

Figure 1.23. Horses in water. Photo courtesy of Opal Fraser.

the directors and his peers to be one of the best sound-effects artists in radio.

Figure 1.22 is an excellent example of how sound effects were done prior to the introduction of sounds effects on records. Al Van Brackels (CBS, New York) rotates a heavy iron disk on wheels to give the effect of a railroad car traveling over steel rails during a broadcast of CBS' "America's Hour."

The art of sound effects could get pretty messy as Figure 1.23 shows. This photo shows Monty Fraser (left) crouching in water doing horses hoofbeats, while Virgil Reimer, stripped to his undershirt, lends a third hand and the all-important script. Perhaps it was shows like this that made

Figure 1.24. Marching feet. Photo courtesy of Walter Pierson.

the art of sound effects less appealing to women. After all, standing ankle deep in dirty cold water with your blouse off would hardly qualify as a glamorous job.

It was difficult enough to get some producers to hire even a second or third artist on the busiest of shows, and no producer worth his credit would hire a *dozen* extra artists just for the sound of marching feet. As a result, artists became creative. For example, the sound of marching feet was made by the ingenious effect shown in Figure 1.24. A series of wooden pegs were suspended by wire or rawhide strings to a wooden frame. By rhythmically moving the pegs up and down, or sliding them back and forth, a convincing marching sound was created. When the police, G-men and government agents on "Gangbusters" joined forces and "marched" against the underworld, this is how they got there. And just in case one of them got out of step, Vic Rubei (CBS), on the left in Figure 1.24, was prepared to shoot them in the foot.

One reason many directors insisted on having the same sound effects artist work their show each week is evident by this picture (Figure 1.25), taken during a "Bob and Ray" rehearsal. As Ray Erlenborn goes through

Figure 1.25. Bob and Ray. Photo from Ray Erlenborn file.

the ritual of looking at the director for a sound effect cue, the director, secure in the knowledge that the experienced Erlenborn doesn't need a cue, sits back and enjoys the comedic brilliance of Bob Elliott and Ray Goulding.

During a broadcast, things were usually too hectic for anyone to even think about taking pictures. What makes Figure 1.26 so extremely rare is that it was taken during an actual broadcast of "Gangbusters." Cueing up the records (left) is Byron Wingett, while his partner Jerry McCarty is busy with the manual effects. If you think live radio was one big party, look at the strain and intense concentration on Byron's face. On the other hand, we can't see Jerry's face and he might be laughing his head off. Under the prop table is a stack of berry baskets used for the effect of a "splintering wood crash." When the G-men called out, "Come out with your hands up or we'll break the door down," this is what did the breaking. The two seltzer bottles were for mixing orders of scotch and soda. It's funny, but as insistent as some directors were for authenticity, they never insisted that soundmen use real scotch.

I have said that sound-effects people were separated into four categories. As you might suspect, the networks did not recognize these various

Figure 1.26. Byron Wingett and Jerry McCarty. Photo courtesy of Jerry McCarty.

classifications of artists. To them, all artists were created equal. It made little or no difference to them whether you graduated with an engineering degree from MIT (Stuart McQuade), had played drums with Paul Whiteman (Jerry Sullivan), had danced on the Broadway stage with Mae West (George O'Donnell), or had done comedy in silent films (Ray Erlenborn); all of these people with such disparate backgrounds were desperately needed by sound effects.

The problem was, how does the network best cost-effectively utilize such diverse talents? Is it reasonable to expect an engineer that was hired to design equipment to be equally adept at squeaking open the door to a show as difficult to do as "Inner Sanctum"? The networks thought so. Or at least they tried to make everyone believe that it was so.

As if the art of sound effects wasn't a mystery enough in those early days, the networks insisted on trying to further disguise the artists' identity by labeling them with such names as "engineers." Although being called an engineer was somewhat flattering to someone who flunked high school math two years in a row, it became embarrassing when some of the newer cast members began asking me why they didn't get better radio reception at home, or what to do about a rear-end shimmy in their new 1948 Buick.

Thank goodness the producers and directors knew who we were. And despite how hard networks tried to convince them that one artist was as capable as the next, the producers continued to make demands for the people they wanted. They knew which people they could trust on a show as difficult as "Gangbusters" or "The Man Behind the Gun." They also knew that if they had to get a laugh from something as commonplace as a door knock, the one doing the knocking better be one of the more audience responsive stars.

Although I refer to them as stars, a CBS vice-president was less charitable when he raised his voice in profanity and screamed, "Just who in the hell do those goddamn bunch of prima donnas think they are?"

Now you are about to find out.

CHAPTER II

COLBEES

COLBEES WAS A DELIGHTFUL little restaurant in New York City on the ground floor of 485 Madison Avenue. Although its doors were open to all with an appetite or thirst, it catered to people who worked in radio. This was understandable because 485 Madison was also home to the Columbia Broadcasting System.

The front half of the restaurant was a combination fast-food counter that served an excellent cheddar cheese soup on Thursdays and an ice cream soda fountain that served the best banana split in New York anytime, day or night. In the back was a restaurant for more leisurely dining and, of course, *le bar*. What made the latter area of ColBeeS such a popular watering hole was its proximity to the imminent and frequent disasters that went on daily in the studios above.

In addition to its good food and even better drinks, ColBeeS provided a unique service for the radio actor. Situated above the cashier and in full view of the customers was a large blackboard. When the cashier received a call for an actor, she would first page him or her, and if she didn't get a response, she'd chalk a brief message on the board. Normally these messages would be simple: "Lipton call regist," for example. This translated to "Billy Lipton call Radio Registry." Radio Registry was the answering service then used by most actors. Although this paging service was extremely useful to the working actor, it served the out-of-work actor as well.

The six most dreaded words for an unemployed actor are "What show are you working on?" This is especially true if the asker happens to be a director. Perhaps the only thing worse is sitting at home waiting for the phone to ring. And that was the dilemma of the actor looking for work: To be seen where it was important to be seen, and to appear successful without going into too much detail. One thing you didn't want to do was lie about what you were doing. Not only would this not help your situation, but you didn't have a prayer of getting away with it. At the time, nothing escaped the eyes or ears of the radio community. How could it? An actor who worked on "Rosemary" at CBS in the morning might do "Young Widder Brown" at NBC in the afternoon and finish up with "Mysterious Traveler" that night over at Mutual. Multiply the shows that one actor did by the number of actors he or she worked with, and then multiply that number by the number of coffee breaks they were all involved in, and the result gives some idea of the efficiency of the gossip hotline during the live days of radio.

Many actors used ColBeeS to solve this problem of appearing successful without actually being successful. They would go to the restaurant and make a quick, furtive surveillance of the room to see if anyone was there who might help them get work. If there was, they would call a friend and set it up for the friend, pretending to be from registry, to call at a prearranged time and have the actor paged. The actor would then "drop by" the table of the person most likely to get him a job, and try to time his conversation so it was just long enough to be interrupted by the all-important phone call without being so long that he had to buy a drink—or, God forbid, drinks.

Although this got an actor seen and his or her name heard, it didn't always work. A friend of mine tried this once but unfortunately the cashier didn't hang up the phone properly and all his co-conspirator got was a busy signal. This left my friend sitting at a table buying drinks and wondering which would happen first, his call from "registry" or going broke.

The soundmen who came into ColBeeS were mostly CBS staff members and therefore had little need or use for the paging service. In fact, the last thing a soundman in need of some libation wanted was to be noticed. Not that CBS had any rules against drinking, but if it affected the quality of your work, the artist could be fired on the spot.

Rarely did soundmen ever allow themselves to get into an advanced condition of inebriation, and certainly not at ColBeeS. ColBeeS was more of a genteel bar and sound-effects people only used it to smooth out the rough spots. Take, for instance, the time on "Gangbusters" when Orval White only had two sound effects.

Orval White was the first black sound-effects man in live radio. He had started out as an equipment man and worked his way up to the sound department. After a reasonable breaking-in period, he was assigned to work with Jerry McCarty and Byron Wingett on "Gangbusters." Realizing how nervous he'd be, they only gave him two effects to do—footsteps and a match strike. However, these were two very important effects.

The steps were those of an undercover G-man who uses the match strike as a signal for his fellow G-men to attack. That meant that the match strike was the cue for Jerry and Byron to supply a veritable cacophony of sounds, including machine guns, gunshots, glass crashes, sirens, car crashes, the works. But it was that match strike that started it all.

During rehearsals, Orval received nothing but praise for his steps and match strike, but on air it was a different story. As Orval did the slow and measured footsteps of the G-man walking down the city sidewalk, he reached for the box of matches. Carefully sliding back the cover, he made a sickening discovery: The box was empty. Not a single match was left. Where before there had been so many, now there were none! His first reaction was to fake the match strike by just running his fingernail across the sandpaper on the box. But he knew that would have sounded as if the match didn't strike. A match strike without the "whoosh" sound of sputtering sulpher held close to the mike was worse than no match at all. Out of the corner of his eye he saw the director wildly gesturing for the match strike. To his credit, Orval resisted the strong temptation to run out of the studio and not look back. Instead, he forced himself to lift and drop his feet in slow, measured steps while his mind raced wildly for a way out of his terrible predicament. Appealing to Jerry, he quietly mouthed the words, "Have you got a match?" Jerry, with equal slowness and distinctiveness, mouthed back, "No."

Orval suddenly realized how difficult it was to do slow, measured steps while your mind was racing, but he continued the steps, which were now getting a little on the wobbly side. Next he motioned to Jerry to ask Byron. Byron turning slightly at Jerry's tap on the shoulder and silent request, shook his head but trying to be helpful, whispered back, "Ask Orval."

Perhaps it was the look on Orval's face, or perhaps it was perfect timing, but at that precise moment, Jerry "discovered" a second box of matches on the shelf under the prop table.

Afterwards, Orval good-naturedly laughed it off. He even made a joke out of it, claiming that his first job on "Gangbusters" was "matchless." They all had a good laugh at that one. But as they walked arm-in-arm to the elevator for the trip down to ColBeeS, both Byron and Jerry knew it would only be a matter of time before Orval retaliated. How or when or where was pure conjecture. They just knew that someday, when they least expected it, he would.

Although this may seem like a cruel way to break in someone doing their first network show, it was all done by design. This was Orval's trial by fire. If he was going to panic at the unexpected, better he do it when there were two artists to take over for him than wait until he was doing a show alone.

Despite the thousands of other effects we were asked to do, footsteps

Figure 2.1. Footsteps across a floor. Photo courtesy of Malachy Wienges.

was one of the most requested. To accommodate this popular sound, everybody had their own special "walking" shoes.

Footsteps gave the radio story movement and perspective. This was especially true if a scene had little dialogue. In such cases, it was vital that each step be heard distinctively because it helped the listener at home visualize exactly the comings and goings of the various characters.

One time during the air show of "Casey, Crime Photographer," an actor carelessly stepped out his cigarette near the sound-effects area. Later, during a scene requiring a long pattern of footsteps, the sound man accidentally stepped on the cigarette butt, causing it to stick and silence the effectiveness of one of his heels. For the rest of that sequence, as Casey (played by Staats Cotsworth) hurried down the long hallway on another adventure, audiences at home wondered about how Casey could move so

Figure 2.2. Footsteps on stairs. Photo courtesy of Malachy Wienges.

rapidly on just one leg. Obviously, the injurious effects of cigarette smoking to the health and sanity of sound men were known many years before
it was announced by the surgeon general's office.

In the studio, we could always tell who was doing the manual effects
by the condition of their shoes. If they were unpolished, scuffed, and
cracked but had new heels and double soles, he or she did the footsteps
and manual effects. Because it was so important that the heels of these
shoes not become worn down, they were only worn in the studio.

To make these steps even more distinctive, different surfaces were
used. Figures 2.1 through 2.7 show the most common devices.

Steps across a floor were done on ½-inch thick pieces of plywood
called, appropriately enough, floor boards. To give the steps a good, solid,
realistic sound, pieces of carpet were tacked to the back of the boards.

Figure 2.3. Footsteps on sidewalk. Photo courtesy of Malachy Wienges.

Figure 2.2 shows how the sound of footsteps moving up and down stairs was created. Although it would seem logical to use one of the portable staircases for these effects, most artists found the stairs too limiting. For the illusion of steps going up the stairs, the artists put his full weight on the soles of his shoes and scraped them in a stepping cadence over the top edge of the board. For the sound of going down the stairs, weight was shifted from the toe to the heel in a stepping fashion that gave the heel of the shoe the dominant sound.

Figure 2.3 shows how the sound of steps on a sidewalk, street, concrete floor, or any similar surface was created using a small marble slab. This same marble slab had a different function in comedy. After a large crash, when it was time to drop the spoon, the marble slab gave the teaspoon a wonderful "tinkly" sound.

Figure 2.4. Preparing for footsteps in the snow. Photo courtesy of Walter Pierson.

In Figure 2.4, John McCloskey (CBS, New York) is seen getting ready for a mid-winter romp in the snow. Normally, the sound of walking in the snow was created as the sound-effects person squeezed a small box or pouch of cornstarch rhythmically by hand. However, if the sound person was working alone and had to do other effects by hand, the only way to do the footsteps was with the feet.

The large box shown in Figure 2.5 was used not only for the sound of footsteps on gravel but also for any sounds involving gravel or dirt. This included everything from digging for gold on "Death Valley Days" to digging a grave on "Lights Out." Figure 2.6 shows an alternate way of doing

Figure 2.5. Footsteps in gravel: the gravel box. Photo courtesy of Walter Pierson.

footsteps on gravel. It was designed for those sound-effects persons who didn't want to get their walking shoes dirty.

Figure 2.7 shows most of the materials used to create the sound of footsteps on a show. In the foreground are palm fronds and broom corn, used for footsteps in the woods or jungle. Also visible are the floor board, marble slab, and gravel boxes and a portable staircase. Ray Kremer is in the background playing the records, Jim Rogan is in the center, and Al Binnie is in the foreground.

Although all artists were required to know how to do these manual and recorded effects, it was natural that most artists preferred one job over

Figure 2.6. Footsteps in gravel: the gravel bag. Photo courtesy of Malachy Wienges.

the other. That was what made a good team—one with a steady hand able to place a needle between two grooves at just the right spot under pressure and the other ambidextrous and quick enough to do four things at once.

Figure 2.8 is an extreme closeup of a stainless steel needle being placed at the exact cue mark. The white mark is a chalk spot to help the artist locate the cue during a busy show. Because of the steel shortage during World War II, needles then were made of sharpened slivers of bamboo.

In Figure 2.9, Virgil Reimer (NBC, Hollywood) listens to make sure the level of his records are acceptable for the studio while Bud Tollefson checks over his manual effects. Now the trick for both of them is to combine the records and manual effects in such a way as to create a vivid picture for the mind's eye of the listening audience at home.

Figure 2.7. Footsteps in action. Photo courtesy of Walter Pierson.

Splash tanks were another important effect. Figure 2.10 shows Tom Buchanan (CBS, Hollywood) with a portable splash tank. Although splash tanks all operated the same, they varied in size according to what they were going to be used for. The tanks used in radio work were pretty much like the one shown in the photo (although some film post-production rooms used splash tanks the size of a small swimming pool). By turning paddles connected to the handle, you could create various watery sounds, from a storm at sea to water gently lapping against the side of a boat. This paddle arrangement was designed to be easily removed in case we needed the large tub for another effect such as blowing underwater bubbles. Because the tank was made out of metal, canvas was used to eliminate the hollow metallic sound.

These tanks, although extremely useful, were a pain in the neck to get ready. First they had to be loaded on an elevator and taken to the floor where the studio was. Next, they were wheeled into the men's room and

Figure 2.8. Hitting the mark. Photo courtesy of Robert J. Graham.

filled with water—bucket by bucket by bucket, a very slow and messy procedure. This was not one of the sound team's more popular effects.

Splash tanks could cause problems in use, as well. For instance, one time Al Binnie and Al Hogan were working on "Mr. and Mrs. North." This particular story had several long scenes of a diver searching for clues underwater. To make these underwater scenes as realistic as possible, the director wanted the sound of bubbles. Lots and lots of bubbles. And that required both Binnie and Hogan to blow air through straws into the water contained in the splash tank.

When the show broke for dinner, the two Als went downstairs to ColBeeS for a couple of drinks and perhaps dinner. If they had only

Figure 2.9. A team checking their effects. Photo courtesy of Virgil Reimer.

known what was about to happen, they would have skipped dinner and stayed with the drinks.

Ten minutes before air time, they paid their checks and left ColBeeS. At exactly five minutes before air time, they got off the elevator and walked into the studio. As Hogan busied himself making certain his records were all cued up properly, Binnie put on his walking shoes and checked the manual effects.

Last-minute inspections of the equipment were a ritual born out of bitter experience. On one show, a child actor had been told by his mother to play in the cute little sound-effects "sand box." This "sand box" actually contained pebbles, small pieces of gravel that were vital to the show's opening scene set inside a coal mine. The sound of handfuls of these pebbles dropping into the box of gravel created the warning to the coal miners of an ominous cracking in the ceiling. The box was also used for all the digging and footsteps sounds. In short, the whole first scene depended on these pebbles.

Sound effects that are that important to a show are usually locked up or, if they are small enough, carried around by the sound team. But no one thought of taking a box of rocks to dinner.

When the team came back from dinner, just prior to air-time, the gravel box was empty. Looking around in panic, they suddenly saw several of the precious pebbles on the floor. Searching further, they found a few more . . . and a few more. With no broom available and the mining scene only minutes away, they fell to their hands and knees and desperately scurried about retrieving the stones. The ragged trail snaked around the large studio, under the piano, under the chairs, behind the curtain, and finally over to where the child actor was sitting. At this point the child demanded indignantly, "Hey, leave my pebbles alone, you're spoiling my Hansel and Gretel game!"

There were other horror stories about times when the sound men didn't check their equipment. John McCloskey, for example, was doing "Ma Perkins" and the only effects he had were a door-opening sound followed by a long scene involving footsteps. On air, John opened the door when the cue came and dozens of Ping Pong balls cascaded out onto his walking board. Recovering from the shock, he spent the next several minutes trying to do footsteps through this mine field of potential noise.

Another time, Jimmy Dwan was doing "Aunt Jenny" and the only effect he had was a door being opened. When the cue came, Jimmy casually turned the knob and got a lesson in sound effect preparedness: Someone had locked the door.

A couple of veterans like Al Binnie and Al Hogan were only too familiar with such stories to ever let anything like that happen to them. Their splash tank was ready and filled to the brim with the all-important water.

Air time got closer, and because the bubble sounds were so important, they decided to give the audio man a final sound-level check. As they picked up their straws and placed them in the water, a woman suddenly screamed. Turning, they saw a group of actors excitedly pushing their chairs back and jumping up from a conference table. While lighting a cigarette, someone had set fire to a whole book of matches and let them fall on the table. An actor, thinking fast, used his script to sweep them off the table into an ash tray filled with cigarette butts. He then gingerly picked up the ash try and was carrying the smoldering mess out of the studio when the matches suddenly flared up again. Again the actor thought fast and dumped the smoldering cigarettes, ash tray and all, into the sound-effects splash tank. As the ash tray slowly sank to the bottom, cigarette butts bobbed to the surface, rapidly staining the water a nicotine brown. Hogan and Binnie, still holding their straws, could only stare in

Figure 2.10. A portable splash tank. Photo by author.

disbelief as the butts shed their papers and spread a scum of tobacco granules over the water. At that moment, the team's preoccupation with the disaster was interrupted by the audio man cheerfully announcing, "I'm ready for your level check on the bubbles, guys."

This was an unfortunate accident, but it is another example of the "liveness" of live radio. And so, the show most certainly did go on, nicotine bubbles and all. If this had happened a few years later, after radio became transcribed (recorded), the director would have waited until the water had been changed. But this wasn't "then" yet, this was "now," and radio was still very much live.

The cumulative effect of these accidents, mistakes, equipment failures, and practical jokes made nervous wrecks out of people in a business that didn't need any help in making people nervous wrecks. What was worse, even the *thought* of accidents, mistakes, equipment failures, and practical jokes was enough to make a body nervous. In those days, watching a sound-effects artist preparing to go on air was not unlike watching a commercial pilot readying his aircraft for takeoff. First the artist had to check the script to see that all the pages were still there and that they were in proper order. (Often this step was unnecessary. Most soundmen, like actors, never let their script get out of their hands.) Next came the records. After making sure they were still all there and in proper order, most artists felt it was a good idea to make certain the labels and the records matched. At the opening of one important dramatic show, a soundman played what he thought was a screeching car crash, only to hear a fife and drum corp's rendition of "I Wish I Was in Dixie."

For the artist doing the footsteps it was a good idea to inspect their walking shoes as well. Foremost was to make certain that neither one was nailed to the floor with a six-inch spike. Next, it was important to make certain that no foreign material—axle grease, cold cream, shaving cream, strawberry jam, or an order of ColBeeS' famous cheddar cheese soup—had been dumped in the shoes. Sometimes it wasn't only the shoes you had to worry about. Take the time an actress brought in her pet cat, Boots. The show they were doing took place in the desert and involved scene after scene of footsteps in the sand. Guess where little Boots went potty?

A lot of other things needed checking too, including the electrical set-up. It was always wise to see that all cables were plugged in where they were supposed to be plugged in. Reseating the power supply amplifiers was a must, as was changing the needles in the pickup arms and replacing all the batteries in the bell, buzzer, and telephone boxes. This last step was more a preventative measure against battery failure than a guarantee these effects would work on air.

For example, one time Virgil Reimer changed his telephone bell battery just prior to broadcast time of the "Jack Benny" show. But when the telephone-ring cue came on the air, the battery, for some strange reason, was dead. Desperate not to spoil the timing of the joke, Virgil sang out loud and clear, "Ding-a-ling-a-ling!" The audience reacted with whoops and howls of laughter. Benny, trying hard not to break up, turned to Virgil and echoed incredulously, *"Ding-a-ling-a-ling???!"* More howls from the audience. Cast-member Phil Harris, trying to help, jumped in with, "That's some phone call you got there, Jackson." Still fighting for control, Benny ad-libbed, "I know ... it's *person-to-person!*"

Later, Benny thanked Reimer for his quick thinking and told him it was one of the biggest laughs they had gotten all season.

Mistakes that turned into compliments were part of the charm of live radio ... a very small part. Most mistakes ended up with the director screaming, "You'll never work my show again!" And because so much of what could happen was out of the sound artist's control, it is little wonder that some—not all—of the soundmen who worked the big shows liked to partake of a bit of schnapps to help quell some of that old-time live-radio charm.

Drinking by anyone doing live radio was an extremely serious offense. Even if you *weren't* drinking, it could be a serious offense if someone suspected you were. A chocolate milk shake could be exaggerated into two double martinis if you screwed up on a show and had been seen coming out of ColBeeS prior to air time.

In radio, a five-minute rehearsal break usually meant the rest room followed by a coffee and a cigarette in the hall. However, there wasn't anything in writing that said we *had* to have coffee and a cigarette, or for that matter, go to the men's room. Therefore, some of us chose more challenging ways to spend our fives—like getting down and up from Col-BeeS in under five minutes. In order to accomplish this, it was necessary to plan these fives with the precise timing of the nefarious Willie Sutton robbing a bank.

The floor plan was ridiculously simple. Studio One, where we were, was on the eighth floor. ColBeeS, our destination, was on the ground floor. This meant that the soundman with the least to do was given the job of phoning down and ordering the drinks. The number of drinks and their varying strengths was an extremely accurate indication of how difficult a particular show was.

The next step involved the elevator. At precisely five minutes before the official five-minute break, the designated soundman would ring for the elevator. In those days there were elevator operators, and they were in our camp. However, if outsiders came along, the operator was powerless to exclude them, and sharing a car with passengers meant frequent stops. It was the last thing we wanted when critical timing was so important.

One highly successful method for reserving an elevator was to tell would-be passengers that an actor had suddenly become ill and there was an ambulance double-parked out front waiting to take him to a hospital. Another good technique was to take a dummy microphone and hold it near the open elevator door. When any "undesirable" personnel approached, they were given the "shush" sign and told we were about to record some elevator sounds and would they please use the stairs?

In all honesty, I think the calming benefits derived from those mad dashes for one or two drinks were quickly expended in the nervous energy it took getting them. But however questionable the benefits were, it certainly helped break the monotony and tedium of a long day. Besides, no one to my knowledge ever really overdid it to the point where it affected their work. However, there was a time one New Year's Eve during "Cimarron Tavern" when Al Binnie, while doing the paddling sounds for an Indian's birchbark canoe, fell into the splash tank. After the show, when the director demanded to know what happened, all three soundmen swore that the poor man had slipped on some spilled water and lost his balance, which was true. The fact that it was the scotch in the water that caused the slipping never came up and was never volunteered.

Not everyone participated in these frenzied flights for momentary respites. Jerry Sullivan is an example. Jerry was a former drummer with the Paul Whiteman Orchestra. When the rest of us were out making our big rush to the first floor, he was content to sit in the hall sipping his black coffee and chatting amiably with the actors or musicians from the show. I always envied Jerry's calmness under fire until one day I inadvertently got his black coffee mixed up with my black coffee.

The first inkling I got of the mixup came just prior to my first sip. As I brought the paper cup near my mouth, my nose was suddenly awakened to an unusual and yet not totally unfamiliar aroma. Sniffing suspiciously at the cup, I concluded that the aroma I was smelling was not so much Colombian as it was Hennessy Four Star. Not being above the perverseness of my fellow workers, I left my coffee where Jerry thought he had left his coffee and then eagerly awaited his return.

When Jerry finally returned to the studio, he picked up his black coffee, took a sip and his brow wrinkled slightly in a slightly suspicious scowl. After taking another slight sniff and small sip, he put the innocent brew down and began casually and somewhat surreptitiously sniffing every unattended black coffee in the immediate vicinity. I waited until Jerry had his back to me and then I reswitched the coffees. Only instead of putting it on top of the prop table I placed it under the table where he kept his cigarettes. When he finally came back for a cigarette, he was somewhat bewildered to discover his missing coffee. Picking it up carefully, he gave it first the sniff and then the sip test. It was the sip test that brought the smile. Then he drained the cup and left the studio. When he returned, it was immediately obvious that he had learned his lesson: Written in large letters on the paper cup was the word JERRY.

The situation reminded me of a famous old W. C. Fields story. The wily old comedian's drinking habits were legendary. To satisfy his thirst, Field employed a hundred different ruses, one of which was the so-called grapefruit-juice ploy. He let it be known that his doctor had insisted that he increase his vitamin C intake. To comply, he was bringing grapefruit juice in a thermos bottle and would be sipping out of it "now and then" while he was on the movie set.

This of course fooled absolutely no one. But as far as Fields was concerned, it was the gospel truth and he would never admit otherwise. One day, while Fields was busy doing a scene, a mischievous prop man discovered that Fields had forgotten to leave his "vitamins" in his trailer. When Fields was finished shooting, he immediately went to the thermos for a shot of his medicine. Lifting the thermos to his mouth, Fields suddenly let out a roar of disbelief, "Godfrey Cambridge!!! Some sonofabitch put grapefruit juice in my grapefruit juice!!!"

Not everyone in the sound department made ColBeeS their home away from home. The more serious drinkers preferred the more obscure watering holes that dotted Lexington or Third Avenues. The Blarney Stone on Third Avenue, for instance, served a very respectable roast beef, ham, or corned beef sandwich for a mere 50 cents. Equally important, a shot of whiskey was 25 cents and a double was 35 cents. The problem with the drinks was that the amount of whiskey the bartender poured never seemed to measure up to what the shot glass appeared capable of holding. This was due to the unusually thick shot glasses used by the bar. Some argued that these glasses magnified everything, including the size of the drink you received. To prove it, one soundman won a bet by removing his "prescription" glasses (actually there was nothing wrong with his eyes) and "reading" through a shot glass from a script he had already memorized.

Having worked at CBS in New York for so many years, I am naturally partial to the cheddar cheese soup, ice cream sundaes, and extra dry martinis served at ColBeeS. For a change of pace and menu, however, there was a delightful little bar on 53rd Street and Madison Avenue called Pochari's. These two were the favorite hangouts and listening posts for the CBS radio crowd. The good folks at NBC in New York went to Hurleys in Rockefeller Center. At ABC in New York, it was Les Artistes, up at 79th Street.

First based in Hollywood at Melrose Avenue and Vine Street, NBC was home to such shows as "Olsen and Johnson," "Walter Winchell," and "Amos 'n' Andy." Later, when NBC moved its studios, the new address became as famous as that New York corner, Broadway and 42nd Street. Even today, without exactly knowing why, tourists in Hollywood pause and take pictures of the street sign at the corner of Sunset and Vine. Although originally the location for the movie *Squaw Man*, it was the comedy shows of radio that did most to popularize this now world-famous intersection.

Out in that land of sunshine and oranges, the soundmen working at the CBS studios at Columbia Square (6121 Sunset Boulevard) found that the place to lie and lick their wounds was Brittingham's. Nickodell's was a favorite source of respite and sustenance for folks working on such shows as "The Witch's Tale," over at Mutual's KHJ at 7th and Bixel. Although many of the soundmen stayed loyal to Nickodell's, such other spots as Musso and Frank's and the Brown Derby were visited for a more expensive change of pace.

These were not the only restaurants or bars that radio soundmen went to back then, but they were the most popular and famous. Where the soundmen ate was often dictated by a personal budget or a particular schedule. Soundmen with a daytime schedule and short meal breaks often brown-bagged it or ate in a local greasy spoon (now called fast-food restaurants). Others, with a long day of rehearsal and repeat shows (to accommodate listeners in different time zones), looked forward to a meal break as their principal source of relaxation. This was especially true of shows with three or four soundmen, and meals were the time to let off a little steam with friends and tell a few war stories.

Like the time when Barney Beck was working at CBS in New York on a script that called for a bee's buzzing. Well, not actually "buzzing . . . buzzing," more "talking . . . buzzing." For this effect, Barney decided to use a wooden mouthpiece attached to a flat rubber tubing, a device commonly referred to as a Bronx Cheer or the razzberry effect.

By carefully blowing into the mouthpiece, you could produce a very acceptable bee buzz. Blowing too hard got you the Bronx Cheer, or even worse, a very rude flatulent sound. This was not an effect to be fooled around with by apprentices. However, it was the only effect most directors would accept for a busy bee.

When a particular effect was asked for at the last minute, the soundman had to dash out of the studio, get on the elevator, go into the sound-effects room, rummage for the right effect (with luck, it was available), and get back to the studio as quickly as possible.

On that day, Van Voorhees, the head of sound effects, had assembled all the artists in the sound-effects department who weren't working on shows and was giving them one of his patented lectures on the do's and don'ts of acceptable behavior with directors. In those days, there were three work infractions that could get you fired from CBS: drunkenness, thievery, and insubordination. Having covered drunkenness and thievery the month before, Voorhees focused this particular talk on insubordination.

For openers, he referred to the assembled group as "uppity" and "undisciplined." (Later, as a vice president, he would upgrade us to "prima donnas.") As Voorhees continued his tirade about our lack of decorum and proper respect for authority, Barney Beck flew in to get his bee effect. Out of breath, in a hurry, and unaware that Voorhees was addressing his fellow members of the department in the next room, Beck began rummaging around for the bee effect.

Talk about timing! Just as Beck found the right bee effect, Voorhees got to the part where he wanted an answer *now!* Beck, in perfect innocence, chose that precise moment to test the bee effect. Only, he blew it a trifle too hard. So as Voorhees repeated his question, "Well, what's your answer?" Barney, to howls of delight from the assembled artists, gave the future vice president a long and juicy razzberry.

As Barney hurried through the room, he waved the bee effect in the air and called over to Voorhees, "Sorry, Van. That was just a test, not my personal opinion!"

Yes, it was more than the cheddar cheese soup that made ColBeeS so popular. It was a safe and warm haven from the sometimes stormy world of a business that didn't tolerate mistakes.

CHAPTER III

SOME GOOD NEWS
AND BAD NEWS

ONE AREA WHERE PRANKS didn't exist during the days of live radio was on a network news show. Even though the network's termination policy dealt mostly with insubordination, thievery, and drunkenness, I'm sure they'd have made an exception if they caught someone putting a whoopee cushion under Lowell Thomas.

Radio news was a serious and profitable business. And yet, two of the giants among newscasters—Lowell Thomas, and Edward R. Murrow—each possessed a wonderful sense of humor. In fact, Lowell Thomas' producer lived in dread that something in the news would strike Lowell as funny because if it did, Lowell found it difficult, and sometimes impossible, not to break up. And when Lowell broke up, it wasn't over in a moment. Two pages later into the news, he would think about what had struck him funny and he'd be off again. It didn't happen often, but when it did, watch out.

On one occasion, Lowell was given a little "filler" (a short news story to fill time) about the death of Dolly, a former circus performer. So far, not very funny. But Dolly had been the fat lady in a circus, and at the time of her demise, it seems she hadn't been on a diet. As a result, there wasn't a hearse in town big enough to accommodate her.

In desperation, one enterprising funeral parlor operator borrowed his brother-in-law's one-ton pick-up truck, and Dolly was thus carried off to her final resting place.

At this point, something tickled Lowell's imagination and he began a low chuckle. But he quickly controlled it and went on with the news. Two paragraphs later, the chuckle came back, and this time, although he managed to control the chuckle, he couldn't stop an irreverent giggle. And the harder he tried, the worse it got.

As rare as these occasions were, the producer had a firm rule that when Lowell did break up, no one was to encourage him by joining in the laughter. As a result, the audio engineer ducked under the sound console, the announcer turned his back, and the sound-effects artist knelt behind his record console. When Lowell saw everyone (except the stern-faced producer) going into hiding, it only made him worse. The producer, trying to save the day, signaled for the announcer to give the lead-in for an early commercial. The announcer, however, was obeying the producer's rule of not letting Lowell see him laugh, so he had his back to Lowell and didn't see the producer frantically waving his arms. In fact, the only one to see it was Lowell, and it only made the situation seem more ludicrous to him. The only thing that saved the show that fateful evening was that, mercifully, it ran out of time.

Another short news piece that tickled Thomas was, curiously enough, again about circus people. This time it involved the mother of eight children who made her living as a bareback rider. Later in the news story it was explained that, in the jargon of the circus, this meant that she made her living riding saddleless horses. But by then it was too late. Thomas was already giggling to the point that the director had to signal for the standby organist to play some music until the staid and erudite Lowell Thomas could continue.

Such seemingly gross acts of unprofessionalism on the part of Thomas were not entirely his fault. Most newscasters, even today, like to add either a humorous or a human interest story to brighten up their newscast, especially if the news that night was particularly depressing. These stories, as well as short fillers, were usually dug up by the producer, which allowed the newsman—in this case Lowell Thomas—to concentrate on the more serious aspects, that of gathering and analyzing the news that made headlines. Often, because of the seriousness of some late-breaking news bulletin, the newsman didn't have time to read some of these cheerful little news fillers ahead of time. As a result their reaction was automatic.

To his credit, I should mention that in 1929, Lowell Thomas went on the air with Floyd Gibbons in a program titled "Headline Hunters," and after more than 2,000 newscasts, these are the only two stories I came across in which Thomas completely broke up during a newscast.

Sound effects on these news shows were restricted to the various shows' signatures. On Lowell Thomas' show, it consisted of several recordings of Morse code dots and dashes. When the announcer opened the show, he would read off the list of cities mentioned in the stories Lowell would be talking about. After each city, a different cut of code sounds would be played. For years, many people thought this signature held some sort of clandestine meaning. It didn't.

The signature for Edward R. Murrow's show was less controversial. All

it involved was a metronome to tick in synchronization with the words of
Bob Dixon, the announcer. The show was sponsored by the Amoco Oil
Company, so it should come as no surprise that those opening letters were
A–M–O–C–O. The only trick to using the metronome was being sure it
stopped ticking after the last "O." One time, after a Christmas party, the
soundman dutifully stopped the pendulum in time, but in doing so, knocked
the metronome off the table onto the floor in front of the microphone.
Murrow, accustomed to doing live shows during the wartime bombings in
London, continued on with his newscast without ever missing a beat.

Edward R. Murrow was the type of man who commanded your attention by doing nothing more attention-getting than walking into a studio.
He was handsome, well-dressed, and extremely self-assured. Ten minutes
before air-time, he'd enter the studio with his collar open and without a
jacket. He'd give everyone a warm smile and greeting, put his script in front
of the mike, rock back in his chair, light a cigarette, and ask anyone if
they'd heard a good joke or funny story. I was tempted to tell him the one
about Lowell Thomas and the bareback rider, but decided not to.

When Ed didn't get a story from us, he invariably had one of his own.
For instance, consider this true story: while covering the air raids in London, Murrow headed up a small team of CBS reporters. Inasmuch as the
reporters had all been hand-picked by Murrow himself, there was a great
deal of camaraderie among the men. Each respected the others' work, so
everyone was pretty much on his own. The only requirement CBS made
of the group was that in order to get reimbursed for their expenses, they
had to fill out an expense sheet. This presented no problem until one reporter, on assignment in a northern coastal village, sent in an expense ac-
count for the month of January that listed, among other things, this cryptic expense notation:

Booze for January $200.00

Even Murrow, who was accustomed to approving all sorts of out-
landish creative expense demands, felt a liquor bill that came close to
matching your weekly pay was stretching it a bit. He therefore wrote the
reporter, telling him that in the future, he'd have to be more specific if he
wanted Murrow to approve such a large expenditure. The next month,
this came in the mail:

Booze for February . . . . $200.00 . . . . JeeeezCrist it's cold up here!

Ed paid it.

With the proliferation of sports on radio and television today, a baseball game would hardly be considered in the category of news. And yet for the 1921 World Series between the New York Yankees and the New York Giants, that's exactly what it was.

In that year, Sandy Hunt, a sportswriter for a local newspaper, suggested to Tommy Cowan, a radio announcer for WJZ in Newark, N. J., that the station broadcast the game. Desperate for new programming material, Cowan jumped on the idea.

Unfortunately, technical problems made it impossible for Cowan's coverage of the game to be transmitted to the listening audience at home. As a result, it was decided that Hunt should go to the game and represent both his newspaper and the station. He did this by talking to Cowan over a phone and Cowan would then broadcast his interpretation of Hunt's remarks to his listeners.

Not only was this crude sportscast successful, small stations throughout the country were quick to imitate this inexpensive idea. But instead of talking over a telephone to someone at the game, they "listened" to a reenactment over their teletypes.

Realizing there was nothing exciting about an announcer parroting what he hears over a teletype while the machine clacked away in the background, a few enterprising stations decided to flesh out these game reenactments by adding the sound effects of crowd noises between the action—crowds cheering for hits, crowds cheering wildly for home runs, even the voice of a hot dog vendor shouting out, "Get your red hots here!"

One of the most important of all these added sounds was that of the bat hitting the ball. Because this was such an extemporaneous show, the timing of the bat cracks was dictated by the play-by-play announcer who did his own bat-crack sounds by hitting a wood block with a drumstick.

One commentator, however, wanted a more authentic sound of a bat crack, and he gave the job back to the sound-effects artists, in this case, Barney Beck. So in addition to doing all the raising and lowering of the crowd reactions and cheers with one hand, Barney also had to hold and strike a baseball bat with a large wooden mallet. And in order for the bat to have the proper-sounding "crack" (as in "crack of the bat"), Barney had to grip the bat tightly between his thighs.

The commentator would give the cue for these bat hits by a quick and decisive nod of his head. Barney would then strike the bat and produce an appropriate crowd cheer: A short one for singles and a long one for homers.

Everything progressed well through the bottom of the ninth. At that time, with two outs and the bases loaded, Joe DiMaggio of the New York Yankees hit a grand-slam home run. Barney, a Yankee fan, gave the large wooden hammer a mighty swing. Unfortunately, his aim was slightly off. Instead of giving the bat a resounding hit, he gave what was above it a re-sounding hit. The pain shot up from the groin area and suddenly the listeners at home heard a sharp increase in the sound of the crowd cheer-ing. Little did they know that the hysterical level of the cheers was not en-tirely for Joe DiMaggio. Most of it was to cover the howl of pain from the agonizing Barney Beck.

The next day, while waiting for Barney to regain his confidence in his aim, the commentator went back to the less lethal drumstick and wood block.

Some of the most enduring shows on radio were the dramatizations of the news made even more exciting with sound effects. One such show, the popular "You Are There," used modern news-coverage techniques to cover historical events. When Napoleon was defeated at Waterloo, such CBS correspondents as Don Hollenbeck did interviews and gave an "eye witness" report from the scene of the battle.

This innovative news show went on the air in 1947, nine years after Wells' *War of the Worlds*. And although it used a format that seemingly in-volved live newscasts, "You Are There" wisely covered events that already *had* happened, not events that *could* happen.

The pioneer in this format of dramatizing the news was, "The March of Time" (1931–1945). This show featured current events, complete with sound effects. However, because the program made no attempt to hide the fact that it was a news dramatization, it was not considered deceptive. In fact, according to Keene Crockett, who did sound effects on the show from 1943 to 1946, the producers were adamant about sound-effect authenticity. During World War II, this most certainly included airplanes, and if the script called for a dogfight between a Spitfire and a Messerschmitt 109, you'd jolly well better use the recordings of a Spitfire and a Messerschmitt 109! And so, even though it was before the availability of audiotape and recording sounds outside the studio was extremely difficult, sound-effects artists in those early days made every effort to get the most authentic sounds possible.

Figure 3.1, for example, shows Michael Eisenmenger (NBC, Chicago) recording authentic sounds during an Army Battle Exhibition at Soldier Field in Chicago in 1943. And in Figure 3.2, Tom Horan (NBC, Chicago) is seen recording a halftrack truck, also at Soldier Field.

Prior to audiotape and portable equipment, you were limited to what you could record by how far your microphone cable allowed you to move

Figure 3.1. Michael Eisenmenger recording combat sounds. Photo courtesy of Robert J. Graham.

from your recording equipment. Sydney Bean (CBS, New York) is shown in Figure 3.3 using an old Fairchild record cutter. If the artist wanted to record a sound, this was what was used. Although they got the job done, they were about as portable as a bathtub.

Because of the difficulty in obtaining authentic sounds, the artists prided themselves on being able to somehow come up with a reasonable facsimile. This satisfied most shows, but the producers of "The March of Time" insisted on realism whenever possible, and not just for the listeners' sake. They also felt that authentic sounds made the actors more keenly aware that they were dramatizing actual news stories.

This reluctance on the part of radio to deceive the listening public by using contrived sound effects on the news probably stemmed from the notoriety earned by the *War of the Worlds* broadcast.

It did not stop the television news people, however. One of the bread-and-butter sound effects in television was "sweetening"—adding sounds to (presumably) make something better. This was (almost) never done to deceive the viewing public, but simply to give the news a more professional

Figure 3.2. Tom Horan recording army truck sounds. Photo courtesy of Robert J. Graham.

and realistic sound. And usually it was necessary. Unedited news films would come in at the last minute, sometimes when we were actually on the air, and they had to be edited quickly to fit a certain time period. However, the mechanics of sound film is such that by editing these films to make sense pictorially, the sound portion of the film suffered. For example, a film clip of an airline jet taking off smoothly might be edited so that only a portion of the takeoff remained. This meant that the sound portion of the takeoff would sound terrible. To correct this, the director would only show

Figure 3.3. Sidney Bean (CBS, New York) with a Fairchild record cutter. Photo by author.

the picture portion of the film and let sound effects do the jet sounds appropriate to the picture being shown.

The news department always tried to schedule ample time for the soundman to view the various films and select the proper effects, but it rarely worked out that way. It seems that all our rehearsal time was spent waiting for some motorcycle courier to come in from La Guardia Airport with that up-to-the-second-late-breaking-news story. Often we were asked to supply sounds for films we never had a chance to see until we were actually on the air. This worked out fine as long as the soundman was a firm believer that less was more. If the film was a fire story, we knew we could use two particular records without getting into any trouble. One was the sound of fire-engine sirens and the other, curiously enough, was that of an African waterfall.

The use of the siren record should be obvious, but it was the Mogambi Waterfalls record that saved our lives. Depending on the speed we set it at or the amount of high or low frequencies we put into it, this record had the ability to become just about any sound we needed in a hurry. At an extremely slow speed with plenty of bass, I succeeded in using the Mogambi Waterfalls to create the low rumble of an earthquake. I also used it for a jet plane (fast speed and a lot of treble), a steam engine chugging out of Grand Central Station, rifle shots . . . the list goes on and on. One time

I even used the Mogambi Waterfalls for the sound of a waterfall and the director hated it!

The Mogambi Waterfalls' ultimate test came when it was asked to help out during the Korean War. Al Binnie, Frank Mellow, and I were scheduled to do a Korean War documentary. After viewing the film at a studio in Grand Central Station, we learned why three of us were scheduled to do the show. This documentary wasn't just a film about one aspect of the war, it was a film of the *entire* Korean War. And most of the film was shot silent and needed hundreds of different sounds.

After selecting as many records as we could from our studio's sound-effects library in Grand Central Station, we went down to 43rd Street and Park Avenue to get a cab up to Liederkrantz Hall at 58th Street and Park Avenue, where we were to rehearse the show. As we stood on the corner, each of us weighted down with every conceivable war noise, we started discussing the film we had just seen. And the more we discussed it, the more obvious it became that perhaps one small drink from one of the bars that dotted Third Avenue would be appropriate.

Later, as we wended our way up the avenue feeling somewhat better, we discovered that there were certain aspects of this film that we hadn't fully discussed. Inasmuch as we were due to air this show live in a matter of hours, we decided to hold another serious strategy conference over a glass or two in the Blarney Stone.

When we finally arrived at Liederkrantz Hall, we discovered that somehow, during one of our numerous war councils, a goodly number of our records had gone missing. Specifically, we didn't have any tanks, howitzers, and large explosion records. To make matters worse, it was Sunday and none of the equipment people worked after five o'clock, so there was nobody to bring us replacement records. And none of us could go because our only rehearsal was about to start. A fine war this was going to be without large explosions, tanks, and howitzers! We hurriedly decided that we would let the viewers' imaginations help us out. Instead of trying to match a sound effect for everything that was shown in the film, we agreed we'd only do sounds for the most obvious things and let the audience's imagine they heard the rest.

For the scene of a platoon of Marines trudging wearily through the snow, for instance, we only put in the sound of some wind and "presence." "Presence" is what you hear when you put your ear to a seashell or cup your hands over your ears. It isn't the sound of anything distinguishable and yet, unlike silent film where there is absolutely no sound at all, presence gives the listener a feeling that something is going on.

Although this technique was working well for us, we were all happy when a clip of film came up that had actual war sounds on it. The clip was a rare piece of film showing a squad of Marines engaged in a close-quarter battle with some North Koreans. As the combatants moved stealthily through the field, an occasional rifle shot could be heard. Suddenly, one of the North Korean soldiers straightened up from the tall grass, grabbed at his blood-smeared face, and fell to the ground. It was a remarkable piece of footage, available because some cameraperson had infiltrated the enemy lines to film such a dramatic and stark view of the horrors of war.

But the director had been brought up watching John Wayne war movies and felt that the scene "needed some pizzazz!" Instead of leaving the actual sound on the film alone, he insisted on machine-gun fire in the background and, of course, explosions, BIG explosions. After giving him what he wanted, his comment was, "Now that's more like it! When I see a war, I want it to *sound* like a war!" It may come as a surprise to that director that his "real" war was, for the most part, an obscure African waterfall.

Sound effects added to the news were pretty much left to the discretion of the individual sound-effects artist's taste and ability, based on the amount of time available. Obviously this was not the job for a perfectionist. Since late-breaking news film very often arrived at the studio while the show was on the air, rehearsals were out of the question. Furthermore, a director's vague information that the next story involved a fire, accident, police shoot-out, track meet at Madison Garden, or whatever could wind up with embarrassing results. I remember the time I produced a huge cheer for a New York Giants' touchdown only to learn they were playing at their arch-rival's stadium in Philadelphia, and the number of Giants fans actually at the game probably wouldn't have filled a bus.

These were just a few of the drawbacks of doing the news, satisfying the tastes of the various directors about the amount of sound needed to heighten the dramatic impact of edited or silent film clips without arousing the viewers' suspicions of editorial hanky panky.

Experienced sound-effects artists assigned to do the news made it a strict rule never to try to do too much. They knew that the most basic sounds, even just something to cover the silence, were often sufficient when accompanied by a picture. Every once in a while, however, vacations or illnesses meant that the scheduling department had to schedule someone without this valued experience.

Jim Rogan was one of the top artists at CBS in New York. His credits included every major radio show at the network. In fact, Jim had supplied the sounds for radio's successful news show, "You Are There."

Despite these accomplishments, Jim was new to the world of adding sounds to the news with little or no rehearsal—especially at 5:30 A.M. on the "CBS Early Morning News" hosted by a young Mike Wallace.

The film that morning was about the Korean War. The footage showed some half-frozen Marines returning from a battle, trudging slowly through ankle-deep snow. Ignoring, or perhaps unaware of, the rule about "when in doubt, do without," Jim put in wind sounds and then decided to add some recorded sound of marching feet.

The record Jim selected was produced by Major Records. It was an excellent record and in addition to the marching sounds, the second cut was that of continuous machine-gun firing. This was common practice with record companies in those days. On one side of a recording they might put as many as a dozen cuts of different sounds. If you didn't pay attention to what you were doing, you might have the sound of applause during a thunderstorm. Jim, however, wasn't that lucky. When the film came up on the air, CBS home viewers were treated to the unusual sight of the exhausted Marines marching unscathed and oblivious to a far different drummer . . . the loud staccato of a machine gun!

To make matters even worse, the sound effects added by the artist were never heard in the studio by the news commentator. Therefore, when the film and sound effects were quickly stopped and the camera cut back to Wallace, his comment, "Quite a tragic story," took on a meaning all its own.

The selection of sounds that the record companies decided should go on the same record sometimes boggled the mind. For instance, record #114 from Speedy Q offered these exotic choices: Side A cut 1: applause, cut 2: cheers, cut 3: boos; Side B cut 1: Model T Ford crank start, cut 2: motor sputters and dies, cut 3: flat tire, cut 4: collie barking, cut 5: cat lapping milk.

With such an unusual combination of sounds, you can see how, in the excitement of doing a busy show, it would be possible to make a little mistake. Admittedly, a company of Marines who are somehow impervious to a .30-caliber machine gun doesn't classify as a little mistake.

This wouldn't have been so complicated if we had had just that one record to worry about. But normally, on a busy news show, we had three or more records going at once, as Figure 3.4 shows.

Even when audiotape was common on many television shows, most artists still used records on the news shows, because of the time element involved. From the moment the soundman finished looking at the various silent or edited news clips to the time the show went on the air was often only a matter of minutes. This meant that the artists had to know immediately where more than 7,000 different sounds were on over 1,500

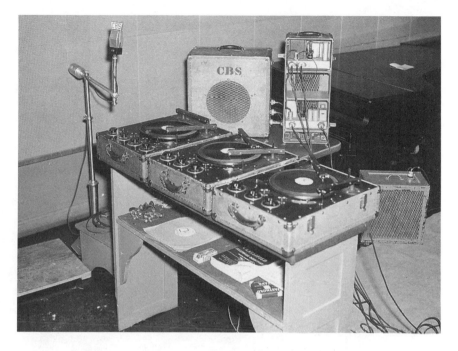

Figure 3.4. Three records cued up on portable turntables. Photo courtesy of Malachy Wienges.

different records. Figure 3.5 gives some indication of how detailed the sound files had to be.

The policy of adding sound effects to the news was common at various networks for years, but at CBS, it all came to an end on the night known forever after as "The Big Splash." Here's how it happened.

One of the problems with doing sound effects on Walter Cronkite's "CBS Evening News" at 7:00 P.M. was that it also required doing the late news at 11:00 P.M. This meant almost three hours of free time (or, perhaps, three hours of boredom).

On a dramatic show, a good portion of those three hours were spent correcting anything that might have gone wrong with the first show. On comedy shows, the time was spent rewriting or polishing those jokes that didn't get a good laugh from the earlier audience. All this, plus hurried rehearsals and even quicker meals, made the three hours pass very quickly.

Doing the news shows on television was different. Since there were no changes to make or rehearsals to attend, the sound-effects artist was pretty much on his or her own. Which was fine for those who lived in the city. They could go home, spend time with the family, have a leisurely dinner,

Figure 3.5. A sampling of recorded sounds. Photo courtesy of Robert J. Graham.

and be back in plenty of time to view the film and sort out the effects needed that night on the show. The problem was, almost no one in sound effects lived in New York City, and besides, venturing too far from the studio could be a little frightening in New York traffic.

Probably the only way of getting around in New York City with any reasonable assurance of arriving on time is to walk. Unfortunately, everything in New York worth going to is either too far, or too dangerous, to walk to from the studios. As a result, artists didn't gamble on getting stuck in traffic in a car or a cab, or marooned underground on the subway. They stayed close to the studio. Even today, after all these years, whenever I have a nightmare, it's always the same—being late for a live show.

That was the problem soundman Ham O'Hara faced five nights a week doing the news. As a result, Ham (or any of his replacements) rarely if ever ventured farther away from the studio than the Slate.

The Slate was television's answer to radio's ColBeeS. It was a cozy little food and beverage establishment located across the street from the CBS television studios on 57th Street. Although the food was good, it was their accommodating way with beverages that drew in the show business folks. In a city and industry not known for its friendliness and hospitality, it was nice to have someone on your side.

On the fateful night of "The Big Splash," the featured story on the 11 o'clock news was a spectacular piece involving a man committing suicide by jumping off the George Washington Bridge. The film was shot by a tourist who just happened to be filming scenes of the bridge when he saw the man standing on the rail preparing to jump.

Everything about the film intensified the immediacy and stark candidness of that troubled man's last few moments. Even the obvious amateurism of the tourist's camera techniques added to the drama—the quality of the film, the lack of lighting, the angles, the lens selection, and of course, the lack of sound, until Ham, feeling the effect of inspiration, or fatigue, or boredom, or Slate camaraderie, decided to heighten the drama of the story.

That night, as aghast television viewers watched the man hurtling through air from the heights of the bridge, they saw the end come as he struck the Hudson River to the accompaniment of the excellently timed, if perhaps ill-advised, sound of a huge splash of water.

Now, to Gertrude Stein, a huge splash may be just a huge splash, but to Dick Salant, the president of CBS news, it was a tad more. Having been one of those aghast viewers watching the film clip, his actions were immediate and decisive.

Phoning the news producer in the studio, Salant proceeded to inform him that he, along with the rest of the CBS audience, appreciated the effort made by sound effects in striving to distract the viewers from the macabre ending by adding a touch of whimsy. He had just one small critique. If sound effects, by adding the splash, intended to lighten the moment of tragedy, why the hell didn't they make a real comedy out of it by following the victim down with a slide whistle!

If this story seems to indicate that O'Hara acted irresponsibly, that was not my intention. I merely wanted to show the hazards of doing a live show without a proper rehearsal. Perhaps what made that splash stand out so dramatically was the fact that the audio man in the control room had O'Hara's volume turned up too high. Whether it would have been an acceptable sound if the volume level of the splash was as O'Hara intended it to be, we'll never know. However, because of that incident, sound effects are no longer added to the news at CBS.

Today, sound effects are not only not added to the news anymore, they are rarely done live for any show. Everything is done by committee in a starship-type room lined with computers and called a post-production room. Here the sound effects are added after the show or film has been given its final edit. The sound effects are all neatly cataloged in computers and are stored on tape. The process of "laying in" (adding) sound effects is a long and arduous process of trial and error.

Laying in these sounds can take months on a high-budget taped show for television or a theatrical filmed presentation. On the live news, whether radio or television, there were no committees and what the audience at home heard usually took only a few frantic minutes to arrange. This was true even on the night that sound effects "sweetened" the atom bomb.

If that effect had to be created for a film, I can only guess at the length of time it would take. But that night on the "CBS Six O'Clock News," the entire effect was created between 5:30, when I viewed the film, and 5:59:30, when I stood ready to go on the air.

Sound effects got involved with "the bomb" because of the important tests that were taking place in Nevada, and although the filmed pictures of the detonation were clear and more than a little frightening, the sound was terrible. There was so much noise and hiss, the soundtrack was unusable, so enter sound effects.

How do you come up with the sound of something that no one has ever heard, especially a sound the magnitude of an atom bomb? There were no sounds in the library to compare with it and so the sound had to be created ... in a hurry.

The first thing the film of the atomic explosion showed was the unusual slowness of the mushroom cloud that lifted skyward after the detonation. This meant that all the dynamite explosions and earthquake rumbling had to be played at a slower speed. The problem with that was that by slowing the speed of the turntables, all the sounds were mushy — they had no impact. To offset that, an extremely versatile record was used for the impact of the atom bomb: not a recording of an explosion, but a constant roaring sound. By slowing its normal speed of 78 RPM down to 40 RPM and cutting off the sound from the pickup arm, the sound level of the record could be raised to its maximum without being sent over the air. Then, when the picture of the detonation occurred, the sound from this record could be suddenly reinstated to become the impact sound of the bomb. That initial explosion followed by all the other sounds mixed together.

As the assistant director alerted me to the fact that the feature news story of the bombing tests was due up next, he added, "and good luck with your atom bomb sounds . . . whatever the hell they are!" And that was just the point. No one had auditioned or even heard the sound I had come up with for the atom bomb, no committees . . . no one.

When the cue came on air, I watched his television monitor and when the picture showed the sudden billowing cloud, I played the records I had selected and crossed my fingers. Fortunately, the reaction in the control room to the bomb sounds was good. However, far more importantly, the printed media the next day didn't suspect that the sounds of the ominous and terrible Atom Bomb had been "sweetened."

Although recording equipment today is much more sophisticated, I wouldn't be surprised if the sound used for the bomb that night is now stored in a post-production department's sound computer's micro chip. But wouldn't they be amazed and perhaps a little embarrassed to learn that this now state-of-the-art atom bomb sound had for its impact a recording of our old friend from live television, the Mogambi Waterfalls.

CHAPTER IV

WHINNY LIKE A HORSE

CONTRARY TO BELIEF, the very first men and women of sound effects didn't make their homes on the East Coast or the West Coast or in Detroit or Chicago. They lived in caves. In order to survive, they learned very early the importance that sounds played. By imitating the sounds made by the animals they hunted, they learned to lure them close enough for their primitive weapons to be effective. Thus they proved conclusively that the art of doing sound effects preceded even the wheel and fire as the greatest boon to humankind.

Unfortunately, most, or perhaps even all, history books ignore this important fact. But Jack Benny knew. He had this to say. "One of the miracles of radio was its power to suggest anything by ingeniously using sound effects. With a few noises your imagination would paint the whole picture." These "few noises" most certainly included those that were created vocally.

A "vocal" is defined as anything done by manipulations of the vocal cords. Included in this group are whistles, snores, animal sounds, bird songs, baby cries, train whistles, bacon frying, explosions.... Actually, its impossible to list all the effects that can be done vocally—if an artist has the talent. That's a big if.

Today, most sound effects are created using computers and digital tape, with a limited amount done manually or vocally. But when Ora Nichols started the business of sound effects for radio, the lack of technical equipment forced her and those other early pioneers to create most of their sound effects either manually or vocally.

To satisfy this need, Ora scoured New York City in search of anything capable of producing sounds. First came the vast array of drummer's traps once used by her husband, Arthur, in the theater. After that, the effects came from everywhere imaginable—junk shops, attics, second hand stores, car wrecking yards ... she even foraged

72

Figure 4.1. An elevator door. Photo by author.

through other people's trash. Nothing was safe from her vigilant ear for sounds.

Soon the shelves of the CBS sound-effects department began to spill over with mechanic's tools, household items, children's toys, medical instruments, business machines, garden tools, luggage, motors, carpenter's tools, and just about anything else that was capable of making a sound.

Even a child's roller skates weren't safe from Ora and her staff. Roller skates were rarely used for the sound of skating, but they were invaluable for the sound of elevator doors opening and closing. (If you don't think the skate in Figure 4.1 is old, take a look at the price on the tip.)

Along the way, sound-effects pioneers discovered alternate, and sometimes easier, ways to produce a sound. The device shown in Figure 4.2, for example, was one of the more genteel ways for the artists in radio to make waves. Unlike the heavy, cumbersome bass drum used in Figure 1.4, this was a small metal cylinder containing BBs. The lightweight device could be tilted back and forth in front of a microphone with little effort and produced the same watery results as the bigger device.

These are two examples of manual effects. Other pictures in this book show many others: battery-powered doorbells and buzzers, train and boat whistles, dry and wet bird calls, duck and animal calls (remember the cave men?), blank pistols, wood and metal creaks, thumb crickets, tear cloths, temple blocks, fight bells, cuckoo whistles, gongs, brake drums, car

Figure 4.2. Making small waves. Photo by author.

horns, dolly sticks, razzberries, triangles, baker bells, tap bells, party horns, fire and police sirens, Chinese tom toms, sleigh bells, bosuns' whistles, horses' hooves, marching feet, thunder drums, chimes, wood blocks, police whistles, mouth sirens, wood and metal ratchets, turn bells, hammers, and twang boxes.

With radio constantly demanding more and more sound effects, storage space was becoming a serious consideration. As a result, effects that defied classification but produced a variety of imaginative sounds were becoming increasingly popular. What made the slatted metal device shown in Figure 4.5 so valuable was its versatility. For instance, if we wanted the effect of a guillotine lopping off the head of Queen Marie Antoinette on one show and the effect of footsteps on a metal fire escape for the next, this was the only effect we'd need.

Despite all of these hundreds of manual effects, Ora and her staff soon found out it was fairly easy to furnish the sound of a piece of wood being sawed by actually sawing a piece of wood, but what do you use for the sound of blood being boiled on "Lights Out"? See figures 4.6, 4.7, and 4.8.

Figure 4.6 shows Ed Bailey boiling up a batch of blood for a story on "Lights Out." This show demanded realism. As a result, Bailey, in 1938, came up with the most blood-like sound he could find: Coca-Cola syrup.

Although these two dissimilar effects shown in figures 4.7 and 4.8

Figure 4.3. Manual effects. 1. battery-operated telephone for rings, clicks, busy signals; 2. oscillator to produce various frequency tones for electronic effects; 3. variable fan for wind effects; 4. telegraph bug for "sending" Morse code; 5. electric door bells; 6. microphone; 7. bells and buzzer board; 8. small motor, especially good for an elevator effect; 9. hot plate for making radio's "hamburgers" (actually fried wet rags); 10. spark gap for electrical effects, particularly mad scientist's lab sounds; 11. rheostat speed controller; 12. 4-way utility box. Photo courtesy of Robert J. Graham.

appear to have nothing in common, they are both onomatopoeic, getting their name from the sound they produce. The object in Figure 4.7 is called a boing box, used primarily in comedy. It consists of a guitar G string attached to a turntable pickup head that is connected to a speaker. By plucking the string and squeezing the handle, we got a very comedic *booooooooiiiing* sound.

The effect shown in Figure 4.8 is called a slapstick. This was another item from vaudeville and burlesque. By snapping the two hinged pieces of wood together, we could get a very convincing whip-crack or slap. This effect was so popular with the comedians who engaged in violent physical humor that that style of comedy is still referred to as slapstick.

You might think that with all the advantages of digital tapes, these effects would long ago have been retired. And yet today, thanks to their distinctive sounds, these same old effects are still sitting side by side next

Figure 4.4. Manual effects. 1. door chimes; 2. door latch; 3. ship's bell; 4. glass scratch; 5. pulley hoist; 6. .22 caliber pistols; 7. lock and key effect; 8. nail pull; 9. wooden cups for horses' hooves; 10. gravel box; 11. & 12. plumbers plungers for horses' hooves or footsteps in water; 13. bit and bridle; 14. slap stick; 15. balloon sticks for crackling brush; 16. broom corn for footsteps in the woods or jungle. Photo courtesy of Robert J. Graham.

to state-of-the-art equipment on "Saturday Night Live" (see Figure 4.9) and "Days of Our Lives" (see Figure 4.10).

Even with the versatility of all these manual effects and an increasing number of sounds on records, some sounds—an irascible cat yowling, or a baby fussing and crying for instance—needed something more. The answer came from the throats of such talented vocal-effects artists as Mel Blanc, Brad Barker, Donald Bain, Madeline Pierce, Sarah Fussell, David Light, Ray Erlenborn, George O'Donnell, Ed Ludes, Earl Keen, Pinto Colvig, Gerry Hausner, Mary Lansing, and the dozens of other men and women who made up a very select group of radio performers.

Today there are dozens of electronic filtering devices that change the characteristics of the human voice. Back then, about the only help these artists had were such mundane props as megaphones, oatmeal cartons, pillows, empty milk bottles, or simply their cupped hands.

Sarah Fussell, for instance, was an accomplished actress who made a second career out of doing baby cries. She often worked on a show in

Figure 4.5. "Off with his head!" Photo courtesy of Malachy Wienges.

both capacities. We always knew when Sarah was going to do a baby cry because she used a pillow to help with the effect. In fact, she had a whole assortment of pillows, each size representing a baby at a different age. It got so that other actors knew how old the child was by the size of Sarah's pillow.

Until the middle 1930s, vocals were considered part of a sound-effects artist's job. Whether the script called for the artist to walk like a woman or whinny like a horse, it was all considered part of the job.

That all changed in 1936. That was when the people in sound effects became members of the actors' union, the American Federation of Radio Artists (AFRA). By becoming members of the union, it was agreed that the ability to do a vocal effect was a special talent apart from sound effects, so whenever a sound-effects artist was required to do a vocal effect, he or she had to be paid a separate acting fee.

Union membership also meant that *any* actor was allowed to do vocal sound effects. An actor in radio was allowed to do three voices for the price of one. He or she might have one major role and in addition play the part

Figure 4.6. Making someone's blood boil. Photo courtesy of Bob Jensen.

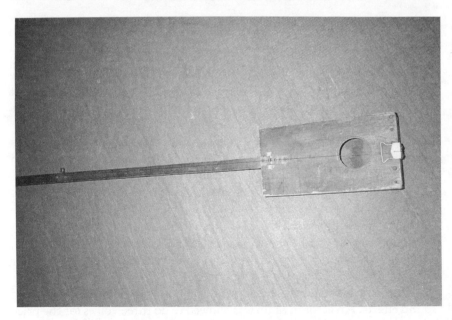

Figure 4.7. A boing box. Photo by author.

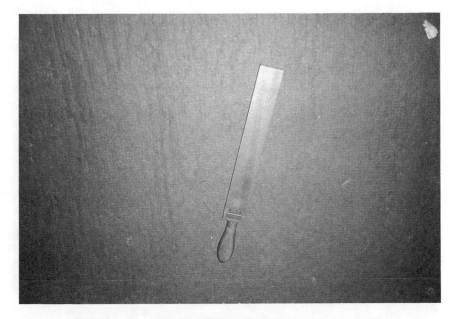

Figure 4.8. A slapstick. Photo by author.

Figure 4.9. Sound-effects props for "Saturday Night Live." Photo by author.

Figure 4.10. Coin drop prop for "Days of Our Lives." Photo by author.

of a cab driver and a salesperson. What determined whether an actor had an additional part was the number of words said. In most cases, these extra parts couldn't exceed five lines.

So suddenly the question was, which effects were sound effects (effects not done vocally) and which were vocal effects? For instance, is the sound of a person snoring a sound effect or a vocal? According to most directors, it was a sound effect. Until the director found out if the snoring sound wasn't on records he would have to pay the sound-effects artist a separate vocal check. At this point, the sound of snoring usually became one of some actor's three roles. Of course, if no one in the cast could snore, and if the director was working with a tight budget or just simply cheap, the character in the story suddenly became a sound sleeper.

To keep up with this increasing interest in sound effects, record companies began coming out with a more extensive selection of sounds and with vastly improved quality. This meant that more attention had to be paid to the sound system on which they were played. And that, as you might have guessed, introduced yet another problem.

As sound-effects record companies began furnishing a wider selection of sounds on records, many were sounds that, before, could only be done vocally. These sounds didn't require the payment of a separate fee. Although this seemed like the answer to a cost-conscious producer's prayers, it wasn't always. For instance, if the director simply wanted the sound of a kitten meowing in the background for her milk, a sound-effects artist played the recorded sound and it was fine—and free. But if the director wanted the sound of a kitten *imploring* her mistress for her milk, it had to be a vocal, and it would cost the director a fee.

For any show looking to save money, the choice might seem to be obvious. But it wasn't. The sounds on the records were fixed, whereas a vocalist could interweave the sounds smoothly with the dialogue. This is why "Mayor of the Town," starring Lionel Barrymore, had Dave Light (CBS, Hollywood) do the sound effects on the show and then paid him extra to do the vocal sounds of the cat and dog that were regulars on the show.

"Mayor of the Town" originated in Hollywood, the place where miraculous things are made to happen. Rin Tin Tin, an early Hollywood wonder dog, gained fame pulling little old ladies and orphans out of burning buildings, and yet never learned to bark on cue for radio. The same was true of Lassie. As many stand-ins as Lassie had for films, it was Earl Keen who came to her rescue when it came time to bark. All these animal impersonators provided a service the talented canine superstars couldn't do—learn lines.

Animals can learn to "speak" on command, but the sounds they make are hardly ever appropriate to what has been said to them. The same is true of recorded animal sounds. There may be a wonderful recording of a dog barking, but the bark is limited as to how it can be used. For instance, consider the following:

> SOUND: *Dog barking happily*
> MAN: Hi boy, glad to see me?
> SOUND: *More happy barks*
> MAN: Didn't you miss me at all?
> SOUND: *Happy barks turn to sad whine*
> MAN: Now come on, I haven't been gone *that* long ... besides, I brought you a little present.
> SOUND: *Whine switches to joyous barks.*

Obviously, doing this type of scene with records (or even tapes) would not only have been a nightmare, it would have sounded exactly like what it was, a man talking to a sound-effects recording of a dog barking. All the spontaneity and timing would have gone right out the window.

Even in films where sounds can be laid in to fit the movement of the mouth, vocal artists are often used to make the animals sound more natural.

In the film *Doctor Doolittle*, Ray Erlenborn made many of the animal sounds. The same was true of the early Tarzan movies. The next time a Tarzan movie turns up on television, listen carefully to the chimpanzee. More often than not, the squeals and screams are coming from the talented throat of Dave Light.

In order to do a chimpanzee, or any animal, successfully, the vocal-effects artist has to think like the animal and act like the animal. Simply making chimpanzee noises with the mouth would never be believable to an audience. Therefore, if acting like a monkey in front of people made the artist self-conscious, the sounds they made with their mouth were rarely convincing.

Doing vocals in radio was no problem as long as we were members of AFRA, the Actors' Union. Later, when we started to acquire more and more technical equipment, being represented by an artists' union made less and less sense. The technical unions, in an effort to become our bargaining agent, began filing grievances every time we plugged our equipment into the wall or changed the position of our microphones. Finally, it became impossible. It was therefore agreed by everyone that because of our increasing involvement with technical equipment, we belonged in the same union as the studio engineers.

This cleared up one problem, but it created another. Because we were now in an engineering union, we weren't allowed to do vocals unless we also belonged to AFRA. Although that was easily solved, the resentment among some of the actors wasn't. They felt that because we were employed by the network, we should leave the vocal work to actors. They didn't realize that the incidental animal sounds on many shows were written in on purpose so that the producers could legally pay their sound-effects artists a fee.

Despite the network's insistence that all sound-effects artists were created equal, producers with a show in the top-ratings, or a producer with a show they'd like to get in the top-ratings, knew better. They knew they had to pay extra to get the best actors, so paying extra to get the best sound effects artists wasn't any different, only sneakier.

Unlike the actors, the sound effects people were staff members of the networks. As such, we were paid a salary negotiated by our union and governed by our time with the company. The only way we could legally make additional money at the network was through overtime.

With this in mind, if you were doing an easy show that paid overtime and were suddenly assigned to do a very difficult show for considerably less money, you might be a little upset with the show making the request. It was therefore times like this that producers tried to make the show-change more appealing by paying a fee.

Unfortunately, the networks didn't see it that way, and any money changing hands between a director and an artist was cause for dismissal. Therefore, to make everyone happy, artists were given various vocals to do for a fee governed by AFRA rates. Some were animals and others were incidental voices, but they required a minimum of acting talent and so posed a threat to no one.

That was not the end of our union problems, however. Now, whenever we hit a gong or cymbal or beat an Indian tom tom, the musicians wanted us to join *their* union! But that's another story entirely.

Possessing the ability to sing beautifully in the privacy of the shower is one thing, but if anyone wants to land a recording contract and go on tour, they're going to have to sing equally as well in front of other people, sometimes millions of other people. The same was true of doing vocals in radio. However, if the artist didn't mind getting dressed up in a tuxedo or evening gown and having a large audience watch while he or she cavorted around the microphone whinnying like a horse (or a damn fool, as some artists perceived it), the hours and pay were excellent.

Two of the very best at this unusual art form were Brad Barker and Donald Bain. Of the two, Donald Bain was by far the nuttier. One time a director thought it would add a nice touch to a night scene to add an off-microphone buzz of a mosquito. Inasmuch as Bain was already on the show, the director saw no problem even though it was a last-minute request. When he mentioned it to the slightly eccentric genius, Bain looked at him thoughtfully and asked, "Is the mosquito male or female?" The director, busy giving last-minute notes to the cast, gave Bain a look of equal parts disbelief and annoyance. "Who cares, Donald? Just give me a mosquito buzz!" But Donald, not to be put off by the director's insensitivities, insisted it made a great difference in how he made the sound, especially if the mosquito was indeed a female. Under normal circumstances, the director would have accommodated Bain by listening to his repertoire of buzzes. But this wasn't one of those nights. Instead, he interrupted the vocal artist in mid-buzz. "Donald, you're a female mosquito. Buzz as sexy as you damn please! If we get letters, we get letters!"

Bain didn't restrict his slightly eccentric behavior to the studio. Very often he shared it with the nonprofessionals of the outside world, specifically with that horde of long-suffering New York City commuters known as subway riders.

Although this underground transit system has been much feared and maligned, it is by far the quickest way to travel if you have to go more than a few blocks in New York City, especially if it's raining, or for that matter even when it isn't. Morning, mid-morning, noon, afternoon, evening, or late night—traffic in New York is always bumper to bumper cars blowing their horns. The trip is bad enough just to go shopping, but when an artist is doing a live radio show and air time is only a matter of minutes away, it can shorten a life.

Bain selected the subway as his means of transportation for two reasons. One, it was an efficient means of transportation, and two, it was an opportunity to create a little mischief. First he would find a seat at the end of the car and slouch down behind an open newspaper. Later, as the train rattled along on its appointed rounds, the riders in Bain's car heard a sound that was totally unique in a subway—the mating call of an English wren. Heads would unbury themselves from the headlines and sport pages, sleepy eyes would open, all conversation would stop and the car would become uncommonly quiet—and so would Bain's little bird.

Not only would Bain's twitterings puzzle the normally blasé commuters, they would do something that is only too rare in the Big Apple. They'd inspire the passengers to smile and talk to their fellow passengers: "Am I goin' crazy or what? I thought I hoid a boidy choipin'."

Bain and Brad Barker both had great vocal mastery over animal sounds. They were also intense rivals in real life, and one director used to fantasize about using them both in a cat and dog fight that would end all cat and dog fights. Asked why he never did it, the director replied that the SPCA wouldn't allow it.

This intense competition between Barker and Bain was common knowledge in radio. Perhaps Keene Crockett said it best. During a rehearsal of "Dick Tracy," the director noticed that Keene was unusually quiet and morose. During a break he came over and asked him what was wrong. Keene looked up with anguished eyes and in halting words said, "Coming to the studio I just saw the most horrible thing imaginable." With this, the concerned cast began crowding around the visibly shaken Keene. "As I began crossing Sixth Avenue, who should come running down the street together but Brad Barker and Donald Bain." Looking confused, the director said, "I admit it's unusual for those two to be together, but why is it horrible?" "Because," moaned Keene, "Barker had Bain in his mouth!"

In addition to his subway habit, Donald Bain loved the food at the Horn and Hardart Automat. This was a famous New York City cafeteria that charged pennies—literally—for its food. Near the door there were attendants who would exchange currency for nickels, and do it without any mechanical device whatsoever. The attendant would dig his or her hand into a huge supply of coins and unerringly slide the correct change across the marble counter. Not a nickel over, not a nickel short!

The food itself lined the walls, behind small glass doors that displayed each selection and gave its price. When the correct amount in nickels was put into a slot, the door would lift up and the customer could take out a sandwich, pot pie, rice pudding, Jell-O, or whatever it was he or she had paid for. This restaurant ranked with the Empire State Building as one of the premier tourist attractions in New York. Not only that, but nowhere in the world could you beat their cherry pie for fifteen cents.

In addition to being a favorite tourist stop, it also had its local regulars. Many were people looking for a job and thankful for a place to sit down and search the want ads, all for the price of a nickel cup of coffee. As a result of this popularity, Horn and Hardart was always busy. Which is why Barker selected it for his little joke on Bain.

Most actors got their work-related calls through an answering service. Because so many jobs in radio came up at the last minute, actors spent most of their free time on the phone calling their services for messages. Wherever there was a phone, there was sure to be an actor lurking about.

On this particular day, Bain made his customary phone call from one of the public phones in Horn and Hardart and was given the number of a producer and told to call him immediately. The "producer" was actually Brad Barker.

The "producer" told Bain he was doing a new show and one of the featured roles was that of a cat with a multiple personality, so they needed someone who could do a whole range of cat sounds. Bain, anxious for the job, said he'd be glad to come to the producer's office and audition. Barker thanked him for his offer, but said there wasn't enough time. In fact, if Bain didn't mind, could he audition over the phone? If it was acceptable, he had the job. Without a moment's hesitation and with the wall phone as a microphone, Bain began doing his repertoire of cat meows.

Most New Yorkers feel that when you live in a city with nine million other inhabitants, there isn't too much you haven't seen. But on this day, in the Horn and Hardart Automat on 42nd Street, the New Yorkers who were present had to admit the city still had a few surprises up its sleeve.

As Bain began his Jekyll and Hyde transition, his free hand began clawing the air with a menacing fury while from his mouth erupted screeches, yowls, and every type of meow imaginable. It was a sight to behold while it lasted. Unfortunately, it only lasted until two New York cops, who had been having coffee in the back, could make their way through the crowd of diners now slowly backing away from the poor little man who thought he was a cat.

Questioned by the two policemen, Bain explained who he was and that he was auditioning for a radio producer, and to prove it, he handed one of them the phone. When the officer introduced himself, the voice on the other end responded smoothly, "Yes officer, how may I help you? I'm Doctor Harris, over here at Bellvue Psychiatric Hospital."

Although people like Brad Barker and Donald Bain did the lion's share of the work, many sound-effects artists were probably equally talented. The problem was, they couldn't have auditioned for a cat part over the phone in Horn and Hardart—even if their life depended on it.

To be honest, many soundmen could do a passable dog bark or baby cry but couldn't do a convincing horse whinny no matter where they did it. There were just a few who were versatile enough to make a career specializing in vocal sounds. Ed Ludes, for instance, was the voice of the penguin on all the Kool cigarette commercials ("Smoke Kooooooools"), and Ray Erlenborn once did a vocal of a washing machine going berserk on the "Red Skelton Show."

George O'Donnell (CBS, New York) was another artist with that rare ability for doing vocal effects, but because of his staid New England upbringing and dignified demeanor, he never fully pursued this God-given talent. Not that George couldn't screech like a baby, snarl like a dog, or trumpet like an elephant with the best of them, but his proper personality just wouldn't allow him. Doing these sounds required more from the artist than just talent. The artist had to *be* whatever vocal he or she was doing, and it just wasn't in George to go through all the body gyrations and facial contortions many of the sounds required.

One of the chief responsibilities that our brain has over our actions is to make sure that we do not look foolish. George took not-looking-foolish and elevated it into an art form. Unfortunately for George, his partner, Art Strand, didn't share George's highly developed sense of propriety.

George and Artie did a wonderfully imaginative children's show called "Let's Pretend," directed by Nila Mack. Hardly a week went by that Nila couldn't have used George's vocal talents, but George refused to get up in front of an audience and, in his own words, look like a "horses arse!" Nothing is forever however. On one particular show, the script called for a child actor to interact with a wise old owl. The child would deliver a line, and the owl would respond with a sympathetic *whoooo* or a knowing *whoooo* or any of a number of wise and understanding *whoooos*. Although we had owl sounds on records, none of these recorded birds had the emotional range of George. It was therefore agreed, after much beseeching on the part of Nila, that George would be the wise, old owl.

Artie, who was George's partner on the show, was an excellent soundman who, in addition to his talent for selecting imaginative effects, was considered by some as not quite crazy enough to be committed. This combination of George's ultra-conservatism and Artie's sometimes bizarre behavior acted as a balance, making the two an excellent team.

The one chink in George's otherwise proper double-breasted suit of armored decorum was the fact that he was extremely "goosey," a fact well known by Artie, and a soft spot he took joy in exploiting. Nila was not blind to either of her two soundmen's weaknesses, so she took Artie aside and issued him a stern warning: This show meant a great deal to her because of the breakthrough in getting George to do a vocal, and she didn't want anyone ruffling her star owl's tail feathers. Had she made her meaning clear?

All through rehearsals, George was outstanding and Artie was on his best behavior. On air, as the show was drawing to a close, the script called for the owl to give three final hoots of farewell. George bent over and leaned into the vocal mike, and the first two *whoooos* were dutifully done with intense and appropriate feeling. But as George cupped his hands to his mouth and bent over for the final, show-ending *whoooo*, Artie was unable to withstand the pressures of temptation and started backing surreptitiously towards George's weakness. And at the precise moment that George began his *Whoo...*, Artie struck with unerring accuracy. To Nila's horror, the wise old hooty owl's hoot suddenly jumped three octaves into a very un-owl like *whoooeeeeeeeeee!*

Today, vocal-effects artists are still a vital part of films and tapes. The difference is, if someone makes a mistake now, they do another take. Back in the live days of radio, your mistakes, whether you were goosey or not, were heard by listeners throughout this great land of ours.

CHAPTER V

THE DIRECTORS

IT WOULD BE NICE to give you the impression that everyone in live radio welcomed sound effects with open and loving arms, but it would be a lie. Some directors actually resented the need for sound effects and used them as sparingly as possible.

Earl McGill, a prominent director and author of *Radio Directing*, was quite outspoken on the subject when he wrote, "Sound effects are a great temptation to a director because they offer a fine chance to impose upon a radio production a literalness that mere words alone cannot achieve. For example, what a temptation there is to put footsteps into a radio play! If one were to believe radio producers, there isn't a house in the whole of the United States that can boast of having rugs or carpets on its floors. This is the most uncarpeted nation in the world. Board floors are mandatory not only in a mountaineer's shack in Tennessee, but in my ladies' boudoir on Park Avenue." So says Mr. McGill.

Although these views sound somewhat petulant, some new directors accepted them without question. In fact, whenever a director said, "No footsteps sound effects. The people in this story can all afford carpets" we knew two things about them: They were new and they had read Mr. McGill's book.

These directors who abhorred the deceptive and artificial use of sound effects saw nothing deceptive or artificial about a white male actor playing a black female or middle-aged women playing the parts of young boys.

Directors with different opinions about the footstep controversy were equally vocal. Asking these directors if they wanted footsteps on their show usually got this sarcastic response: "How else do they get across the room ... float!??"

My first bad experience with a director occurred while I was still attending New York University. Each Saturday afternoon, the students

88

from the various acting classes would do a live weekly broadcast over WGYN, a radio station owned and operated by the city.

All functions on the program except the directing and engineering jobs were performed by the students, including the sound effects. The trouble with this arrangement was that students who enroll in an acting class expect to act, not do sound effects.

For the first two years of the broadcasts, this was not a problem because an engineering student had volunteered to build some of the equipment and had stayed on to do the sound effects. But after his graduation, no one in acting looked upon the sound-effects vacancy as a step towards stardom. As a result, the director asked and then begged for volunteers without success.

Just when it looked like the NYU Playhouse would start the fall season without benefit of sound effects, the instructor heard me audition for an acting role. Even though we were separated by distance and the control room window, I heard him breathe a deep sigh of relief.

With the passage of time, I became more and more proficient at doing sound effects, and less and less skilled at acting. It was therefore by mutual consent that I dropped one of my acting courses and switched to a class that included sound effects.

Figure 5.1 shows the NYU radio studio. That's me standing behind a set of sound effect turntables that had once served as a credenza for bowls of waxed fruit. The two gentlemen to my left were also acting students. The one in the middle is obviously already proficient in the art of upstaging. Seeing that a picture was about to be taken, he grabbed the sound effect prop telephone leaving the two of us with nothing more exciting to do than to turn the pages of our scripts.

Al Schaffer's sound-effects class was part of the advanced radio-acting course. Because it counted for credits, students attended more out of obligation than interest. Except me. Once I began doing the sound effects for the Playhouse, I found that I genuinely liked the job. It also occurred to me that my chances of being able to eke out a living as an actor were exceedingly small. Therefore, when it came time to graduate and Schaffer offered me a job in his freelance sound-effects company, I jumped at the chance.

During the early days of radio, soundmen worked a 40-hour week. This meant that if you were on a show such as "Lineup," which started at 8 A.M. and didn't finish until 1 A.M., you would have already logged 17 hours towards your 40-hour week and once you reached the 40 hours, you were given the rest of the week off.

One result of this arrangement was that many artists had lucrative freelance accounts that paid more than their network salaries. Such was

the case with Barney Beck and his partner, Al Schaffer, two of station
WOR's top soundmen.

Figure 5.2 shows Schaffer (left) and Beck (right) at work. In addition
to being partners on "The Shadow" and "Bobby Benson's Adventures,"
they also had a busy freelance business. In their free time they often enter-
tained at Veterans' Hospitals and for shut-ins at convalescent homes.

Their problem was that, because they both had heavy schedules at
WOR, they often ran into conflicts with their freelance accounts.
Therefore, my job with them was to answer phones, set up equipment in
the different studios, and do effects on shows that weren't too busy.

One of their regular accounts was "Radio Free Europe." This series was
similar to "Voice of America." Each week a program dramatizing the evils
of communism was beamed to countries behind the Iron Curtain. These
countries included Hungary, Bulgaria, Romania, Yugoslavia, Poland, and
Czechoslovakia. Although the sound effects on these shows were fairly
simple, knowing when to do them, or for how long, was not.

As might be expected, the shows were written in the languages of the
various countries and used actors who were fluent in those languages. Inasmuch as neither Barney, Al, nor I understood the languages, nor did the
actors for those countries understand English, all of us were totally dependent on the directors for our cues. The problem was, sometimes, because
of illness or scheduling problems, the replacement director assigned to the
show didn't understand the language either. In that case, he received help
from a production secretary who understood the language but didn't know
what sound effects were.

On one particular show, the only sound effect I had was that of a manual typewriter. I was to supply the typing sound for a communist labor boss
who was dictating a letter to his secretary. On the actual show, the director, because of the language and sound effects mixup, didn't cue me to stop
typing. As a result, audiences behind the iron curtain heard the typing
sounds start out in the office, continue out in the hall, down the elevator,
into a taxi, and finally into the bedroom. Probably the first time that a man
and woman ever made love to the accompaniment of a typewriter.

The first weeks of my new job were spent trying to learn the WOR
record library and observing Barney and Al in action on shows. Inasmuch
as the WOR library held well over a thousand records and I had only
observed a few shows, my first assignment came sooner than any of us expected or wanted.

Schaffer and Beck worked together on a very profitable freelance show
called "So Proudly We Hail." One week, however, Schaffer had a last-
minute conflict with a show at WOR and I was to fill in for him on "So

Figure 5.1. Radio studio of New York University. Photo by author.

Proudly We Hail." To complicate matters, the director loved Schaffer's work and barely put up with Beck even being in the studio.

As soon as we got to the studio, we headed for the men's room where we made some last minute plans. We both agreed that whatever happened, Barney would do the talking. It was also decided that, for the benefit of the director, I was the one taking Schaffer's place although, in actuality, I would only be doing the effects that were most obvious to the director from his vantage point in the control room.

We went on into the studio and had just begun setting up our equipment when a voice over the intercom barked, "Where the hell is Schaffer?" It was obvious that no one had told the director about the last-minute substitution. This was not the way to start off a day. When Barney began explaining that Schaffer had a conflict and that I would be working the show, the director replied, "Not on my fucking show, you ain't!"

Despite my lack of experience, I sensed we were in trouble.

Barney, showing his experience, continued smiling toward where the voice was coming from and somehow managed a quick wink of reassurance to me at the same time. "Supposing he just does door knocks and phone rings?"

Figure 5.2. Al Schaffer and Barney Beck with actress Kit Barton. Photo courtesy of Barney Beck.

Again the voice boomed. "Listen to my lips, Barney. No you ain't!"

Barney, still trying to salvage something positive out of the ugly situation, asked pleasantly, "Mind if he just watches?"

"Barney, I'm not talking about him. I'm talking about *you!*"

Much of the director's lame humor was for the benefit of the cast, and yet there was no doubt in my mind that this director really did dislike Barney. Nevertheless, Barney was allowed to stay, but only because the director didn't know who I was.

Fortunately for all of us, the show wasn't that busy with sound effects. In addition, despite what this director thought he knew about sound effects, he could not know which sounds were the most difficult to execute. Therefore, even though I seemed to be doing most of the effects, Barney was doing the ones that required the most experience.

Despite our little deceit, the director managed to find something wrong with everything either one of us did. The thunder didn't crackle enough, the recording of rain sounded like a scratchy subway train, even the door knocks weren't right—either they were too timid or overly belligerent. His comment on the way Barney was opening and closing a desk drawer was, "The secretary is a girl, for Christ's sake, not King Kong!"

As I turned to see how Barney was taking this latest outburst of sarcasm, he managed a small smile and whispered out of the corner of his mouth, "Welcome to big time radio."

Somehow we got through the rehearsals and the air show. When it was all over, we knew we had done a good job because the director left without saying a word—something we hadn't been able to get out of him all day.

I worked with this director on a free-lance basis on several more occasions during the next two years. And whether it was with Barney or without Barney, it never got easier. But at least with experience came understanding. When I realized the pressures that directors were under, I attributed a lot of their emotional flare-ups to tight nerves strung tighter by too much black coffee and cigarettes and not enough rehearsal time. Getting acceptable performances out of a studio filled with individual temperaments, whether they were actors, musicians, or soundmen, was bad enough. Getting a show on and off the air on time could be almost as harmful to your health as the studio's black coffee and cigarettes.

And that tension led to some memorable events. Take, for instance, the case of Bill Robson. Bill was a highly respected director of such shows as "Big Town," "Man Behind the Gun," and "Escape." One time, while directing a scene, Robson realized that if he didn't pick up the pace, the show would be cut off the air before its conclusion. Making some quick cuts in an actor's speech, he cued the next actor to start speaking. Unfortunately, that actor was looking at his script and not at the director. Robson became so excited throwing cues for the actor to cut in that he broke his finger against the control room window!

As a footnote, what happened next is an indication of how much insecurity there was in live radio. As Robson grimaced in pain, the actors doing the scene were mystified about which of them was bad enough to cause Robson to make such painful faces!

In addition to the question of whether or not a director was pro or con footsteps, there were other idiosyncrasies we had to deal with. One time I had to replace Jack Amrhein on a "Philip Morris Playhouse" production of *Rain* starring Sylvia Sydney. Jack (see Figure 5.3) was one of the top soundmen at CBS. It therefore came as a surprise that the rehearsals were fairly simple. The script called for nothing more complicated than thunderclaps, rain, and some exterior jungle sounds. Why this show needed someone with Jack's capabilities was puzzling—but not for long.

All the rehearsals went fine (they always do, don't they?) until just prior to dress rehearsal. At that time the director came over and thanked me for not giving him my "whole bag of tricks" during the rehearsals so he'd been able to focus on the actors. When I asked him what he meant by a bag of tricks, he smiled nonchalantly and said, "You know, what Jack does."

This was a problem with many directors. They assumed that all sound-men thought and worked exactly alike. He felt that by telling me to do what "Jack does," he had answered all my questions. However, since I had never worked with Jack, all it did was create problems: Now, in addition to coming up with the effects that I felt the story needed, I had to keep reminding myself, "Is this the way *Jack* would do it?" And, of course, be-tween the way I would do it and the way Jack would do it came the direc-tor's way of doing it.

His first complaint was that my recorded rain didn't sound wet enough. I solved that by bringing in a portable sink and, by running water along with the recorded rain, achieved the necessary wetness to please the direc-tor. Then came the footsteps. There were steps on wood, steps up a squeaky set of stairs, steps on mud. Some were men's, some were women's, and some were even barefoot. And as an added touch, instead of using music the director decided that I should add appropriate sounds to accom-pany the clergyman's heart attack. Naturally, this too occurred outdoors in the rain and climaxed with the stricken man falling to the ground in thick, oozing mud.

After the dress rehearsal, the director told me he wanted the mud oozier for broadcast. Having run out of real mud, he finally settled for my adding hundreds of paper towels saturated with water, but he insisted I do the actual body fall in this sodden mess and make convulsive body sounds to match the heart-attack dialogue!

To this director, doing the recorded effect of a clap of thunder was no different than doing a body fall in mud. The fact that one sound required a great deal of preparation, had to be done physically, and required a live microphone whereas the other was on record had totally escaped his notice. To him, all sounds were the same. How you did them was of no concern to him. Just as long as you did them to his liking.

After the show, the director thanked me for my effort, and casually asked, "Oh, by the way, when does Jack get back?"

Perhaps the most difficult directors to deal with were those who looked upon sound effects as something you put on a scale and weighed. If they paid for a pound, they damn well expected to get a pound. Their idea of a busy sound-effects show was determined by the amount of sound effects they heard. Our idea of a busy show depended on where these sound effects occurred. For instance, doing the sound of typing on a typewriter and a series of angry door knocks hardly qualifies as difficult sounds, unless the director wants them to happen at the same time. Then they become

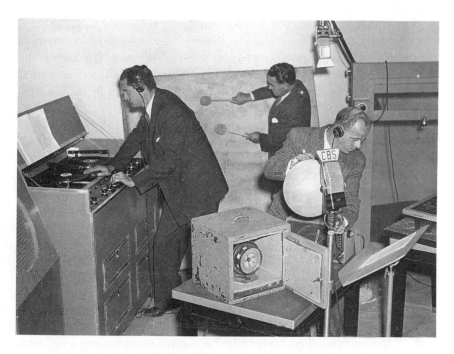

Figure 5.3. Bob Mautner, Jimmy Rinaldi, and Jack Amrhein. Photo courtesy of Walter Pierson.

very difficult. If you don't believe me, put down this book and pantomime typing continuously with one hand while knocking on the door with the other. Kind of makes tapping your head and rubbing your stomach a piece of cake.

Doing even just two effects can sometimes be extremely difficult if they happen simultaneously, and especially if they involve the use of hands or feet. Unfortunately, very few directors ever took the typing-knocking test, so they couldn't understand this. The complaint sounded like this: "You don't do a damn thing for the whole show and now you want a second man for one lousy page! You guys have some racket!"

And yet, despite how talented an artist might be, some scripts were impossible to do alone. Consider the team shown in Figure 5.3. While Jack Amrhein (CBS, New York) is in the foreground making explosive sounds with a balloon containing some BBs, James Rinaldi is in the center striking a thunder drum, and Bob Mautner is playing records. How could a lone soundman manage all that without the quality of the show suffering?

A soundman's nightmare was to work with a director who was a combination of the two types: In addition to adding last-minute effects, he wanted to see you busy on every page and wouldn't pay for a second man.

Jim Rogan was another of the top soundmen at CBS in New York. He and his partner, Ray Kremer, were responsible for the sounds on many of the network's leading shows, including Welles' "Mercury Theater on the Air." Robert Lewis Shayon, who directed "You Are There," requested Rogan for an episode about the famous horse stampede in Calgary, Canada. The script didn't read that busy so Rogan was working alone.

From the beginning, things did not go well. The fact that Jim was working alone didn't dampen Shayon's penchant for realism one bit. With each rehearsal he would add more effects.

In the beginning he just wanted a "few more horse whinnies," but as the day progressed, things started getting out of hand. The small stream mentioned in the script was now a turbulent river. Even Rogan's recording of a stampede of horses was unacceptable. According to Shayon, it lacked the "presence and immediacy of the hoofbeats done live." By the time Shayon got finished adding an effect here and an effect there, the show was busy enough for three soundmen. What made it even more difficult was that most of the effects happened during the same three-page sequence.

During dress rehearsal, Rogan tried valiantly to accomplish the director's impossible dream. Standing barefoot in a laundry tub of cold water with his trousers rolled up, he thrashed about trying to make his two bare feet sound like a turbulent river, all the while drumming coconut shells in dirt for the thundering herd of horses.

When dress rehearsal was over, the director was less than pleased with the sound effects. "This is supposed to be an exciting stampede of wild horses," the director complained angrily, "with herds of horses galloping over the plains and plunging into a flood-level river! Why the hell can't you make it sound that way?"

Jim, still knee-deep in the wash tub of water, answered in as patient a voice as he could muster, "Because up in Canada, they have real herds of horses and real rivers. All you have here is one soundman standing in a tub of cold water, knocking coconut shells together in fifty cents worth of New York City dirt!"

The one type of director in radio who defied all logic was the so-called visual director. These were the ones who had to see what effect you were using in order to know if they liked its sound.

Figure 5.4 shows the lengths to which some of them would go. There were probably dozens of effects that Walt Guftason could have used for the sound of $100,000 worth of jewelry. However, the director not only wanted to hear $100,000 worth of jewelry, he wanted to see it as well. As if it wasn't nerve-wracking enough doing a show live, Guftason had to have two Pinkerton guards looking over his shoulder the whole time!

Visual directors had another annoying habit. In addition to actually seeing the effect, they also wanted to see how it was used. For example, take the case of a body falling down some stairs. When there was a visual director involved, it often meant that the soundman actually had to fall down some stairs.

Portable stairs like those shown in Figure 5.5 were a staple item in sound effects, and they were fine for a variety of different effects. There were two big exceptions: using them for stairs (except on a comedy show), and falling down them (except on a comedy show). And if it was dangerous to fall down one flight of these portable stairs, it was nearly suicidal to fall down a stack of three of them.

But a three-flight fall was exactly what was called for one time on "Columbia Workshop." The show had made one of its infrequent visits to CBS in Hollywood to do an episode called *Man with a Gun*, written without dialogue and totally dependent on music and sound effects to tell the suspenseful story. The director was a visual type.

Because of the number of sound-effects cues, there were seven sound-effects artists assigned to the show. One of them, Ray Erlenborn, was elected to do the fall because of his experience doing pratfalls on comedy shows. Three portable staircases were stacked up to a height of over ten feet—two feet more than the height of an average ceiling. If Ray had been a stuntman in the movies, he would have been paid a bonus for doing a hazardous stunt.

The fall occurred at the end of the show, when the character gets shot and tumbles down a long flight of stairs to his death. After Ray rehearsed the fall for a sound check with the audio man, everyone was pleased with the way he did it except Al Span, one of the seven sound-effects artists on the show. Al thought Ray's method of coming down the stairs head first was too dangerous. The proper way, he explained, was to come down the stairs sitting on your butt. Ray disagreed, but Al was adamant. And to prove he was right, he proceeded to the top of the stairs and demonstrated the proper procedure. Everyone agreed that Al's method was more spectacular and even sounded better. But this was little solace to poor Al who had to be rushed to Hollywood Presbyterian Hospital with a fractured tail bone!

I found myself remembering Al Span's backside mishap one time when I was reading the script for *The Lost Weekend*, an episode on "Philip Morris Playhouse." I was the soundman, and the script called for the sound of a body tumbling down a flight of stairs, ending with a bottle breaking.

Despite the fact that we were doing radio, Charles Martin, the director, wasn't so much interested in how the fall sounded as he was in what

Figure 5.4. Walt Guftason making the sound of a $100,000 dollar bracelet. Photo courtesy of Mrs. Walter Guftason.

I looked like doing the fall. This meant falling down the portable stairs. I stood my ground (my stairs, really) and refused to work on anything higher than a single staircase unit. This was not, as I discovered, the easy way out. Falling down five stairs and trying to make them sound like three flights of stairs was one of the most difficult effects I ever did. After a fall like this, even though the director didn't rave about the stunt, sometimes not breaking your neck is applause enough.

Working for visual directors was never fun, but working for a visual director in front of a large audience was lunacy. In addition to pleasing the director with how an effect looked and sounded, you also had to keep the audience in mind. In a serious dramatic show such as *Lost Weekend*, doing that fall in a way that would cause even one person to laugh would have destroyed the entire mood of the show.

A studio audience was essential on a comedy show because of the support it gave to the comedians' timing. On a dramatic show, however, an audience could be trouble, especially if the script involved gunshots (or falling down the stairs). To avoid any noisy disturbances from the audience every show, both comedy and dramatic shows, had a warmup.

As the name implies, a warmup occurred just before the show went on the air and was used to familiarize the audience with what was expected of them. Very often, to make these warmups more interesting, the producers used sound effects.

Perhaps the most unlikely show to have an audience was "The Shadow." The show was done at the Longacre Theatre, at Broadway and 48th Street in New York. Included in the warmup were the soundmen, Barney Beck and Al Schaffer, and the announcer, André Baruch.

To make the audience more comfortable with the sound of the gunshots, Baruch would have Beck come out on stage and demonstrate what the audience could expect when they heard the sound of gunshots on the program that evening. He would then suggest that everyone in the audience put their fingers in their ears to muffle the loud noise.

Beck would then produce the .38-caliber pistol, hold it in the air, and pull the trigger. Instead of hearing the much-promised loud gunshot, the audience heard a soft click. The embarrassed Beck pulled the trigger again and again, the results were always the same.

Finally Baruch, removing the fingers from his ears, would call out, "We're on the air in 30 seconds, Barney. Can't you see what's wrong?"

Barney would then obediently look down the barrel of the gun, to the accompaniment of a very loud gunshot, provided by his partner, Schaffer, from offstage.

The real purpose of a warmup was to deliver a talk on the do's and don'ts of live radio, but a little nonsense was always welcome . . . even on "The Shadow."

The most famous of all visual directors was Orson Welles. It seems incredible that a man of Welles' accomplishments and experience in radio

Figure 5.5. The Lost Weekend *stairs. Photo courtesy of Malachy Wienges.*

would be so influenced by what he saw rather than by what he heard, but apparently that was the case. In 1938, on the strength of his strong showing on such diversified efforts as "The Shadow," and "The March of Time," CBS offered Welles a radio show of his own called "First Person Singular."

Recruiting the help of John Houseman, his theatrical partner, Welles' first episode was based on Bram Stoker's *Dracula*. The show was an immediate success. Over the next two months he followed up with radio versions of *The Count of Monte Cristo, Julius Caesar, A Tale of Two Cities, The 39 Steps, Abraham Lincoln* and *The Man Who Was Thursday*. The show became so successful that CBS continued it on into the fall season, up against Edgar Bergen and his witty little monocled friend, Charlie McCarthy.

When it was decided that the program should have a more prestigious title, Welles added the words "on the Air" to his already successful theatrical endeavor, Mercury Theater.

Between the theater and the radio show, Houseman and Welles were putting in a minimum of 20 hours a day. As a result, they added several people to help with the work load—at the princely salary of $50 a week. One was Howard Koch. Koch would soon make headlines with his script

Figure 5.6. A lawnmower for the New York Times. *Photo by author.*

adaptation of H. G. Wells' *War of the Worlds*, proving he had been worth the expense.

Despite the 100 percent effort Wells was giving his theatrical work, he managed to juggle the percentages so that he still had 100 percent left over for radio. As a result, Welles and radio got along just fine. Welles and sound effects was a different story.

In one of the shows he was doing for his radio series, a scene called for a man to cut his lawn, nothing too difficult. That sound effect was requested all the time. Figure 5.6 shows how the sound-effects department usually went about it.

We took a piece of equipment and stripped it down to its barest necessities because, unlike a visual director, a sound-effects artist wasn't concerned with appearances, only with how a thing sounded. As an added bonus, stripping a prop down to its sound conserved much-needed space on the sound-effect shelves and made the props more convenient to handle. But somehow the sight of a stripped-down lawnmower being fed shredded newspaper rather than its normal diet of grass was too much for the sensitivities of Orson Welles. He demanded, and got, half a studio covered with real grass, and a real lawnmower, pushed by real actors, doing the real mowing.

Although this touch of realism gave the studio a wonderful spring-like aroma of newly mowed grass, the results were disastrous. First of all, a prime-time show requires many rehearsals on a live mike using sound effects, and even Orson Welles didn't have it in his power to make a new lawn grow between rehearsals. The difference between the sound of a lawnmower cutting grass and a lawnmower just spinning its blades is unmistakable, even to a visual director.

So after hours of not hearing grass being cut and of watching the lawnmower get stuck between the sods of grass, Welles capitulated to the lowly and homely one-wheeled mower and the shredded remains of yesterday's *New York Times*.

Part of a visual director's problem was explained by author-director Earl McGill (of uncarpeted floors fame): "To a certain degree a microphone lacks discrimination. A dishpan falling on the floor and the same dishpan falling in a sink are one and the same dishpan making a clatter." The part about a microphone lacking discrimination is absolutely true. However, a dishpan falling on the floor only sounds the same as a dishpan falling in the sink if both surfaces are similar.

But such subtle distinctions were never the concern of visual directors. To them, a dishpan was a dishpan was a dishpan. How close an effect was done in reference to a microphone, what the surfaces were, what the ambiences were—all these made little difference.

The only time subtle shadings of sounds were not an issue was in comedy. In comedy, it didn't matter much where the dishpan clattered as long as audiences knew immediately that the clattering sound was indeed that of a dishpan. Which is why, to ensure at least getting a laugh from the studio audience, an experienced soundman would always use a bed pan because a bed pan is visually funnier. And as long as it was the clattering sound that was funny to the listener at home, why not use a prop that would get the biggest laugh from the studio audience?

We all thought that Welles had learned his lesson, but that was far from the case. Several weeks later he made another valiant effort to introduce realism to the sounds of radio. (I'm certain that Orson Welles demanded the same perfection of himself that he did of the world he lived in, which must have made the job of being Orson Welles one very tall order.)

This time Welles' critical eye focused on that very simple and yet functional effect that had been a standard in sound effects since its inception, the gravel box. In practice, these shallow, square trays often contained not gravel but dirt or even cornstarch. In this case, because we were working on a desert story, the box contained sand ... and Welles hated it. When Welles hated something, he didn't go to the corner and sulk. He let you know about it.

"I'll be damned if you're going to do the footsteps for my desert story in a box cats use to poop in!"

The soundmen, wishing to please, offered a compromise. They would spread a bag of playbox sand over a piece of canvas and use that to simulate the footsteps in the sand. Orson retorted that *he'd* use a hundred bags of sand and let the actors do their *own* footsteps in the sand. And so it came to pass that the sands of Coney Island were dumped on the floor of the "Mercury Theater on the Air" studio.

When Orson Welles did a desert story, he did a desert story!

"Of course, there were things wrong with this idea, and they became apparent almost immediately. First, there was the technical problem that actually walking on sand doesn't sound like walking on sand. It's one of the very few effects that—literally—must be seen to be heard. It's similar to walking on water. You have to see it to believe it.

Furthermore, if the audio man raised the level of the actors' mikes to hear the footsteps, their voices became deafening, and so did every cough, and chair scrape. Even the pages of the actors' scripts being turned were magnified to such a point of loud distraction that the show would sound terrible.

Therefore, one gravel box of sand, near a floor microphone, was worth a ton of sand spread over the length and breadth of a studio.

To Welles' credit, he realized he had made a mistake, and when the soundmen returned from their dinner break, the sand had been removed.

I keep referring to the effects artists of those days as men, and indeed most of them were. But there were also a few women who made a tremendous contribution to the art. The most notable was Ora Nichols. She and another pioneer, Henry Gauthierre, often did the sound effects on Welles' show.

Once, in a fit of anger during a dress rehearsal, Orson referred to Ora as a screwball. Henry saw the tears in Ora's eyes and, slamming his headset down, led Ora out of the studio and down to the ground-floor bar of ColBeeS.

Walking out on Orson Welles was unheard of. Not only were Orson Welles and John Houseman shocked, but so were the members of the cast, and even Fred, the bartender at ColBeeS. People did not challenge Orson Welles. And they most certainly didn't walk out on him just before a live broadcast.

After a series of phone calls to the sound-effects department demanding either their return or their replacement, Orson was told it would be impossible to replace them at that late date. This was sobering and humbling news at best, and as air time got closer, Orson agreed to apologize to Ora if they would both return.

As the two artists returned to the studio, Welles sidled over to Ora and whispered his apologies. Ora, a woman that took a great deal of pride in her profession, looked up at the young genius through her pince-nez glasses and this time the tears were replaced with fire.

"Mister Welles, I've always treated you with a great deal of respect and in return I expect the same. You insulted me loud enough for everyone in the studio to hear you and you're just going to have to apologize just as loud!"

Which he did. But whether he ever forgot the incident is something else again, because that Christmas, Ora received a holiday telegram that read:

Orin—you deserve everything that I'm wishing you—Orson Welles.

There is no way of knowing whether the misspelling of Ora's name was intentional or a Western Union error. What is known is that although Ora and Welles continued to work together, they could never be mistaken for the "Ethel's and Albert's" of live radio.

During rehearsals for a show entitled *The Bridge of San Luis Rey*, Welles spent hours with Bill Brown, an excellent sound-effects artist, getting just the right sound for the collapse of a primitive rope bridge that spanned a deep chasm.

In order to satisfy the authenticity of the sound, Bill accumulated dried vines, branches of wood, and even rattan laundry baskets. By walking on these assorted materials, Bill was able to produce a very realistic crunching and creaking sound. However, the most important sound effect for the show was the collapse of the bridge, sending hundreds of peasants hurtling to their death in the ravine below. For this effect, Bill cut wide strips of an automobile's inner tube. He then wrapped them with dried leaves, palm fronds, and vines. By stretching the inner tube and suddenly releasing it against the studio wall, the resounding "snap" was just what Welles wanted.

The sound of this effect was so important to the success of the show that Welles agreed to the expense of having the effect fed to an outside recording company and recorded on acetate. (Even during the live days of radio, networks had contracts with outside recording companies to record their programs in the event of plagiarism law suits. These recordings were referred to as air checks, and because they were not played frequently, they were put on records made of acetates. Acetates were a cheaper and more

convenient method of recording, but they lacked the durability of a conventional record.)

Although Welles was tough on sound-effects artists, he was equally
demanding of everyone else on the show, including the actors. To make
the bridge disaster scene even more realistic and horrifying, for example,
Welles wrote in terrified screams from all available cast members to show
the townspeople reacting to the tragedy.

One scream in particular was meant to show the listening audience
just how long this fall from the bridge to the canyon floor was. To do this,
Welles used the sound of one long, agonizing scream. The length of the it
was too much for one actor, so he used two. He had Everett Sloan start
the scream and continue it for as long as he could hold his breath at a
forceful level. Then Welles would cue the second actor, who would blend
the intensity of the first scream and trail it off into eerie silence. It was indeed a startling effect and the stuff that creative radio was made of.

On air that night, the cue came for the bridge to collapse, and Bill's
snapping effect, combined with vines creaking and a slight wind sound,
was even more realistic than in any of the rehearsals. Welles, standing tall
on his studio podium, then threw a decisive cue to Sloan to begin the long,
climactic, heart-stopping scream. What he got, however, was something
that first surprised, and then shocked, and then caused the blood to rush
from the face of the young genius. The second actor, in panic and thinking
that the cue to scream was for him, jumped the first actor's cue and did
the abbreviated second half of the scream first! Hearing his brilliantly or-
chestrated scream cut exactly in half, Welles leaped from his podium,
streaked across the studio, delivered the errant actor a quick and well-
directed kick in the behind, and got back to the podium in time to cue the
orchestra proving Orson Welles was not only an innovator and genius, but
also quick on his feet.

In addition to all of his many contributions to the theater, radio, and
films, Welles also possessed a somewhat bizarre sense of humor. One night,
he was doing a script that called upon his talents both to narrate and to
act the leading role in the story. That meant he was at the microphone
from the time the show went on the air until it went off. As the studio clock
clicked away the seconds to air time, Welles strode confidently up to the
microphone, gave the control room a small smile of acknowledgment,
and tripped on the microphone cable, sending his carefully edited and
marked script flying in the air. As the chests in the control room tightened,
actors and actresses scurried around on all fours trying to collect the pages.
There were cries of "I've got page 10 . . . I've got 12 . . . Who the hell has
page 11?" With that, the theme music began. And as the actors continued

to scramble about in silence retrieving pages, an unusually unruffled Welles reached in his jacket and produced a carefully marked script—the real one.

Although Welles' little practical joke may seem a little on the cruel side, it was quite mild compared to what another director, Dick Standwich, did to one of his cast members.

When the television soap "The Edge of Night" was on CBS and still live, Standwich decided to get even with an actor who was noted for his practical jokes.

Fifteen minutes before air time, Standwich found out that his show was going to be pre-empted for a late-breaking news story on the crisis in the Middle East. He confided this information only to his assistant director and told him to keep it a secret.

Now there was a rather well known fact about Standwich: he did like to partake in a toddy or two prior to air time, sometimes more.

The scene involving the actor was at the very opening of the show. The scene took place in a hospital room where the actor was confined to a bed with tubes coming out of every visible orifice.

As the show went through all the normal hectic preparations of going on the air live, Standwich appeared in the doorway of the actor's hospital room and gave the actor a rather unusual smile, unusual, that is, for a man to smile in just that special, musing manner at another man.

The actor, perhaps because of the maize of tubings and IV bottles he had to look through, failed to recognize this subtle danger signal. Instead, he shifted one of the larger tubes in his mouth and called over to Standwich with nervous impatience, "Hurry, Dick, if you have a note, give it quick!"

Dick, swaying slightly from side to side for the benefit of the actor, moved slowly towards the actor, who was now becoming increasingly alarmed by the rather unusual look on Standwich's face.

Arriving at the bed, Standwich gently picked up one of the actor's bandaged encased hands and whispered, "My note to you, you big lug, is that I love you!"

With that tender announcement by Standwich to the now alert and wide-eyed actor, the floor manager began calling out the seconds to air time. "Five-four-three-..."

As the horrified and speechless actor could only listen to his once-promising career tick away and make gagging sounds with his mouth, Standwich supplied the coup de gras. Leaping into the bed and throwing his arms around the cast embalmed neck of the cataplexied actor, Standwich waved his hand to the camera and shouted out in unbridled glee, "Look at us America ... wheeeee! We came out of the closet!"

By now, everyone in the studio was in on Standwich's subterfuge and the only one that didn't howl with delight was the actor. He was too busy chasing the suddenly sober Standwich. He would have caught him if his one leg wasn't in a full cast.

Incidentally, such sudden and mysterious illnesses that confined an actor to bed on the soaps were usually an indication that the actor's contract was being negotiated, which in turn meant that his illness could go either way. If he went along with the producer, he was miraculously cured from even the most incurable illnesses. If he insisted on more money, he died.

On one soap, a group of actors tired of this cavalier treatment decided to form a coalition for their contractual dealings. Convinced that there was safety in numbers, the disgruntled cast members made their demands to the producer. By way of response, the producer reminded the group of the script's upcoming town picnic.

"You all remember the terrible automobile accident we had last year? This year it could very well be a crowded bus!"

The actors quietly left the room and the coalition was dissolved.

Much of what I have written so far has shown the directors with the upper hand. This was true in most cases, but by no means in all.

Jack Keene (ABC, New York) is, to my knowledge, the only soundman who had a twin brother. Jack is shown in Figure 5.7 peering deeply into a young lady's eyes, or perhaps it was Jack's twin brother, Frank. Walt Guftason of Pinkerton fame (Figure 5.4) is at the right, calming her fears. Unfortunately, neither of the actresses in the photo are identified.

One night before a very busy show, Jack Keene came up with a gag that almost gave the director a nervous breakdown. Jack hid behind a triple turntable in the studio while his twin, Frank, stormed into the control room with a stack of old sound-effect records and demanded that some of the show's sounds be cut. The director, seeing his only soundman on the verge of hysteria, gave him that special smile reserved for drunks or the hopelessly insane.

He explained in as slow and well-modulated a voice as he could muster that it was only three minutes until air time and it was just a teensy too late to be talking cuts. But he'd be glad to loan the soundman a tranquilizer.

With that, "Jack" took two steps forward in a menacing fashion. "If you won't give the cuts, I'll just take them!" Then he began punctuating his sentences by smashing a record. "There goes the wind! 'KERSMASH!' There goes your thunder! 'KERBOOM!' There goes the rain! 'KERPOWY!' There goes the car starting! 'KERCHUNK!' And here goes your whole damn

Figure 5.7. Jack Keene and Walt Guftason with two gun shy friends. Photo courtesy of Mrs. Walter Guftason.

show!" And with that, Frank dumped the entire stack of records at the feet of the now-horrified director and stomped out of the control room. The director, pale and shaking, could only stare in speechless disbelief.

And with seconds to air time, the real Jack Keene rose up from behind the turntables and gave the director a friendly little smile and wave.

Needless to say, Jack and the director never worked together again. The good news, however, is that the director didn't have Jack fired.

Ray Erlenborn (CBS, Hollywood) had many accomplishments to his credit, but patience with a visual director wasn't one of them. Once, while he was working on "Dr. Christian," the director, made a last-minute request for the sound of checkers.

Of all the hundreds of sounds the CBS sound-effects department had on its shelves, in drawers, in boxes, checkers was not at that moment one of them. If time hadn't been a factor, Ray would have gone shopping. But it was early Sunday morning, and Ray felt his chances for success were not promising. He therefore did what all soundmen had to do in those days: he improvised.

Hurrying out into the hall, he made a quick inspection of the janitor's closet. Selecting the broom that looked the most used, he took it back to the shop and sawed off half a dozen pieces of wood from the handle. Then he returned the now considerably shorter broom to the closet and rushed up to the studio to begin dress rehearsal.

When the cue came for the game to begin, Ray did all the things that were required of a checkers game, including a triple jump. Suddenly his moves were interrupted by the director on the intercom. "Stop the watch. Ray, what the hell is that you're doing?"

"Playing checkers, ma'am."

"They sure as hell don't look like checkers!"

"I couldn't get real checkers so I cut some pieces off a broomstick."

"That figures," the director responded sarcastically. "In here the checkers sound like a cookie cutter!"

"Well, if that's the case, ma'am," Ray answered brightly, "why don't I just get a real cookie cutter for the checker sounds!"

The checker sounds were cut and so was Ray. He and the director never worked together again on "Dr. Christian" . . . or any other show.

"Buck Rogers in the 25th Century" was a popular science fiction show even before the term science fiction had been coined. This imaginative program was heard first on CBS (1931) and then on Mutual (1939). The problems confronting the sound-effects artists on those shows were enormous. It was their responsibility to come up with all the futuristic sounds that were only in the imagination of the writers and directors. The scripts were overflowing with such sounds as rocket belts, ray guns, rocket ships, sparkle static, dream water, repellent guns, reducer rays, and various and sundry zips and zaps to ward off Killer Kane or dispose of all those hideous outer-space monsters.

The opening and closing theme of the show was the combination of a drum roll on the sound-effects thunder drum and the announcer's voice (with lots of echo) intoning, "Buck Rogerrrrs . . . in the twenty-fifth century!" Having the announcer say the line into a microphone placed near the strings of a piano would make the strings vibrate in a way that gave his voice exactly the eerie, futuristic sound the show was looking for. Figure 5.8 shows how we set it up.

It is interesting to note that more than 50 years later, this piano effect was still being used in Hollywood for such films as *Raiders of the Lost Ark*.

Because of the technical difficulties involved with doing these early radio shows and insufficient rehearsal time, most directors made it a rule that there were to be no visitors in the studio at any time. This most certainly included sound-effects men who were not assigned to the show. Even allowing an apprentice soundman to ring a telephone during one of the early rehearsals was discouraged. According to one director, "My studio is no goddamn schoolroom!" and that kind of says it all. It also ex-

Figure 5.8. An early echo chamber. Photo courtesy of Malachy Wienges.

plains why apprentices had such a difficult time acquiring studio experience.

Although the "no visitor" rule might seem somewhat stern, the director of "Buck Rogers" would argue it wasn't stern enough, not by half.

It was during the closing of one of the Buck Rogers shows that an actress came into the studio to visit Virginia Vass, who played Lt. Wilma Deering on the show.

Quietly opening the outer and inner studio doors, the actress waited patiently while the announcer finished reading the closing into the microphone in the piano: "Listen again next week to . . . *Buck Rogerrrs in the twenty-fifth century!*"

Then, thinking the show was over, she excitedly waved and called to her friend, "Hi, Virginia!"

Everyone, including Virginia, whirled around with withering looks and signaled for her to be quiet. Meanwhile, the announcer continued speaking into the live mike: "This is CBS. . . ."

Flustered and embarrassed, the visitor sputtered her apology, "Holy shit! Am I sorry!" as the announcer continued: "The Columbia Broad-casting System."

And all over America, people turned to one another and asked, "Did you hear what I think I heard?"

To which the response was assuredly, "No, it couldn't have been, not on *radio.*"

CHAPTER VI

THE COMEDIANS

COMEDY SHOWS WERE THE HOME of the sound-effects stars. In fact, many of the soundmen who did these shows thought they *were* the stars. What's more, there is evidence to prove they were right. From the many years that the "Fibber McGee and Molly" show was on the air, what joke comes to mind that could top the famous closet-crash sound effect?

On "The Jack Benny Show," the sound effects created for Benny's visits to his subterranean money vault have little competition from the spoken jokes. And when you multiply the number of jokes told in anticipation of hearing these sound effects, the argument becomes even more convincing.

You would think, because of their exalted position in the sound-effects hierarchy, that these comedy soundmen were something special. They were, but very often only on comedy shows. Put some on a show with as many sound effects as, for example, "Gangbusters" and they would have had a very difficult time. Despite their title of sound-effect artist, in their hearts they were really comedians who used sound effects to get their laughs.

In Figure 6.1, Ray Erlenborn (CBS, Hollywood) demonstrates the two attributes all comedy sound-effects artists had in common. One was the ability to do a variety of effects at the same time, while the other was the ability to get up on the stage and get laughs with these effects. Obviously, Erlenborn was not shy in front of an audience. Frank Loughran, on the other hand, was of a different sort. Shown in Figure 6.2, Loughran was an excellent sound-effects artist at NBC in New York. And like Erlenborn, he possessed the talent to be able to do two things at once. But unlike Erlenborn, he would rather put that pistol to his head than get up in front of a comedy show audience.

All sound-effects artists had to possess a good imagination and a sense of timing. The few who were in demand to do comedy had that and more.

112

Figure 6.1. Ray Erlenborn. Photo from the files of Ray Erlenborn.

They also had a total lack of inhibitions that would let nothing get in the way of getting laughs. (Unfortunately, this sometimes included the star of the show.) Perhaps their greatest asset was a highly developed and often bizarre sense of the absurd.

Jackie Gleason once said that comedy was whatever you get a laugh with. Other people, also known for their appreciation of humor, were a little more elaborate:

> "Laughter always arises from a gaiety of disposition, absolutely incompatible with contempt and indignation." *Voltaire.*

> "I laugh because I must not cry, that's all, that's all." *Abraham Lincoln.*

> "Of course they are often sympathetic with me while they laugh! Playful pain, as you say, that is what humor is. The minute a thing is over-tragic it is funny." *Charlie Chaplin.*

> "Everything human is pathetic. The secret source of humor itself is not joy but sorrow. There is no humor in heaven." *Mark Twain.*

Figure 6.2. Frank Loughran. Photo courtesy of Frank Loughran.

Those are just a few opinions about what humor is. Jimmy Durante, on the other hand, tells us what humor "ain't." Durante started out in the beer halls of Coney Island and moved on to vaudeville and eventually to radio to co-host, with Garry Moore, "The Camel Caravan." It was here that Durante first began closing the show with his intriguing "Goodnight Mrs. Calabash, wherever you are." Although there was much speculation as to the identity of the mysterious Mrs. Calabash, the truth of the matter is, she never existed.

Durante was impressed with John Charles Thomas' famous sign-off, "Good night, Mother," and wanted something equally punchy for his sign-off. After listening to and discarding hundreds of names, Phil Cohan, Durante's producer, puffed thoughtfully on his Calabash pipe, and as he watched the smoke curl to the ceiling, suggested, "Calabash ... Mrs. Calabash."

Durante loved it, not realizing it was said more out of desperation than inspiration. And when the American public heard it, they loved it, too. Soon Jimmy's closing message, "Goodnight, Mrs. Calabash, wherever you are," became one of the most famous closings in all of show business.

Durante had a reputation for being good natured and easygoing, but even so, on one of his early television shows he and his producer got into a rather heated argument over a comedy sketch involving a large crash.

Durante wanted a hundred cardboard boxes to fall on him, with appropriate sound effects. The producer argued that a hundred boxes would be too expensive, and pointed out that using a hundred boxes would require extra men in the grid above, special-effects people to do the rigging, extra stage hands to clear the boxes after the drop (this was live television), and besides, where would they have room for a hundred boxes backstage for the rest of the show? Durante reluctantly agreed to have the number reduced from 100 to 15.

That night on air, when the 15 boxes dropped on Durante, the audience greeted them with stony silence. After the show, Durante angrily confronted the producer with this insight on humor: "Ya see? It's just like I told ya. Fifteen boxes just ain't funny!"

This business of what made certain things funny was a serious one. Why for instance, did the small tinkling sound of a small bell (see page 267) following the Fibber closet crash, never fail to get bigger laughs than the huge closet crash it followed? Was it the sound of the bell, or knowing when to ring the bell? Therefore, was it the number of Durante boxes, or knowing when to drop them that was the real culprit?

There's a saying that the three most important ingredients of comedy are timing, timing, and timing. And what is timing? It's recognizing that particular instant in time when all conditions are working together to bring about the most desired results. In comedy, it was laughs, and no one knew this better than the comedy sound men.

Russ Gainor (CBS, New York) was used mostly as an assistant on the busier dramatic shows because of his lack of experience. However, put him on a comedy show and few could touch him for ingenuity and that elusive quality called timing.

For the early "Ernie Kovacs" television show, about the only thing CBS gave Kovacs was the air time. When a television star has to use the backs of old Captain Kangaroo cue cards for *his* cue cards, it's a sure bet there isn't a budget for writers. Desperate for material, Kovacs allowed Gainor to ad lib anytime he felt the urge. As a result, both Gainor and Kovacs used this loose format to challenge one another's ability to get laughs, without a script and with the pressures of being on live television. But then, both of these comedic combatants knew the value of timing.

One day while on the air, Kovacs found himself with time to kill and nothing more important to do than sit at his desk, puff thoughtfully on his cigar, stare into the camera, and wonder, what the hell he was going to do next. At that moment, Gainor ad-libbed a sound-effects door knock. Without missing a puff, Kovacs called out, "Come in." Gainor did a sound-effects door opening and started doing footsteps on a wooden floor. Four footsteps, five footsteps, ten footsteps, twenty footsteps ... and still they kept coming. Not too slow and not too fast ... simply unhurried and precise, like the beat of a metronome or like Gary Cooper going to face the killers in *High Noon*.

As the steps continued, Kovacs continued to stare at the camera in a detached, unconcerned manner, puffing slowly on his cigar. Finally the footsteps stopped. It was Gainor's way of saying, "Make something funny out of this." Kovacs removed the cigar from his lips in a calm, unhurried manner, smiled, and in a voice meant to be helpful rather than critical said, "You forgot to close the door."

Kovaks, expecting to hear running footsteps followed by a door slam, was totally unprepared for the next sound he heard: a quick and decisive door slam *without* the steps. If Gainor had run back and shut the door, it would have been normal and expected. The ability to somehow close the door without walking back is totally unexpected, and therefore the funny way of closing the door.

Years later, Jack Paar was doing a morning television show at CBS and wanted to do this same footstep routine, which he'd seen on Kovaks' show. Russ Gainor was doing sound effects on the show, and he reluctantly agreed, knowing that not everyone possessed Kovaks' great timing. That morning on the show, Gainor obediently did the sounds, the door knock, door opening, and footsteps. This time, however, Paar only let him get to ten steps and, since no one in the studio was laughing, nervously jumped to the punch line: "You forgot to close the door!" Russ, reluctant, but obedient, slammed the door—to more silence from the audience.

After the show, Paar demanded to know why this routine, so funny on Kovacs' show, got absolutely no reaction on his show. Gainor managed a smile and spoke just one word: "Timing."

The competitive fires that burned so brightly in the breasts of these comedy soundmen often were the cause of friction between the soundman and the star of the show. Henry Morgan once paid his soundman the ultimate compliment and then proceeded to kick him off the show. Morgan later explained, "Sure he was funny. But then I noticed he was begin-

Figure 6.3. Monty Fraser and Bud Tollefson (NBC, Hollywood) cleaning up after a big laugh. Photo courtesy of Opal Fraser.

ning to become confused about what my function on the show was. When I came in the studio, he would give me lines to say so that he could do a sound effect. I finally decided it was too late in my career to become a straight man for funny noises."

That was the big problem about doing comedy in radio. If the effects didn't get any laughs, the soundman was kicked off the show. On the other hand, if the effects got consistently bigger laughs than the star, the sound-man was also kicked off the show. For more reasons than one, comedy was a serious business for sound-effects artists.

Judging by the thoughtful expressions on Monty Fraser and Bud Tol-lefson, shown in Figure 6.3, they can only be discussing one thing: how to get bigger and longer laughs. Fraser, on the left in the photo, holds some dried grass used for the sound of walking through the brush or jungle, while with his left hand, he hands Tollefson a temple block, used for mak-ing hollow wooden head-hits, like those heard in cartoons or in the old Three Stooges movies. (Incidentally, that strange, square banjo-looking box that Tollefson is holding is a boing box. This instrument had only one string that, when plucked, made a loud and comedic "boiiiiing" sound popularized in the film cartoon, "Gerald McBoing-Boing.")

This business of sound effects getting bigger laughs than the stars was a problem even on a show like "Amos 'n' Andy."

When this venerable radio show went to a half-hour length, Freeman Gosden, who played the part of Amos and the Kingfish, became mildly upset over soundman Gus Bayz getting so much attention with his sound effects. Naturally, this was after the show started broadcasting in front of an audience. I say, naturally, because when "Amos 'n' Andy" was a 15-minute nightly show broadcast from a studio, no one watched Freeman Gosden and his partner, Charles Correll, do the show. In fact, no one was even allowed in the studio. That included their wives, and it most certainly included the soundman. Even the audio engineer, who had to be in the control room since that was where his equipment was, could not see into the studio because of large sheets of brown wrapping paper taped to his control-room window.

To my knowledge, no reason has ever been given as to why they were so fanatical about their strict rule of privacy. I can only guess that the powers that be believed that having people watch would disrupt the stars' concentration. To be as believable as these two brilliant comic actors were, it was essential that for those brief 15 minutes, five days a week, both Gosden and Correll did really become those two most listened-to individuals in all of radio, Amos 'n' Andy.

That background of working in privacy might explain why Freeman Gosden felt that having Gus Bayz doing his sound effects on stage was distracting. This was a common complaint, not just of comedy shows but of dramatic shows done in front of a studio audience, as well. When the studio audience listened to the radio at home, they heard a blend of actors' voices, music, and sound effects mixed together and balanced to perfection by the audio engineer. This, plus their imagination, was what radio was all about. In the studio, however, they didn't get this homogenous blend of sounds. Instead, they only got the parts that made up the blend.

Listening to a dramatic show at home and hearing the hero slugging it out with the bad guy could be extremely exciting as the sounds triggered your imagination and the complete "picture" filled your mind. Watching the hero slugging it out with the culprit in the studio, however, was ludicrous. The audience saw two well-dressed actors standing at a microphone while a sound-effects artist created all the sounds — the punches, the bottles breaking, the chairs breaking, the gunshots.

It was for this reason that the audience of a serious dramatic show was always cautioned not to react to the sound effects during the broadcast. This, however, never stopped audiences from looking.

On a dramatic show, that was fine. On a comedy show, it wasn't. Comedy shows had audiences for two reasons: to help with the timing of the jokes and to provide live laughter. And that required that nothing distract the attention of the audience. To some comedy stars, sound effects were a distraction, even though they wanted the laughs they knew sound effects could provide.

Freeman Gosden thought he had the problem solved by having Gus' sound equipment moved to the back of the stage, close to the orchestra and out of the audience's line of sight. This did not make Gus happy, and it had nothing to do with ego. Gus knew, from experience, that audiences enjoyed watching the artists doing sound effects, and when they saw them doing something funny, they just laughed that much more.

Therefore, week after week, Gus would inch his equipment closer and closer to the audience. But just when success seemed within Gus' grasp, Gosden realized what he had done and had him returned to the back of the stage.

This cat-and-mouse game went on for several months until the night when the script called for Gus to do a big Fibber McGee–type crash. This meant a lot of manual effects (no comedy show would ever allow records) and more room than he had been allocated. It was decided that he was to move up, from the area he had been given in the back of the orchestra, to the front of the orchestra, next to the saxophones. Although this new area wasn't much of an improvement, at least he was visible to the audience.

On the actual show, nothing Gus had done in rehearsals had prepared him for the overwhelming response the audience gave his crash. The more items he dropped, the more they laughed.

Then, the worst thing that could possibly happen to a comedy artist happened. Because of this unexpectedly enthusiastic response to his crash, Gus found himself running out of things to drop, and the audience was begging for more!

Seeing one more item out of the corner of his eye, he dove for it in desperation. The trouble was, the prop wouldn't come loose and he couldn't see what was holding it. But whatever it was, the audience loved it. The more he pulled, the louder they screamed. Finally, he gave one mighty tug, and over the pile of rubble came the object, along with its owner, a disheveled and angry musician! In the heat of getting laughs, Gus had been trying to smash a priceless, one-of-a-kind saxophone!

The next week, Freeman asked him to set up at the front, as close to the stage and as far from the orchestra as possible.

Soundmen who had to work alone sometimes created some memorable comedy moments, even on a serious dramatic show. One time on "Mister Chameleon," I had to do the sound of an ear-wrenching train crash. The director wanted not only the crash but also the screeching metal skid of the iron wheels locking brakes on the steel rails and a huge burst of steam when the two trains collided. All in all, the crash, the skids, and all the train sounds leading up to the crash required two record consoles of six turntables and a dozen records.

I couldn't get another artist to help me, because of a scheduling problem. Furthermore, all the little extra sounds the director wanted had to come from all those records, many of which had a wide variety of sounds side by side.

All the records were tricky, but there was one I was particularly worried about. It had crowd noises next to a Model T sound next to an artillery officer yelling, "Ready-fire!" next to an explosion sound. The combination of the two sounds, an explosion of an artillery shell hitting a tank, was ideal—a huge explosion *and* metal. All I had to do was hit that chalk mark on that one groove!

Having to do this sequence alone and live was so frightening, I didn't dare go down to ColBeeS for a shot or two of help. Just as well—it was one thing to screw up on a show but if they had smelled the faint aroma of ColBeeS on my breath, I could have been fired.

When the on-air cue came for the crash, I began the sequence. First the train whistles frantically trying to warn the other train of the impending danger; then the skids, all three records of them. Then came the all important explosion, and although my hand was shaking from nerves, I put the steel needle right on the correct spot. Then came the car crashes and more explosions, and finally a huge burst of steam. And just when I thought I had created one of the all-time great train crashes and my worries were finally over, out from this twisted wreckage came, miraculously, the voice of a conductor cheerfully bawling out, "All *aboard!*"

Perhaps the most famous comedic sound effects in radio were the noises that emanated from Jack Benny's Maxwell car. Because of their distinctive nature, such sounds were not in any library of sounds. They had to be created.

Virgil Reimer, a top NBC-Hollywood soundman who was assigned to come up with the motor sound for Benny's Maxwell car, had only the writers' cryptic description of, "lousy motor" (see script below) to work with—that plus the fact it had to be funny.

To begin with, he listened to every car record he could lay his hands on. The closest sound he could find was a recording of an old Model T Ford putt-putting along, which was fine and authentic but it wasn't funny. And so the search continued.

What made finding just the right automobile sound so difficult was, as usual, the record companies' habit of putting the most incongruous sounds side by side. For instance, instead of grouping all the automobile sounds together, they mixed them in with other sounds—screams, snores, horse whinnies, whatever.

The other problem that Reimer faced with records was that no matter how appropriate the car sounds on records were, he knew a record could only be a small part of the Maxwell car sounds. Because his experience taught him that no comedy show done in front of an audience would ever allow their soundman to play a record if the effect could possibly done in a more visually entertaining manner.

This was a basic sound effects rule. Sound effects on a comedy show had to satisfy two criteria: they had to sound funny and they had to look funny. Virgil knew that no matter what effect he came up with, in order to get laughs with the sound, a part of it would have to be done manually.

To give some idea of the challenge Reimer was faced with, the following is part of an actual Benny script, given to me by George Balzaar, a Benny writer for many years.

> (*Sound: traffic noises and auto motor*)
>
> JACK: Ah, there's nothing like an auto ride on a day like this. . . . Gosh, how time flies . . . here it is, 1936, and I bought this car in 1924 . . . and it was only ten years old when I bought it. . . . Yes sir!
>
> (*Sound: auto horn*)
>
> JACK: I understand the model after this one had the crank in the front. . . . Gosh, what won't they think up next? . . . Well, I guess I'll step on the gas and let her out a little.
>
> (*Sound: lousy motor up . . . coughs and sputters . . . couple of gunshots . . . more coughing and sputtering . . . motor dies with a duck call*)
>
> JACK: Hmmm . . . it's missing a little . . . I wonder what's wrong. . . . Well, there's no use sitting here. . . . Might as well get out and crank it.
>
> (*Sound: creak of car as Jack gets out . . . sound of cranking . . . motor starts up . . . coughs and sputtering . . . two gunshots . . . more coughing and sputtering . . . motor dies with a duck call.*)

That was the sort of description of sounds that Reimer had to work with. Of course, Benny's tight-fisted stinginess was already legendary, so to maintain that image, Reimer tried to come up with a car sound that audiences would accept as something that only someone as cheap as Jack Benny would own.

This is the way Virgil Reimer put it: "It was already established that the car would be a Maxwell. This made the car antique, rather than just badly in need of repair. A car that simply sounded awful could have been relatively new but not taken care of properly. There's a difference. One implies neglect, while the sound we were looking for suggested a lack of sophistication . . . an out-dated sound. A sound that was in keeping with the Jack Benny character."

In his search for just the right Maxwell car sound, Reimer scoured the junkyards of Hollywood for weeks. Some of the motors that sounded right were too big to be handled comfortably; others that were the right size sounded terrible (or in this case, sounded too good). Finally, after weeks of discouragement, Reimer finally came up with an old motor that met all the requirements. It was no larger than a basketball and had just the right awful sound that he had been searching for. In addition, when it was turned on, the whole motor shook and shuddered and even gave off a blue-gray smoke.

Back in the sound-effects shop, Reimer attached a device called a variac into the AC outlet cord. The variac allowed Reimer to vary the amount of electricity that was being fed to the motor and therefore to control how fast or slow the motor vibrated. Next he riveted a metal bucket to the top of the motor and when the Maxwell car was supposed to have motor trouble, Reimer could drop in a combination of nuts, bolts, bottle caps, nails, screws—anything small and metallic. The combination of the vibrating motor and the metal objects being clanked and banged about in the bucket would be just right.

Later, as the popularity of this Maxwell car effect caught on with the audience, Mel Blanc was brought in. Blanc was the genius who supplied the voice of such cartoon favorites as Bugs Bunny and Porky Pig.

Now the Maxwell crash became a work of art. With Reimer supplying the recorded sounds, mixed with the "bucket of nuts and bolts" effect, and Mel doing the wheezes, coughs, gasps, gulps, and snorts, the combination was perfect. Not only was Benny delighted, but so were the studio and home audiences who each week waited to hear those imaginative sounds emitting from Jack Benny's wonderful old Maxwell.

Benny's delight was characteristic of the man. He was one of the most

Figure 6.4. Jack Benny (left) switches roles with Virgil Reimer. Photo courtesy of Virgil Reimer.

unselfish performers in radio. He felt that any laughs generated by individual cast members or by sound effects contributed to the overall success of the show. In Figure 6.4, Reimer is seen doing the jokes while Benny waits for his cue to jump in with a gunshot. It was this type of good-natured clowning between the stars and sound-effects artists that made live radio so special.

Another series of sounds rivaled the Maxwell car effect: Benny's periodic visits to his money down in the old vault. What follows is part of another actual script given to me by George Balzaar. In this particular sketch, Jack has to withdraw some money and he and Ed Kern, playing the guard, are already at the vault.

> JACK: Wait here, I'll go into my vault and get the money. Please turn your back.
>
> (Sound: several footsteps, heavy iron handle turns with creaking of chains . . . heavy iron door creaks open . . . six more footsteps . . . heavier iron door handle turns with creaking chains . . . heavier door creaks open . . . four more footsteps.)
>
> KERN: Halt . . . who goes there . . . friend or foe?
>
> JACK: Friend.
>
> KERN: What's the password?
>
> JACK: . . . Uh . . . a fool and his money are soon parted.
>
> KERN: Oh, it's you, Mr. Benny.
>
> JACK: That's right . . . how have you been, Ed?
>
> KERN: Quite well, sir.
>
> JACK: Me, too . . . and it's sure good to get back home.
>
> KERN: Oh, have you been away?
>
> JACK: Yes, for eight weeks . . . I went to New York.
>
> KERN: Oh . . . it must be nice there now.
>
> JACK: No, no, Ed it's winter.
>
> KERN: . . . Oh . . . well, it's hard to tell in here.
>
> JACK: Yes, I imagine it is. . . . Take out your gun, Ed. I'm going to open the safe.
>
> KERN: Yes, sir.
>
> JACK: Let's see . . . the combination is right to forty-five . . . (light turning sound) . . . left to one-sixty . . . (light sound) . . . back to fifteen . . . (light sound) . . . then left to one-ten . . . (light sound) . . . There.
>
> (Sound: handle turns . . . terrific steam whistles, bells, gunshots, etc., ending with beee ohhhh whistle.)

JACK: I wonder if I need a louder burglar alarm.... Well, let's see ... this ought to be enough money.

(Sound: door shuts ... footsteps.)

JACK: Well, so long Ed.

KERN: Goodbye, Mr. Benny.

JACK: Say, Ed, I've been thinking ... you must be kinda lonesome down there.

KERN: No, no, I don't mind it.

JACK: Well, nevertheless, I'm going to get you a radio.

KERN: A radio? What's that?

JACK: Well ... it's a new thing that people enjoy.

KERN: Well, send it down.... If I like it, I'll eat it.

JACK: No, no, Ed, it's nothing to eat.... Well, so long.

KERN: So long, Mr. Benny.

(Sound: few footsteps and creaking door closes.)

MUSIC: Playoff.

Benny's writers scripted these bank visits, but it was up to the sound-effects artists to translate these words into sounds that would get laughs. This is quite evident by the catchall abbreviation ETC. in the sound-effects instructions that accompany the opening of the safe.

Notice that in the "alarm sounds," in addition to footsteps, iron doors, and chain sounds, there's a call for the "BEEE OHHHH" fog horn. This fine, deep-voiced fog horn gained radio fame when it was used as the signature sound in a series of deodorant commercials—hence, B.O. for body odor. Comedy quickly picked it up, and after that any attempt to use this wonderful old fog horn for anything other than comedy was out of the question. In fact, from that point on no one ever referred to it as a fog horn; it was always the more odorous—"BEEE OHHH horn."

It's of interest that when Benny did these "vault bits" on television, they never got the laughs they did in radio. The TV directors even went so far as to put a moat filled with crocodiles around the safe, but nothing worked to recapture the old magic. Which proves that what the listener imagined about the Benny subterranean vault surpassed anything visual that the set designers could come up with for the cameras. All it took in radio was a few words and some creative sounds.

The difference between doing sound effects on a dramatic show and doing them on a comedy show was the studio audience. On a dramatic show we were only interested in the sounds themselves, but on a comedy show it was the sounds plus the studio audience's reaction to the sounds. The studio audience of 500 people had a huge influence over what millions of listeners heard over the radio.

When "augmented audience reactions," better known as laugh tracks, were still years away, comedy shows used "claques." Claques were people hired to come to the comedy shows and laugh—and not just laugh with the same old laugh each time. These people were armed with an arsenal of hilarity. They had titters, giggles, guffaws, small laughs, long laughs, short laughs, loud laughs, and, of course, the button-bustin' belly laugh. The theory was that laughter was contagious. If the people at home heard the studio audience laughing, then it must be funny. And who wants to be accused of not getting a joke?

To make certain that every man and woman, in the audience was ready to add to the hilarity, comedy shows had their own version of the ritual called warmups. These were less instructional than the dramatic show warmups and concentrated more on getting the audience in the mood to laugh.

Comedy warmups worked well—most of the time. One time sound-man Barney Beck was working on the Beatrice Kay Show on WOR, New York. Barney and the announcer, Jay Jackson, did a routine that ended, just seconds before air time, with the audience laughing hysterically. The routine involved Barney sitting in the audience and heckling Jackson while Jackson tried to do his warmup. Jackson would say things like, "So when I give you the signal to applaud, I want you to applaud as loud as you can. In that way, the audience at home will think its even funnier!"

With that, Barney would shout out, "Who are you to tell me when I have to applaud!"

Jackson would try to ignore Beck, but Beck would continue his harangue. "I go to work and the boss tells me what to do! I go home tired and depressed and my wife tells me what to do! Now I come here to relax and you tell me what to do! Who do you think you are . . . my mother!!!???"

Finally, Jackson had the pages escort the badgering Beck out of the theater. But when they got to the back of the theater, one of them would shout out, "What should we do with him, Mister Jackson?" Jay would answer back, "Anything appropriate!" and the audience would hear the sound of a gunshot.

That was the way the routine was supposed to work. One night, however, the seat that was selected for Barney was behind a woman who took her radio shows very seriously. She was one of those people who would start out with the game shows in the morning and go to every radio show that had an audience. For these lonely people, going to a radio show was more than just entertainment, it was a way of life.

As Barney went into his prepared heckling routine the woman in front of him began bristling with anger at Barney's seeming rudeness. Finally, she couldn't take Barney's words of abuse anymore. Turning around, she began beating him over the head with her umbrella.

Jackson, on stage, began breaking up, and instead of stopping the woman, he actually encouraged the bumbershoot onslaught by shouting things like, "Thank you, madam, for coming to my rescue!"

Barney, in the meantime, figured he'd gotten all the laughs he was going to get from this woman, so he covered his head with his arms and made a beeline for the lobby. Half way up the aisle, Jackson called out, "And don't come back!"

To this, Barney ad-libbed, "Don't worry. After all this, I'm going to shoot myself!"

And to this, the woman screamed out, "Good!"

Moments later, a .38 caliber gun shot rang out, and the woman screamed in horror, "He really did it!"

Jackson interrupted the woman and assured her that Barney was all right. But before he got very far, Barney's voice called out loud and clear, "But I wouldn't be if my aim had been better!"

Interestingly enough, at one time all shows, whether they had an audience or not, were without any sort of audience response. It was felt that it distracted the listeners at home. But after Eddie Cantor allowed his audience to applaud, all the other shows followed suit. Although radio comedians never lost their healthy respect for the home listeners, of course they began playing to the studio audience. After all, how could they ignore 500 people sitting there not laughing at the jokes? Some, notably Ed Wynn, couldn't resist getting dressed up in outrageous costumes to get "sight gag" laughs from the studio audience.

Figure 6.5 shows what soundman Harry Saz (NBC, Hollywood) came up with when asked to develop a sound that would get laughs on a radio quiz show. Naturally, the apparatus was in full view of the studio audience. Every time a contestant got a wrong answer, Harry would throw those huge switches, which in turn triggered a small buzzer sound. Little wonder that audiences at home were mystified to hear laughter from the studio audience every time a wrong answer was given.

One of Jack Benny's routines didn't need funny clothes, claques, or anything else to get laughs. It was, in Benny's opinion, one of the longest sound-effects laughs on his show. It occurred during a sketch about two garbage men picking up Phil Harris' trash. Harris, also nicknamed Curly,

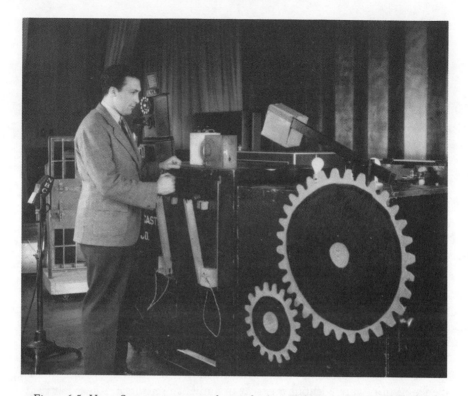

Figure 6.5. Harry Saz creating a comedy sound effect. Photo courtesy of Virgil Reimer.

was Benny's orchestra leader for many years, and the show had a running gag about the quantity of scotch Phil drank.

I've included the script for that sketch, to illustrate that getting laughs with sound effects could be extremely difficult and even get you a traffic ticket.

> (Sound: garbage truck running.)
>
> SAM: Well, just one more stop.
>
> SEYMOUR: (whining) Do we have to?
>
> SAM: That's what you said last time ... and the time before that and the time before that...
>
> SEYMOUR: I keep hoping he'll move out of Beverly Hills.
>
> (Sound: truck stopping.)
>
> SAM: Bad news, Seymour, he didn't.
>
> SEYMOUR: I shoulda listened to my mother and become a doctor.

SAM: Look on the bright side. I read where the Jack Benny Show was out of town most of last week. How much garbage could Curly have?

SEYMOUR: We'll soon know. Help me dump this trash can in the truck. On the count of three. 1 ... 2 ... 3?

(Sound: bottles out of trash can. Start with a few and build to an avalanche.)

The sound-effects rooms in those days were nearly as well stocked as Noah's Ark. If you looked hard enough, you could usually find two of anything. But for Phil Harris' bottles, simply using milk bottles, soda bottles, baby bottles might sound fine for the home audience, but it would be a terrible choice for the all-important studio audience. Adding an assortment of wine and whiskey bottles would help, but it still wouldn't be correct. Phil Harris was a scotch drinker. Therefore, it had to be scotch bottles, and not just any scotch bottles, either. They had to be the most immediately recognizable scotch bottles for all the nondrinkers in the audience.

In those days that meant Haig and Haig scotch. This expensive scotch was packaged in a concave, three-sided bottle bearing the trade mark, Pinch Bottle. The problem was to find 50 empty bottles of Haig and Haig Pinch Bottle Scotch.

Unlike soft drink bottles that carried a reward of 2 cents when they were returned to the store, empty scotch bottles were worthless, and once their amber contents had been swilled, they were discarded. Most people don't want to be reminded of the amount of booze they consume or, for that matter, keep score with empty bottles. But that left Reimer with the unpleasant task of canvassing Hollywood bars.

Unless you're desperate for a drink, going into a Hollywood bar that advertises OPEN AT 6:00 A.M. can be a rather unnerving experience, especially if it's only a little after 8:00 A.M. In the dimly lit cigarette haze, the people huddled over their drinks at the bar give you a wise and knowing look as you make your way over to the bartender. After you inform him in a low voice you don't want a drink, only an empty bottle, he stops wiping a place for you at the bar and looks at you with more critical eyes. "You with the studios?" he asks, "studios" being a catchall word meaning show business. Rather than make a big story of it, you simply nod, reach for your wallet, and try to ignore the curious looks squinting from the bar.

Only in Hollywood do they know the value of an empty scotch bottle. This was true in every bar that Reimer went into and by the end of the day, as he drove back to the studio, he worried about two things: the size of his petty cash voucher, and what he would tell the police if he had an accident with 50 empty scotch bottles in his car.

Doing sound effects on a comedy show required not only a sense of humor and great timing, it also required dedication and hard work. Why else would an artist take the pains to individually select, say, the hundreds of items used in a Fibber McGee closet crash that lasted 30 seconds?

Keene Crockett was one of the few second-effects artists who were equally at home on a dramatic show and doing comedy. He's shown in Figure 6.6, doing effects for "Chandu, the Magician." When Bob Hope came to New York, he always put in a request for Crockett. The following story shows why.

In one of the Hope sketches, the script called for Hope to have a fight with his newly wedded bride, played by Frances Langford. While rehearsing the sketch, Hope felt that the bit needed some action and decided to have Langford start throwing some of their wedding gifts at him. One of the gifts Hope wanted thrown was an entire china service for 12.

This didn't seem to present any problems to Crockett or to the NBC sound-effects department, since the shelves were stacked with old, random dishes. But despite the fact this was radio none of them were acceptable to the visually minded director. So Crockett, on his lunch hour, had to go to the nearest five-and-ten-cent store and shop for new dishes that matched. Unfortunately, New York City was having a thunderstorm and when it rains in New York City, two things happen automatically: the taxicabs vanish from the streets and everyone in the city goes shopping.

By the time he located a cab, he was already running behind schedule, and of course the store was jammed with people. Having no other option, he agonizingly waited his turn in line, with one eye on his watch.

When he finally got a saleslady, he quickly told her that he wanted dishes, a service for 12 in any color she had handy. The woman gave Keene a look that sales people in New York are famous for: they aren't surprised or dismayed, they just nod and plunge ahead. She asked him if the dishes were to be used for "good" or for everyday, and Crockett, preoccupied with the thought of being late for the next rehearsal, shook his head impatiently and replied, "Neither. Just something cheap to throw at Bob Hope!"

One of the problems facing sound-effects artists in New York City was the International Alliance of Theatrical Stagehands and Electricians (IATSE). This union represented many of the behind-the-scenes theater workers. These people raised the curtain, built and moved scenery, lit the stage, and saw to it that props were in the proper place for the actors. This last group, known as prop men, were the union members that sound-effects artists had all the trouble with.

Most disputes between rival unions are solved in the same way mothers decide ownership of playthings among squabbling siblings: "Who

Figure 6.6. Keene Crockett. Photo courtesy of Keene Crockett.

had it first?" In unionese, this is known as precedence. When the New York stage world fell on the same hard times as the rest of the country, many IATSE members lost their jobs. However, the networks began leasing or buying many of these empty theaters for radio use, and IATSE was determined to get as many members back working as possible. That meant being very protective over its jurisdictional rights, and one area that became exceptionally sensitive involved the care and handling of props.

Loosely speaking, theater props consist of anything that is used to decorate a scene. The use of props by an actor is an important part of any play, but the union rules stipulate that they can only be handled by an actor while there is an audience in the theater and the curtain is up. Otherwise, anytime a prop is moved, even if it's only a chair or a glass of water, members of the prop union must move it. The union could get pretty tough about this.

When radio took over theaters for their audience shows, many of the duties once handled by these prop people were no longer necessary. Instead, their primary duties were to see that the radio actors' needs were attended to, including putting area rugs around the microphones to deaden footsteps, and providing folding chairs to sit on. But their job did include moving anything that came or went on the stage, even if it was as seemingly insignificant as a glass of water for an actor's dry throat.

Into this rather touchy union atmosphere came the intrepid sound-

Figure 6.7. The kitchen sink. Photo courtesy of Walter Pierson.

effects artists with their myriad assortment of manual effects, right down to and including the kitchen sink. And I mean that literally, as Figure 6.7 shows. This useful prop was invented by Stuart McQuade. Equipped with a recirculation system, it could always be counted on for water to wash dishes, for getting Junior a glass of water, or for filling those countless pitchers of lemonade, coffee pots, or tea kettles for the genteel ladies of the soaps. The prop also gave a good watery sound to those early radio rainstorms.

Naturally we called this vital piece of sound effect equipment a manual effect, but the prop people had other ideas.

"Manual effects, hell," the stagehands screamed, "they're props! And any props that come into this theater are our jurisdiction! End of discussion ... period!!"

Of course we argued that they weren't props, they were manual effects and they were *our* jurisdiction! End of discussion and *double* period!!

The bickering back and forth was finally settled when our union allowed their union to move our equipment across the stage to where the sound-effects area was. Once there, we were free to move it around as long as we didn't move it across the stage.

Although this seemed a satisfactory solution, not all the stagehands agreed with the ruling and especially not the old timers in IATSE. They were afraid it was "just the beginning. You let them guys from sound effects get away with something and the next thing you know we'll all be out in the street!"

Into this hornet's nest of jurisdictional dispute walked soundman Vic Rubei, then with CBS in New York. Rubei's talents were very much like the little girl's in the nursery rhyme: when he was good, he was very, very good, but on the few occasions that he screwed up, he gave directors sharp pains in the chest area. Like Norman Corwin, for instance. Norman Corwin was one of the brilliant innovative geniuses of radio, not only as a director but as a writer as well. His imaginative blending of voices, music, and sound effects were always an example of the potential listening joy that dramatic radio was capable of producing.

On one show, Corwin chose to open and close a show with music he had composed especially for the program. The opening music depicted Satan ascending from Hell and the closing music accompanied Satan back into the infernal fires of Hell. It's important to understand that with the opening music, Satan comes out of Hell, and with the closing, Satan goes back to Hell. On air that night, as Corwin rose from his chair to throw the all-important opening cue, a hush came over the control room. The only sound was the big clock on the wall ticking off the seconds. Corwin, resplendent in his trade-mark red suspenders, then lifted his arm and extended his pointing finger. Lowering his arm slowly but decisively, he pointed to Vic Rubei for the music of the devil rising from Hell. Rubei complied, but the music was not the devil rising but the flip side, the devil returning to Hell. Slowly, ever so slowly, Norman Corwin sank, like the devil, into his own private Hell, a somewhat older man.

Norman Corwin somehow survived those terrible moments of live radio. Figure 6.8 shows him, many years later, directing a recreation of a radio show that was presented for the enjoyment of fans of old-time radio.

Most sound-effects artists wouldn't have survived a mistake of that magnitude, but Vic Rubei was so good he was always in demand, albeit a sometimes nervous demand. The real problem with Vic was that he was never satisfied with mere excellence. He demanded perfection. It was this never-ending quest that often got him into hot water.

One such dip into hot water happened the evening he was assigned to one of the converted Broadway theaters to do "The Phil Baker Show." The script called for a Fibber McGee–type crash. Asking Rubei to copy an effect was tantamount to waving a red flag in front of a bull. He'd create

Figure 6.8. (Left to right) Bob Dryden, Norman Corwin, Burgess Meredith, and the author, recreating the magic. Photo by the author.

his own crash, thank you, and it would be one that Fibber himself would sell Molly for!

The radio control room in that theater was built on the stage itself, out of the line of vision of the audience. Rubei decided that the roof of the control room was the perfect spot to set up his fabulous crash, and he went about the painstaking job of piling the roof high with aluminum pots, pans, lids, old golf clubs, tennis racquets, rubber boots, cups, saucers, dishes, just about everything that wasn't nailed down in the sound-effects department. Then, because all this junk was on top of the control room roof, he threaded a rope through all the effects and the net bags containing all the crockery. As soon as he pulled that rope, all the stuff would come showering down onto the stage. Any delay would kill the laughs.

During dress rehearsal, the crash of the stuff cascading down from on high proved what a comedic genius he was, and he promised the director that, on air, it was going to be even bigger and better!

True to his word, Rubei set it up again, climbing up and down the ladder with load after load of new effects, each one chosen either for its funny sound or its funny looks. An oversized pair of red bloomers may not make much of a sound, but to a studio audience, anything of a risque nature ensured laughs, and just to be sure, Vic threw in a couple of giant enema syringes and two hospital bed pans. As the air time neared, the director became increasingly nervous about the crash. Was Vic sure it would work? (Of course it would.) Was he absolutely *positive* it would work? (Are you kidding?)

With that assurance, the director went off to give some last-minute notes to the large cast and the orchestra leader.

However, because of its importance and magnitude, Vic secretly checked and rechecked the crash. To make sure that everything would come down on cue but not all at once, the thin, strong rope was carefully strung in and around all of the effects. As he gave the rope a gentle tug, the line straightened out and the effects inched closer to the edge of the control-room roof. Everything was in readiness.

On air, Vic moved smoothly through his series of phone rings, door knocks, door slams, door bells, with each effect bringing him closer to *the* effect.

As the cue neared, he clenched the thin rope with cold, nervous hands and waited for the precise moment.

He followed every word of his script as it inched down to his cue.

> FATHER: Can you reach it?
>
> SON: *(with effort)* Just boost me up a little higher...
>
> FATHER: *(effort)* Be careful, all your sister's wedding gifts are piled in front of you ... all her bone china dishes, crystal glassware...
>
> SON: There, I reached it ... whoaaaaaaa
>
> FATHER: Watch out, you numbskull ... you're going to fall right in your sister's...
>
> *(Sound effects: the biggest dish, glass, and whatever-else-you-got crash and keep it coming!)*

Rubei gave the rope a tremendous yank as if he were setting the hook in a trophy sailfish. The rope straightened out obediently, but nothing happened! He gave it another yank, and another, and another! Not even the red bloomers budged! Somehow the rope had gotten snarled around something! But how could this be?? He had used such care in setting the effects, and when he'd tried the rope just minutes before air time, the items, including the bloomers, were literally teetering on the edge of the roof!

The director, in an apoplectic rage, cued the orchestra and the comedy show limped off the air with the big crash still sitting on top of the control room roof.

After the show, the irate director demanded to know what happened. Poor Rubei sputtered a bewildered apology and explained he hadn't done anything different on air than he had done all day. And by way of illustration, Vic again gave the rope a yank. This time the crockery, glasses, bedpans, bloomers, everything, came crashing down onto the stage, narrowly missing the even angrier director. Rubei, the rope still in his hand, just stared in open-mouth bewilderment.

CHAPTER VII

AND NOW – A WORD
FROM OUR SPONSORS

THE WORLD OF ADVERTISING and sponsors at first seemed to have little to do with sound effects, but its influence on everything that was done
in radio was far-reaching and final. If the sponsors wanted a certain sound-
effects man or woman on the show, they got them. Of course, the opposite
was just as true: for the slightest reason, or even no reason at all, they could
have a sound-effects artist removed from a show, and if the real or imagined offense was heinous enough, it would mean from *any* show where the
sponsors pedaled their wares.

This iron-fisted autonomy often infuriated the network heads. After
all, *they* were the ones paying our salaries. However, when you consider
the $42.9 million the sponsors paid the networks in 1933, and the $86
million by 1935, it's not surprising that the sponsors had clout. When the
sponsors pouted that they wanted a certain sound-effects artist, they got
the artist . . . period.

Sound-effects artists are no different from any other human being, and
being wooed by one sponsor when you've already been wooed by another
puts you in an excellent negotiating position. Soundmen who were in demand were able to make extra fees that often exceeded the $37.50 they
were being paid weekly. The networks, of course, hated having the sponsors running their sound-effects department. The trouble was, they
couldn't find anyone willing to tell this to the sponsors. As a result, the
practice continued.

By the 1940s, radio was riding the crest of its popularity. The networks
began constructing huge studio complexes to accommodate eager audiences
demanding to see their favorite shows in person. So great was this interest
that in New York and Hollywood, stage theaters and movie houses were
converted or sold as well as rented to this latest thriving industry, radio.

And that was fine as far as the sponsors were concerned. Studio

audiences were a highly reliable and visible demonstration of the popularity of a show they were sponsoring. In fact, many sponsors attended
"their" shows on a regular basis. If the show was high in the ratings, an invitation to be their guest was somewhat like getting a preferential seat at the
World Series. So popular and chic was this practice that separate booths,
usually adjacent to the control room, were set aside as so-called client's
booths.

In those days, sponsor identification was often tied in with the title of
the show: "The Philip Morris Playhouse" (cigarettes), "Imperial Time"
(margarine), "Hallmark Playhouse" (greeting cards), "Gulf Screen Guild
Theater" (gasoline), "The General Electric Theater" (appliances), "Fleisch-
man Yeast Hour" (yeast), "Molle Mystery Theater" (shaving cream), "The
Cliquot Club Eskimos" (soft drink), "Lux Radio Theater" (soap), "Coty
Playgirl" (cosmetics), "The Bell Telephone Hour," "Campbell Playhouse"
. . . the list went on and on.

In addition to show identification, some sponsors carried it even fur-
ther and allowed their product to be strongly identified with personalities—
Bob Hope with Pepsodent toothpaste, for example, and Jack Benny with
Jello puddings.

So strong were these tie-ins that the products were incorporated into
the show and were used as frequently as possible by the stars. Jack Benny,
for instance, opened his show by substituting the more conventional
"hello" with, "Jello again, this is Jack Benny."

Bob Hope was even more liberal with his toothpaste plugs. He made
Pepsodent his middle name: "This is Bob Pepsodent Hope" became a catch
phrase and was used at the close of his shows, along with such pithy observations as, "This is Bob Pepsodent Hope saying, if you want a safe and sane
July Fourth, stay away from those sometimes explosive fifths."

Benny and Hope weren't the only practitioners of free-wheeling plugs.
Mel Allen, the voice of the New York Yankees, used to refer to a home
run as a "Ballantine blast," Ballantine being the brand-name of the spon-
sor's beer. Another sportscaster, sponsored by the breakfast cereal
Wheaties, would have this to say about a home run: "Wow, look at it go.
It sure looks like *he* had his Wheaties today!"

This Wheaties line became so popular with the public that it became
synonymous with an excess of power and energy—or the lack of it.

One favorite device that sponsors used to attract listeners was the
catchy opening. It was generally believed that if you could hold the
listeners' interest for 15 seconds, you had them hooked for the whole show.
As a result, sponsors were always looking for ear-rousing openings such as
this:

SOUND: *big glass crash—shrill police whistles!*

SOUND: *scream of police sirens*

SOUND: *gunshots and machine guns—sneak in marching feet.*

ANNCR: *Sloans Liniment presents, Gangbusters!*

The excitement created by this opening became so popular that it coined the phrase: "Coming on like gangbusters!" Figure 7.1 shows some of those effects. The whirling device on the right is a fan used for the sound of wind. Frank Blatter, on the left, is handling this manual effect and Harry Bubeck is in the background, doing the records. During 1941–43, "Gangbusters" was broadcast from Studio D in Chicago.

Although "Gangbusters" was in a class by itself for exciting openings, there were others.

ANNCR: Faster than a speeding bullet!

SOUND: *gunshot and ricochet*

ANNCR: More powerful than a locomotive!

SOUND: *locomotive effect*

ANNCR: Able to leap tall buildings at a single bound!

SOUND: *burst of wind up full*

MAN: Look! Up in the sky! It's a bird!

WOMAN: It's a plane!

MAN: It's Superman!

The opening for "Superman" is self-explanatory. Even people who'd never heard of "Superman" were tempted to listen just a little longer. And that was the whole idea behind these so-called show signatures: grab the audience that was spinning the dial looking for something appealing to listen to.

One of the problems of having a strong sound-effect association with a certain product was that no other sponsor wanted that particular sound used on their show. That was even true of sound effects that were strongly identified with a particular show itself and not a product. (Although actually that's just another way of saying the same thing.)

MUSIC: Sting

SOUND: *hoofbeats*

Figure 7.1. Harry Bubeck and Frank Blatter in a hurricane. Photo courtesy of Robert J. Graham.

> ANNCR: From out of the West comes America's famous fighting cowboy—Red Ryder!
> SOUND: *rifle shot and ricochet*

The rifle shot-and-ricochet sound was so identified with "Red Ryder" that other shows refused to allow you to use this effect. So was the squeaking door effect on "Inner Sanctum." Actually, the squeaking sound of that door was made with an old, dilapidated office tilt-back chair salvaged, like so many other sound effects, from the trash pile. But despite how good this squeaking door effect was, it could only be used on "Inner Sanctum." Other shows were afraid to use it for fear they'd be compared to, or confused with, "Inner Sanctum."

Limiting the shows that certain effects could be used on was a serious matter, especially since we didn't have that many good effects to begin with.

One such effect was an excellent fog horn. It had just the right mournful sound to set the scene for any mystery story that took place near the water. However, some clever advertising writers decided that the sound was also perfect for that most heinous of all human disgraces ... BODY ODOR!

In those days, no commercial in its right mind would mention such an offensive subject. So instead, the Lifebuoy soap commercials let sound effects do their dirty work. Taking the "B" from body, and the "O" from odor, the sponsor's clever little rascals came up with perhaps the most famous two letters in the English language, B.O.

> ANNCR: So why use perfumey soaps that only cover up the problem? Use mild and refreshing LIFEBUOY SOAP and you'll never have to worry about...
> SOUND: *fog horn*

The commercial and fog horn sound-effect caught the nation's imagination and suddenly, everyone in America was doing sound effects. Friends in the locker room and on the street chided each other about the dangers of . . . BEEEEE OHHHHH! If you couldn't get a date, it was because of BEEEEE OHHHHH. If your car wouldn't start for you, it was because of BEEEEE OHHHHH.

So identifiable was this effect with an unspeakable personal hygiene problem that the mournful fog horn was elevated out of the mist and into the glare of instant recognition. That made the people at Lifebuoy ecstatic, of course, but it made the sound-effects artists foam at the mouth. Another excellent effect had just been taken away from us. But that was the name of the game with sponsors: sell the product any way you can.

A good example of how ingeniously the writers in radio utilized vocal sound effects is illustrated by this American Tobacco Company commercial for Lucky Strike cigarettes, from the "Jack Benny Show."

> JACK: Now, Don, put that apple on your head and stand by that tree . . . and I'll knock it off with this arrow.
>
> DON: Okay.
>
> JACK: Ready . . . aim—
>
> MEL: *(chirps merrily)*
>
> MARY: Wait a minute, Jack, don't shoot.... A bird just lit on Don's head.
>
> JACK: Oh, yes . . . I'm glad you stopped me, Mary.... I wouldn't want to hurt a poor little bird.
>
> MEL: *(chirps merrily)*
>
> JACK: Go away, birdie.
>
> MEL: *(chirps merrily)*

JACK: *(mad)* Birdie, birdie, go away.

MEL: *(angry chirp followed by razzberry)*

JACK: Hmmm . . . Don, get rid of that bird, will you?

DON: Go away, birdie, go on, go away.

MEL: *(chirp chirp . . . chirp chirp chirp . . . chirp chirp . . . chirp chirp chirp)*

DON: What's that, birdie?

MEL: *(whistles: ls/mft . . . ls/mft)*

JACK: Well, what do you know . . .

DON: That's right birdie, Lucky Strike means fine *tobacco.*

MEL: *(whistles: yes, Lucky Strike means fine tobacco.)*

JACK: Say, you're a smart little bird.

MEL: *(whistles: "I know it.")*

JACK: Now, go away, birdie, fly away, go, go, go.

MEL: *(chirps merrily and then goes into "Love and Bloom.")*

JACK: Well!

(Applause)

The "Mel" in the commercial was, of course, Mel Blanc, who in addition to being a vocal effects genius, did many comedy roles on the Benny show. Perhaps one of the more memorable ones was that of the train announcer who could get screams of laughter with just announcing the names of three small towns in California: "Train leaving on track nine for An-a-heim, A-zusa and Kook-a-monnnnnnnnnga!"

The "Mary" in the script was the enormously talented, Mary Livingstone, Jack Benny's real wife.

Being able to integrate the often-despised commercials into a program by involving the stars was a tremendous help in selling the sponsors' products. But there were also disadvantages. What if the star did a show that was offensive to some listeners? There was a greater likelihood that the people at home would blame the sponsor if the show bore its name. And what if the show was doing poorly in the ratings? That might be seen as a direct reflection on the merits and prestige of the product, especially by such trade papers as *Daily Variety.* If the writers of this well-read paper could describe the Wall Street Crash of 1929 as "Wall Street Lays an Egg," wouldn't they be just as likely to write, "Beer Producer's Ballgames Go Flat" or "Cereal's Broadcasts Go Soggy?"

There were other serious concerns as well. Supposing the spokesperson for your milder-than-mild cigarette got lung cancer? Or the host of your highly rated Saturday morning kiddie show turned out to be a pervert? Who would have thought that lovable old Uncle Don (Don Carney), thinking he was off the air, would remark to the shocked children and parents of America, "That should hold the little bastards"? (That was the end of Uncle Don.)

Sponsoring those early radio shows, where so many things could go wrong, was a risky and expensive operation. As a result, the ad agency people who handled the accounts of these various sponsors took every precaution to preserve the integrity of the shows that bore the sponsors' names. Some of these precautions were necessary, while others seemed just a trifle overkill.

For example, I was scheduled to replace vacationing Jack Amrhein on "Philip Morris Playhouse" for a brilliant comedy, *Three Men on a Horse*. During the first reading, an actor read the line, "Gee, this has to be my lucky day!"

The actor no sooner got the words out when an agency man interrupted the rehearsal to inform Charlie Martin, the director, that the word "lucky" was to be cut from the script. Lucky Strike cigarettes were one of Philip Morris' biggest rivals in the cigarette market, so on a program that was sponsored by Philip Morris, the best anyone could hope to be was "*fortunate*," never "lucky."

When Charlie Martin balked at the request, the agency man smiled and countered that he'd allow the word lucky on the show the same day that the "Lucky Strike Hit Parade" hired a featured singer named (you guessed it) Philip Morris.

The problem was how to do a show like *Three Men on a Horse*, which involved a lot of talk about horse racing, without ever using the word lucky.

Later, Charlie observed, "Thank God, we're not doing *Beau Geste*. How the hell could we get the people around the desert if there was no such thing as a camel?!"

When it came time to let the audience in for the dress rehearsal, the same agency man came over and gave me a package of Philip Morris. I thanked him for his generosity but told him I used Chesterfields, "the cigarette, not the coat." If he heard my little attempt to lighten the atmosphere, he ignored it. Instead, he fixed me with the same congenial sneer he had used on Charlie. "You can smoke whatever you like, but the only cigarettes we'll ever see in this studio are the ones that pay the bills. And by the way, if you cough on air, you're off the show."

Next week, Amrhein was still on vacation and I was still on the show. Which indicates not how good I was but merely that when the show was

Figure 7.2. Christmas on "Blondie." Photo from the files of Ray Erlenborn.

on the air, I didn't cough. Nobody ever said the job of doing sound effects was easy.

Sponsors got pretty creative about plugging their products. Figure 7.2 shows the cast, crew, and staff of the "Blondie" show at the annual Christmas party. In the center is Arthur Lake (Dagwood) having a tug-of-war over a gift with Penny Singleton (Blondie). Soundman Ray Erlenborn stands behind Penny. Notice the tree, decked with pretty red and green bows, and that other traditional symbol of Christmas—Camel cigarettes.

Let me add one final word about the "Philip Morris Playhouse." The cigarette company had as its spokesman a midget dressed in the red uniform of a hotel page-boy. He was called Johnny, and his picture was everywhere that cigarettes were sold. So identifiable was Johnny, in his red page's uniform, that he was the only performer I ever saw in radio who dressed up for his part.

At the opening of the show, the announcer would intone, "And here he is, stepping out of millions of store windows to say . . ." and at this point Johnny would step up to the mike and cry out, "Call for Philip Morrrrris!" And that was it. Four words, and he was finished. Four rather simple words, actually. And considering how much he was being paid by Philip Morris and how many times he said it each day, it seemed a little like getting paid to say your own name, or like Mickey Mouse saying "Come to Disneyland." But evidently it was more complicated than that, because that evening on air, Johnny not only stepped out of millions of store windows, but when he sang out "Call for Philip Morris," he read it from a *script!*

After the show I asked him about it. After all, if I could get fired for smoking Chesterfields, how could he get away with using a script for four words, two of which were the sponsor's name? He smiled and said that the agency, rather than objecting, insisted on it. It seems that one night, he got up to the mike and when the cue came, he went completely blank. He remembered nothing! The announcer had to do his part in falsetto! Fortunately, his face was so recognizable they couldn't fire him, but from that night on, he had to carry a script with him everywhere—just in case.

Back then, the networks had extremely strict rules about mentioning products that weren't paying for the air time. They referred to these "plugs" as "giving away what they were in the business to sell." Sportscasters were not even allowed to give the scores of a game being broadcast by a rival radio station. And no wonder: If you were sponsoring a dull, uninteresting baseball game, would you want your sportscaster reporting that "they're having a tight barn-burner over in the Polo Grounds. It's a scoreless tie, with Carl Hubbell pitching a no-hit game"? Who in their right minds would stay with a game where the New York Yankees were clobbering the St. Louis Browns, 12–0?

As strict as the network watchdogs were, some products were constantly being named by writers and performers, without any thought of payola (the term used to indicate the payment of money for the illegal plugging of a product). This practice was acceptable because these products were identifiable not so much for what they were but for what they represented. The Cadillac automobile, Tiffany diamonds, the Waldorf-Astoria hotel—all were synonymous with affluence. Products such as these were often used on comedy shows because they didn't need explanations. Others included Stetson hats, Greyhound bus lines, Macy's department store, and Rolls-Royce.

The only involvement sound effects had in these plugs for pay was to create the sounds for the written script. If for instance a script specifically called for the sound of an electric razor over the more popular (at the time) shaving brush and hand razor, or an electric mixer was called for rather than mixing a cake batter by hand, or a powered lawn mower was specified rather than the manual mower, we knew the writers would soon be receiving a visit from the person that delivered the mail (or packages).

This practice of plugging individual products or whole industries

(Idaho potatoes or Florida oranges) was hated by the sponsors (unless of course it was their product that was getting the free plug), but they were powerless to stop it. This was especially true when the plugs were the payoff to a joke. And that's what made getting these plugs on the air so much of a challenge for the writers.

Bob O'Brien, Joan Davis, Jack Benny, Eddie Cantor and Izzy Elinson became the toasts of the comedy writing community with this coup.

It happened on the Eddie Cantor show. The dialogue was between Cantor and a snobbish social climber. As Cantor politely listened to the woman flaunting the extent of her art treasures done by the old masters, Cantor, not to be outdone, mentioned that he had three masters at home in his kitchen. When challenged by the bore to name them, Cantor responded: a Mix-MASTER, a Coffee-MASTER and a Toast-MASTER!

Because this was a rare triple plug, in addition to getting Elinson and O'Brien in the comedy writer's hall of fame, it also got them the appliances.

Although all this sounds a little silly, I can assure you it wasn't. In the movie *It Happened One Night* starring Clark Gable and Claudette Colbert, Gable removes his shirt and, to the delight of the female film-goers, he is bare-chested! The impact of this rather scandalous exposure was felt immediately, not only by film critics, but by the underwear industry on Wall Street as well. And the next day, when the male population took off their shirts, most of them had, like Clark Gable, stopped wearing underwear tops. Many years later, when Jacqueline Kennedy made it fashionable not to wear a hat, the millinery industry suffered a loss from which it still hasn't recovered.

If you still think it's silly, try this one. I once wrote a pantomime for Dick Van Dyke to use on the prestigious television program, "Armstrong Circle Theater," sponsored by Armstrong linoleum. The payoff of the sketch came when Van Dyke hurled his imaginary champagne glass into an equally imaginary fireplace accompanied by the sound effects of a glass crash. An agency man immediately informed me that the glass smashing incident would have to be cut. When I explained how important it was to the sketch, he gave me the same congenial sneer the man from Philip Morris had given me and replied, "Armstrong also makes glass."

Thinking there was more, I waited. But that was it: "Armstrong also makes glass." I looked at him, completely puzzled. "Are you saying that because Armstrong makes glass, glass isn't breakable?"

"No, what I am saying is that because Armstrong makes glass and is sponsoring this show that pays your salary, on "Armstrong Circle Theater" glass doesn't break." And he was right. The glass-breaking bit was cut. No, let me re-word that. The glass-breaking bit was dropped from the sketch. As we now all know, nothing ever got "cut" on the "Armstrong Circle Theater," at least not in the Never Never Land of advertising on radio and television.

CHAPTER VIII

GUNSHOTS AND
OTHER STRANGE SOUNDS

IF I HAD TO SELECT the one sound effect that caused us the most problems and embarrassments, it would undoubtedly be the gunshot. To fans of old-time radio, probably the first thing that comes to mind when gunshots are mentioned is this sound-effects story.

During a live radio show, the sound-effects pistol used to deliver the show's most important gunshot suddenly jammed. The quick-thinking actor, not hearing the shot, blurted out this brilliant ad lib.

"On second thought, shooting is too good for you. Instead, I'll use my knife and stab you . . . like this!"

At which point the startled actor heard—a gunshot!

Although this story is by far the most popular, it is only one of many embarrassing stories concerning gunshots.

The pistol shown in Figure 8.1 is one that CBS had designed to satisfy the demands both of directors and of a safety committee from the New York City Police Department. One feature that appealed to the police was that the gun's barrel was plugged with a metal rod and therefore could only fire blank cartridges. Billed as being fool proof, the pistol made its debut over the CBS network on July 8, 1938, and immediately starting things off with a bang by misfiring on air.

There were two major things that could go wrong with a sound effect gun—the mechanism and the ammunition.

Problems with the mechanism of the gun itself were rare, but they did happen. As a preventative measure, soundmen with free time were regularly assigned the job of maintaining and cleaning all the guns in the department's arsenal.

And those arsenals were ample, as Figure 8.2 shows. That's Ray Kremer (CBS, New York) taking inventory and cleaning some of the CBS weapons arsenal, while an unidentified gun moll looks on admiringly.

148

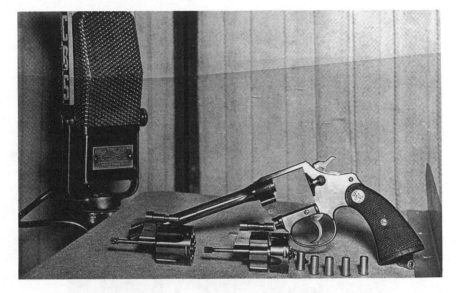

Figure 8.1. Sound-effects pistol. Photo courtesy of Walter Pierson.

It's doubtful that John Dillinger or Pretty Boy Floyd or even Scarface Al Capone had as many guns at their disposal back in the 1930s. The networks as well as police officials constantly worried that these hand guns might fall into the wrong hands and be modified back to their original capabilities. So, in addition to worrying about whether a gun would fire on cue, a soundman could lose his job if one was lost or stolen.

Faulty ammunition was by far the most frequent cause of a pistol malfunction, and the most difficult to prevent. Out of any box of shells, there might only be one bad blank cartridge, but if that one faulty blank came up on a vital cue, not only was it extremely embarrassing but the timing of the scene was destroyed as well. There could be other blanks in the gun and you might even have a backup gun, but if the shot didn't occur at the exact moment it was supposed to, the believability of the scene would be destroyed.

One of my first jobs at CBS, as the number three man on "Gangbusters," was to help out with the gunshots. Normally the third man on a show was either the newest or the least experienced. Although I had done sound effects freelance for two years, I was certainly the newest and least experienced compared to Jerry McCarty and Byron Wingett, the two regular sound-effects artists on the show.

Figure 8.3 was taken during a dress rehearsal of "Gangbusters." Firing the guns is Byron Wingett, while Jerry McCarty prepares to knock over

Figure 8.2. Ray Kremer with some prop guns. Photo courtesy of Malachy Wienges.

the victim's chair. Voorhees, head of the CBS sound-effects department, is the interested party in the center.

Incidentally, Figure 8.3 also shows a strange piece of equipment in front of McCarty that has nothing to do with pistol shots, but illustrates the constant challenges to the artist's ability to create sounds. It's a dry cleaner's press for ironing clothes. To create the sound they first had to C-clamp an iron mechanism to a step ladder. When the lever was pulled, the heavy metal rod would strike against the padded board and give the sound of the press hitting together. The sound of the accompanying steam was supplied by the air tank in the foreground.

Although firing guns off was all part of the sound-effects artist's job, not everyone did it with the same joie de vivre. In Figure 8.4, Orval White (CBS, New York) has his ears covered and his eyes tightly shut as he bumps off a few more bad guys on "Philip Morris Playhouse." Charlie Martin, the show's director, kept complaining about Orval's choice of effects for a New York street scene. Finally, in exasperation, Orval said that he'd given him everything in the CBS library, so just what was it he wanted? Martin answered, in a tone that was both irritating and patronizing, "Is it so very difficult to give me the simple sound of an everyday New York

Figure 8.3. Bryon Wingett, Van Voorhees, and Jerry McCarty. Photo courtesy of Jerry McCarty.

City street scene?" So, at dress rehearsal, Orval played his normal traffic sounds, but at one point added the terrified scream of a woman.

Busy shows (with ample budgets) required at least two soundmen. One did the recorded effects and the other did all, or most, of the manual effects. These latter sounds included everything from "punches to the head" (hitting a sponge, a wallet, or a head of cabbage) to gunshots. Normally, the soundman with the most experience was delegated "first man," and if the show was very busy, he might have three or four assistants helping out. As the newest member of the team, I was in the number three spot. This meant I would be doing the least critical sounds, helping out with the gunshots and, most important, going down to ColBeeS for coffee, or the equally crucial cigarettes.

Prime-time shows in those days could take anywhere from a day to a week to prepare. "Gangbusters" was a three-day call for the sound-effects people. On Thursdays we set up the equipment and selected the effects for the show. On Fridays, everyone sat at a table and the director had the actors read their parts while he took a rough timing. Then he gave them cuts, corrections, and notes, and after that, the cast had their first rehearsal using the microphone and sound effects.

It was my job to fire two guns simultaneously. Before I had a chance

Figure 8.4. Orval White.

to get too nervous, Jerry McCarty, the number one man, told me that for
this rehearsal I wasn't to fire the guns but just to say, "bang–bang–bang."
I couldn't believe my ears. My very first cue on radio's top-rated crime show
and all I got to do was say "bang–bang–bang!" Despite my disappointment,
I said my gunshots loud enough for everyone to hear them. I think even
the director liked the way I did them, because I never saw anyone smile
quite so hard.

That night, I didn't even mind the ride home on the crowded subway,
because while other New Yorkers had to settle for their mundane newspapers, I had my very first network script to read. And since New Yorkers
can be pretty blasé, I made certain that no one within arm's length missed
the fact that it wasn't just *any* script, it was a genuine CBS "Gangbusters"
script.

During Saturday's rehearsal, Jerry sent me to the Gold Room (where
all the valuable effects were kept) to sign out my two guns. Back in the
studio, I cleaned and recleaned my guns while everyone was getting script
changes prior to dress rehearsal. Then, just before the dress rehearsal, Byron Wingett decided he needed another record to add to an already complicated 4-record car-crash sequence and, as third man, it was also my job

to get last-minute effects. They also asked me to bring back three containers of coffee from ColBeeS. I started to take the pistols with me, but Jerry convinced me that riding down in the elevator with two .32-caliber pistols sticking out of my back pocket might cause some concern among the other passengers. I agreed with his logic, hid the guns under the prop table, and hurried out of the studio.

When I got back, dress rehearsal had started. Despite the fact that I had only one short scene for my gunshots, I was starting to get a bad case of nerves. My hands gripped the pistols so tightly that the muscles in my arms began to ache. With only one page to go, I had to force myself to breathe deeply to get some oxygen in my lungs. My neck was so stiff that when I moved my head, I turned my whole body. Jerry looked over to see if I had cocked both of the pistols; I had. The problem now was to keep my shaking hands from accidentally pulling the triggers.

As I watched the director, Leonard Bass, lift his arm for my very first network cue, I sucked in my breath and held it, just like I had been taught in the Marine Corps. Suddenly he jabbed his finger at me! I squeezed the triggers and never before did silence sound so loud! Jerry and Byron whirled around to see what was wrong. The director kept frantically stabbing his finger at me. Even the actors tried to cover for me. One shouted, "Shooting's too good for him . . . give me that knife!" Another cried out, "Throw him in the river!" An actress got into the act, screaming, "Hang him!" During all this bedlam, I just kept pulling the triggers as fast as I could . . . still nothing! In the control room, Leonard Bass was jawing obscenities while the mouths of Jerry and Byron had fallen open in mutual shock. In the midst of my disaster, all I could think was, "This can't be happening to me. I was a sharpshooter in the Marine Corps—with real guns!" Suddenly, in the midst of my hysteria, I heard a final smart aleck actor yell out, "Hell, let's not do anything. At this rate, he'll just die of old age!" At that point everybody in the studio collapsed with howls of laughter!

I learned an important lesson that day: when the first man sends you out for a record and three black coffees, make certain your guns are still loaded when you get back.

My second serious encounter with guns happened when I filled in for the vacationing Jimmy Lynch on "Perry Mason." That show was technically a soap, but it had enough sound effects to qualify for a prime-time slot. Especially gunshots—lots and lots of gunshots. So many, in fact, that I needed two guns.

During the rehearsals, I would simply hold the guns in the air and say, "gunshot," instead of firing them. As a result, I had absolutely no problem with the gunshots. I would have preferred to fire the guns, but the cast preferred that I didn't. So I didn't. But the minute we had a break, I gave the audio man a sound-level test, partly to see how loud they would be but more importantly, to make certain they were working.

With almost half an hour left before we went on the air, I decided to cash my first CBS pay check at the bank across the street.

Normally, small sound-effects props, and this certainly included guns, were carried in a CBS sound-effects briefcase. But since I had only been with the company a few weeks, my bag was still on order. Not wanting to risk leaving the guns in the studio (already I was getting like Mark Twain's cautious cat!), I jammed them into my hip pocket, put on my jacket, and went to the bank. I should have taken into consideration that because it was pay day, the line would be long. As I inched closer to the teller I began to get concerned about the time. When I finally stepped up to the window, the teller wanted to see my CBS ID card before she would cash my check. Reaching for my wallet, I found it was blocked by one of the guns. I pulled the gun out and put it on the marble counter, and noticed out of the corner of my eye that the teller's mouth had dropped open in shock. Thinking she was going to scream, I quickly stammered out that it was only a blank pistol and I was using it on "Perry Mason," and to prove it was blank, I pulled out the other gun!

"See, this one is just like the other one. They're *both* blank!"

I perhaps have done more stupid things but I doubt it. The only thing that saved me from further embarrassment (and perhaps getting shot) was that the bank guard was engrossed in a conversation with a customer over by the doorway.

The other thing that worked in my favor was that this particular Chemical Bank was across the street from the sometimes strange goings-on at CBS. (Hadn't police invaded those very same studios the night of Welles' Martians Invasion?)

As I mumbled my apologies to the understanding teller, I hurriedly made my way for the door. I hadn't taken two steps when the crowd in the bank and especially the bank guard, were more than a little startled to hear the teller calling out calmly, "Mister Mott, you forgot one of your guns!"

In addition to all the misfiring and gun jamming things that could go wrong with guns, there were the actors to consider. Most of them were afraid of the harm that even a blank gun could do, and all of them hated the noise. Therefore, for some strange reason, the way gunshots were done in New York was not the way they were done in Hollywood.

The rivalry between the actors on the two coasts began when those in New York who had theater background looked upon themselves as superior to those in Hollywood with only film experience. Being able to do a three-act play straight through could hardly be compared with the Hollywood film method of doing a scene over and over until you got it right: So said New York. "Baloney," argued Hollywood.

So it went, back and forth. It is therefore understandable that when an actor from New York walked in to do a radio show in Hollywood, the air became somewhat fraught with tension.

On one such occasion, a New York actor had to do a fight scene involving gunshots. Dutifully facing the director in the control room for his cues during the first rehearsal, his back was, unfortunately, towards Gus Bayz, the Hollywood sound-effects artist.

As the fight scene approached, Gus produced a large .38-pistol, loaded it with blanks, and waited for his cue. The New Yorker, still unaware of Bayz or of his pistol, growled the cue line: "You'll have to come and get me, copper!!!"

Gus did indeed come after him, with three very rapid and loud gunshots. The astonished New Yorker let out a yell of surprise, threw his script in the air in shock and whirled around angrily to confront Gus.

"My God, man, for rehearsals in New York, we just say bang–bang–bang, we don't shoot the real gun until we're on the air!"

Having been caught in this New York-Hollywood snobbery before, the soundman gave the ruffled actor a benign smile and replied, "In Hollywood, we do things a little differently. Out here, we fire real guns in rehearsal and say bang–bang–bang when we get on air!"

In 1974, Gus was involved in another gun incident of a somewhat more serious nature. Although it happened long after the live days of radio, it was still radio.

Hy Brown, the veteran radio producer of "Inner Sanctum," was doing a remote broadcast from the Biltmore Hotel in Phoenix, Arizona, as part of a convention for the CBS Network's radio affiliates. To help with the entertainment, he agreed to do an episode of his popular syndicated radio program, "Mystery Theater."

These affiliate conventions were thinly disguised attempts to increase business for the CBS Network, so no expense was spared. In addition to various radio and television stars from the CBS Network, there was always a prestigious speaker from outside the entertainment world. That year it was the U.S. Secretary of the Treasury, William Simon. The show that night on "Mystery Theater" included a great many gunshots. To conserve his supply of blanks and in kindness to the other cast members, Gus decided to wait until dress rehearsal to actually fire his .38-caliber pistols.

Dress rehearsal began promptly at 4 P.M. and, in the audience waiting for his part in the program, sat Secretary Simon. The story moved smoothly into the scene involving the gunshots. As Gus raised the two .38-caliber guns and began blazing away, secret service agents, whose job it was to protect Secretary Simon, materialized from nowhere and wrestled a startled Gus to the floor. After snatching the two guns from his hands, they ordered him up against the wall at gun point ... at *real* gun point.

Hy Brown, along with actors and actresses and staff members, rushed across the stage protesting Gus' innocence. They quickly explained to the officer in charge that Gus was the sound-effects man on the show and that the guns he was using only shot blanks. To which the now thoroughly embarrassed agent lamely replied, "Oh yeah ... well, I don't care if they're blank or not. What I want to know is, how he got them past my men without them detecting them!"

Although I wasn't there, I'm going to guess that Gus just walked in. Something similar happened to me at an "I Like Ike" testimonial dinner for President Eisenhower. The dinner was held at the Mayflower Hotel in Washington, D.C. My effects on the show consisted of playing manual boat whistles during a sketch in which the Broadway and film actress, Thelma Ritter, was to be the Statue of Liberty.

In addition to President Eisenhower, the main ballroom was filled with cabinet members and foreign diplomats. Naturally, with such an assemblage of important people, everyone had to pass a security check before the FBI would let them enter the ballroom.

After being cleared by security, I went to one of the agents and requested my security pass. In return, he handed me a paper clip. When I continued to wait for something a little more official, he told me there wasn't anything else and I was to put the paper clip on my lapel.

As the time of the telecast drew closer, there were more and more people moving about with paper clips attached to lapels or dresses. And paper clips that hadn't found a permanent home on somebody could be found on tables, on the floor, or in someone's unfinished drink. It got so bad that if I hadn't known that those bent pieces of wire were the security passes that allowed us all to be with the President of the United States and his cabinet, I'd have sworn I was at my high school junior prom.

On my flight back to New York after the telecast, I began checking my CBS sound-effects briefcase to make certain I hadn't forgotten one of the smaller boat whistles. As I rummaged around, I made a rather startling discovery: Wedged in a corner and wrapped in an oil-scented cloth was the .32-caliber pistol I had used on a show in New York the day I left for Washington. I had spent a whole evening with President Eisenhower and his cabinet with a .32 pistol in my bag! As I sat looking at the pistol in my hand, I couldn't help thinking how lucky I was to have made the discovery of the gun in the safety of a an airliner at 30,000 feet.

One of the most bizarre gunshot incidents happened to George O'Donnell, one of the gentlest and most dignified of all the sound-effects artists at CBS in New York. George began his career as a dancer in vaudeville and was one of the pioneers in sound effects.

In addition to being fastidious with his personal appearance, O'Donnell always took great pains to see that the equipment he used on a show was in excellent working order and before a rehearsal he would meticulously check each item.

On one particular show (forever after referred to as the night of the "Big Boom"), O'Donnell was assigned to work with a man who had the reputation of being a loner and of being difficult to get along with, particularly when it came to touching his equipment or making suggestions. No matter how innocent the offers of help might be, the man perceived them as critical attacks on his competency and wouldn't hesitate to let you know they weren't appreciated.

The show they were doing was a documentary about the assassination of President Lincoln. Although the script was extremely busy, it came as no surprise to O'Donnell that he was given only one effect, the sound of thunder which, because this was in the early days of radio, was made by striking a huge drum. All other sounds, including the important gunshot that assassinated the great man, was to be done by the loner.

Despite the loner's refusal to be friendly, the rehearsals went smoothly. The director even complimented the thunder-drum effect, but still O'Donnell was worried: The loner had brought only one gun for such an important effect, and that, to O'Donnell, was just plain foolish. However, the loner's sour disposition left O'Donnell with little choice but to put his tongue between his teeth and clamp down hard.

On air, as the terrible moment arrived, the actor playing Edwin Booth delivered the appropriate cue line. And as the huge cast, a 30-piece orchestra, the director, and millions of breathless listeners waited for the fateful gunshot, there was only an awful silence. Not even a click. Nothing. The sound-effects gun hadn't merely misfired, it had jammed!

Other soundmen might have relished this moment of sweet revenge, but not O'Donnell. Despite what he personally thought of his co-worker as an individual, to him the show was the thing. So without a moment's hesitation, he reacted to the crisis quickly and decisively. Raising his mallet, he struck the huge thunder drum a resounding BOOOOMMMMM!!!! There are moments like this that spawn greatness. This, however, was not

Figure 8.5. Vic Rubei. Photo courtesy of Walt Pierson.

one of them. Although his quick-thinking effort to save the day was laudable, the radio critic for the *New York Times* had other, less charitable things to say: "This is the first time in American history that Abraham Lincoln was ever assassinated with a *cannon!*"

One of the most difficult enemies that all sound-effects artists faced was boredom. A soundman could do an impossibly busy show and never make a mistake but screw up a show's single cue of a door knock just through boredom.

Fortunately, on most shows a little boredom would have been a welcome change. Figure 8.5 shows Vic Rubei caught in a moment when boredom wasn't a problem. For this job, he had to bring a car to a stop (with a recorded sound), then open the door for the occupants and do their footsteps — sometimes for as many as three people.

Vic was a fine sound-effects artist at CBS in New York, and was assigned to do sound effects on a show not noted for its need of sound effects, the "Kate Smith Show." Rubei had only a single sound effect — a gunshot. And the only thing worse than doing these one-cue shows at all was to have the single cue come at the very end of the show.

To fight off boredom, a soundman sought the distraction of a crossword puzzle. If that was too easy, or too difficult, he might balance his checkbook, or perhaps clean out his wallet or update his address book. The soundman *knows* he has the cue line seared in his mind, but somehow, by the time he gets to the K's in the address book and realizes how many old friends have moved away—have *really* moved away—he gets to thinking about his own tenuous mortality and. . . . Vic Rubei suddenly noticed that Kate had stopped talking and the show had become very quiet. He looked up and the director in the control room was on his feet frantically pointing his finger at Rubei and jawing unmentionable obscenities! Vic shot into action; unfortunately, his gun didn't do the same. All that was heard over the awful quietness of the studio was an ominous click–click–click.

The wonderful part about doing a show as relaxed as the "Kate Smith Show" was that nothing was that big a deal. With her unflappable poise, Kate covered for the absent shot by pointing a finger in the air and ad-libbing a vocal BANG. The audience loved it and the incident was forgotten as Kate began singing her theme song, "When the Moon Comes Over the Mountain." The audience may have forgotten, and Kate may have forgotten, but Rubei hadn't forgotten. It was bad enough to be late for a cue, but to miss it completely because of an errant gun? He would get to the cause of that problem, now!

Kate Smith had just finished singing the first line of her theme song when she, along with the studio audience of hundreds and the listening audience of millions, were shocked to hear a loud and distinctive gunshot! Kate's voice jumped an uncharacteristic octave and CBS's telephone switchboard began lighting up.

"Was that a shot I heard?"

"Is Kate Smith all right?"

"Did they apprehend the one that did it?"

They must have, because Vic Rubei never worked the "Kate Smith Show" again.

It would seem that a simple solution to the missing-gunshot problem would be to bring extra guns to the show. This was sometimes done on prime-time shows that required several artists, but it often created as many problems as it solved.

We used only blanks, but because the guns were the real thing, they had to be registered with the police and kept under lock and key. If we needed a gun on a show, we had to sign out for it and be responsible for its care and safety.

There were other problems as well. To begin with, the network's legal department didn't want us using any guns, period, let alone having a sound-effects locker filled with backup guns. All that their legal minds could visualize was guns falling into the wrong hands with horrible consequences: "EXTRA! EXTRA! Prominent citizen gunned down with the same pistol used on CBS' "Gangbusters" show!" As a result they, and the police, agreed that CBS would limit and carefully monitor the number of guns it had in its possession.

Although this next gunshot story also involves George O'Donnell, I don't mean to imply that he made any more mistakes than the rest of us. In fact, if O'Donnell, or any other artist I mention, hadn't been excellent at the job, they wouldn't have been in the sound-effects department long enough for me to write about them.

O'Donnell was a gentle man and extremely considerate and polite. I have never met a man where the term "gentleman" was more appropriate. His manner of dress and deportment were impeccable, and the only time he would get mildly upset was when some member of the department looked, in his words, "scruffy," which could mean anything from not wearing a tie to wearing shoes that needed polishing. When someone new joined the department, O'Donnell always had time to answer questions or give some much-needed advice.

O'Donnell had had a long and successful dancing career, and didn't enter sound effects until he was past middle-age. That did not stop him from becoming one of the best however. If he had any weaknesses, it was not his age, it was his strict New England upbringing. He hated, with a passion, to feel or look foolish. This was unfortunate, because in addition to his capabilities as a soundman, he could have been one of the best vocal-effects men in the business. But doing vocals and being dignified do not go hand in hand, so he turned down all vocal offers and concentrated on sound effects.

It is ironic that one of the most embarrassing of all the gun stories should involve this proper gentleman.

The incident occurred while O'Donnell was working on "The March of Time." This highly acclaimed show was broadcast from 485 Madison Avenue in New York. The studio was to the right of the elevators, and the restrooms were to the left. The closest restroom was the ladies' room, which was just down a short flight of stairs from the studio. It is important to keep this in mind.

The rehearsal of the show was progressing fine until the gunshots were cued. The director felt that they didn't have the proper perspective and wanted them more off-mike, more distant-sounding. O'Donnell obliged by firing the guns in a "shot box," an insulated box the size of a television set. But that sounded too far off. So he began slowly moving away from the microphone, firing off a blank at each new location. Still it wasn't right. Finally, he reached the studio door, and in one last, desperate attempt to please this finicky director, O'Donnell opened the studio door and went down two of the five steps leading to the hall and ladies' restroom. He then pulled the trigger and the .32-caliber gun boomed loudly, followed almost immediately by an explosive flatulent sound and a terrified scream coming from the restroom.

Red with embarrassment, O'Donnell mumbled his apologies to the unseen lady and rushed up the stairs, back into the studio. As he slammed the studio door, the director called over in a genial voice, "Your gunshot was perfect, George, but you're going to have to lose the scream and fart!"

Trying to please directors with the sound of our gunshots was a never-ending battle for a number of reasons. One of the most important was the way gunshots sounded in the movies. A director would see a movie where Edward G. Robinson bumps off Humphrey Bogart, and want to know why we couldn't make our gunshots sound like that! Or he would see John Wayne gun down a few black-hatted hombres and whine about how swell *those* shots sounded! And so it would go. Despite all the explanations we gave, both technical and emotional, the directors wouldn't listen.

But our explanations were valid. Part of radio's problems with gunshots could be blamed on the visual directors of radio, those who insisted that what they heard had to match what they saw. For instance, when early radio tried to adopt the theater's technique of doing gunshots by striking a leather seat with a drumstick, it was flatly rejected. It wasn't that it made an inferior sound, it was, as one visual director put it, that "It just doesn't look like a gunshot." As a result, sound-effects artists found themselves relying on what *looked* like a good-sounding gunshot—the blank pistol.

Nothing quickened the pulse of a visual director more than seeing his sound effects artists brandishing a pistol in the air—no matter how bad the resultant gunshots sometimes were because of poor acoustics, or insufficient rehearsals. In Figure 8.6, Donald Mihan does the pistol waving and Robert Graham does the records on "The Fibber McGee and Molly Show." Mihan never worried about a gun misfiring. In addition to doing sound effects, Mihan moonlighted as a personal assistant to Jim and Molly Jordan in Chicago in 1938.

There is nothing wrong with the sound of a blank pistol under ideal conditions. But a radio studio was not an ideal condition. They were designed for the actor's voices, not gunshots. Gunshots need reverberation. It's the difference between the way your voice sounds in the shower compared to a clothes closet. One makes your voice reverberate, the other soaks up your voice and deadens it.

While the networks in New York were converting movie theaters and

Figure 8.6. Don Mihan is not taking any chances with his gunshots, while Robert Graham does the records. Photo courtesy of Bob Jensen.

legitimate theaters into radio stations, WXYZ in Detroit decided to do the networks one better by moving into the intarmacy, and therefore more easily converted, Mendelsohn's Mansion.

To begin with, the ballroom on the third floor became Studio A. This was used to accommodate large orchestras and small combos. On the first floor, what had been the library was now Studio B.

Studio C was on the second floor. It had once served as a bedroom, and clients assigned to "Aunt Minnie's bedroom" knew they would be working in the less imaginative Studio C. Also on the first floor, next to master control, was Studio F, the announcer's booth. The carriage house behind the Mansion became Studio G, and contained the station's large theater pipe organ.

From the sound-effects point of view, the most important of all the studios at WXYZ was Studio D. Studio D had once served as a living room and still contained the large fireplace, a massive hand-carved mantel, and walls covered with dark mahogany paneling. Although these appointments were in keeping with the rest of the mansion, they hardly seemed an appropriate setting for such high adventure stories as "The Lone Ranger," "Sgt. Preston of the Yukon," and "The Green Hornet."

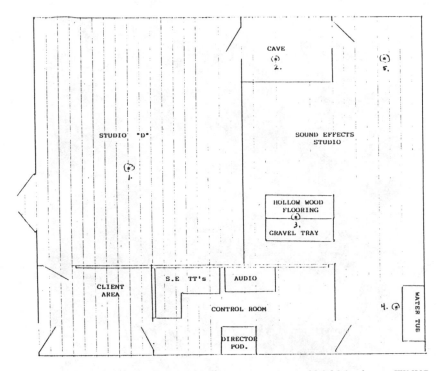

Figure 8.7. "Home of the Lone Ranger." Illustration courtesy of Mel Morehouse, WXYZ.

Although the management saw to it that nothing in this room was removed, the engineers soon had the ceiling acoustically treated and the room draped with heavy curtains to make the room suitable for broadcasting.

The floor-plan of the Studio D area is shown in Figure 8.7. The sound-effects studio had been a large solarium with double doors leading from the living room through an area designated "The Cave."

This Cave area was isolated from both the main studio and the sound-effects studio, and so was used for off-mike sounds, those heard away from where the principal action was taking place. These sounds were normally crowd effects done by whatever actors were not actually saying character lines during the scene.

The asterisks in Figure 8.7 indicate microphone locations. Recording engineers, especially those who work with rock bands and use as many as six microphones just to mike the drums, might be interested to note that only one microphone was used for each of the different areas. This included Studio D itself, where the actors worked. No matter how large the cast was, all the lines were said into one mike, an RCA 44, hung from the ceiling by its cable. If the microphone had to be adjusted

Figure 8.8. Fred Flowerday and Tony Caminito. Photo courtesy of Jerrell Frederick.

to varying heights, it was simply raised or lowered by pulling on the cable.

This single-mike arrangement was the same for the sound-effects area. Mike #3, for example, was used for all the manually done horses' hooves and footsteps. Mike #4 was used for all water effects. And mike #5 was used for the wooden-door effects on "The Lone Ranger" and for the car-door effects on "The Green Hornet."

Each of these shows had five sound-effects artists, four in the studio doing the live manual effects, and one in the control room doing the recorded effects.

Pictured in Figure 8.8 are two of the regular sound-effects artists on

Figure 8.9. Double-arm system. Photo courtesy of Robert J. Graham.

"The Lone Ranger," Fred Flowerday, seated, and Tony Caminito. After years of doing sound effects, Flowerday moved into the director's chair. Caminito worked in the control room doing the show's recorded sounds.

For his job, Caminito needed three 78-RPM turntables and two transcription tables with mixed 33/45/78 RPM speeds. The three sound-effects turntables were used for such recorded sounds as birds, thunder, waterfalls, and artillery cannons, while the transcription tables were used for musical bridges and—surprise—recorded gunshots.

Notice that there are two pickup arms on one record in Figure 8.9. This allows the artist to play one record cut continuously. When the needle on one pickup arm is about to come to the end of the cut, the artist closes the volume control (the potentiometer, or pot) for pickup arm #1 and opens the volume control to pickup arm #2.

The audio booth was elevated about four steps above the studio floor to give the director an overview of both the actors and the sound-effects studio.

And finally, there was the client's booth, with 10 theater-type seats mounted on risers for the comfort of the sponsor and the sponsor's guests.

The attention that WXYZ gave to the special needs of sound effects was unusual, just as it was unusual to have five sound-effects artists on all their shows. What was even more unusual was that all three of the shows produced at WXYZ were created by two people, George Trendle and Fran Striker. Trendle and Striker collaborated on "The Lone Ranger" and "The Green Hornet," while Fran Striker came up with "Sgt. Preston of the Yukon" on his own.

Having just two people responsible for the production values of all three shows was a big help for the sound-effects artists. They knew what these men expected from sound effects and they gave it to them.

This was especially true with the gunshots and footsteps. No matter which director did the show, they knew the sounds had been approved by the producers and couldn't be changed. Therefore, it didn't matter who wrote or directed the show, there was a strict sound-effects format that was adhered to on all the shows.

Knowing what sounds they were going to be using from week to week was a privilege not granted to the network artists. They had to be ready for anything, especially with the gunshots. If every network show had used the same recorded gunshots, all the gunshot problems would have disappeared including those caused by the network's "limiters."

Limiters were designed to set parameters on the volume of sound that went out over the air to the home receivers. If the limiters weren't taken out of the circuit at the time of the gunshot, the sound would be compressed.

The studio audio man had the job of making sure that a show's overall broadcast sound wasn't too loud or too soft. And that's part of the reason why everyone in Figure 8.10 is smiling even though their show CBS' "Gangbusters," is about to go on the air live. The soundmen are Jerry McCarty (left) and Byron Wingett (right); in the center is Artie Irons, the show's audio man, whose job was to see that the overall sound level was just right. Soundmen, of course, always complained that their sound-effects levels never got loud *enough*. As a result, they all played a little game. The soundmen would use one level for their effects during rehearsals and then, when they got on the air, they'd make their sounds ever so slightly

Figure 8.10. Jerry McCarty, Artie Irons, and Byron Wingett. Photo courtesy of Jerry McCarty.

louder. The audio men knew this, of course, and on air, they would make the sound-effects level ever so slightly softer. Ah yes, live radio . . . now you know why they're all smiling. Incidentally, you can tell how old this picture is by the WWII "shelter" (as in air raid) sign over the door.

Although all artists wanted their gunshots to sound realistic, there were other considerations—like not causing your partner to go permanently deaf. Doing gunshots on a show could be extremely dangerous. Normally, when the shots occurred, there were other sounds to do as well. But despite this, where gunshots were concerned everyone was usually where they were supposed to be at the time of the shots.

But not always. On "Silver Eagle, Mountie," Jim Jewell, the director-producer-writer, decided he would do the sound of a screaming eagle. Although this was a sound effect, it was also a vocal effect and therefore could be done by anyone, including Jewell, who had an actor's union card.

As his eagle cue approached, Jewell came out of the control room and began warming up for his big moment by running around the studio flapping his arms. Unfortunately, in his zealous attempt for realism, he flew too close to the sound-effects area, and as soundman Curt Mitchell fired his gun, Jewell let out a scream that was a cross between a bald eagle and a deafened producer. But because they were on the air, Jewell couldn't say

Figure 8.11. Burt Lancaster and Keene Crockett. Photo courtesy of Keene Crockett.

what was really on his mind. Instead, he fled out of the studio and moments later, despite the studio's sound proofing, the cast and Curt Mitchell heard the muffled howls of a wounded bald eagle.

I've mentioned that directors often complained that our radio gunshots didn't compare favorably with the gunshots heard in films. Well, often they were right, and the reason could be traced to Hollywood's postproduction studios. In those studios, directors had a choice of dozens of different-sounding shots, each of them on film and meticulously labeled. And if the directors didn't like anything there, they'd order up a camera and sound crew and record some different shots. These shots would be fired in the mountains, in the valleys, in canyons, in empty 50-gallon drums, in Paramount restrooms — any place that might enhance the sound of the gunshots. Furthermore, during post-production they might combine five different gunshots to make one great-sounding gunshot. (Incidentally, that was the technique [over dubbing] used to enhance the sound of the MGM lion roar and the Tarzan yell.) After these film gunshots were accepted, they were added to the picture of the gun being fired, with frame-by-frame accuracy.

Figure 8.11 shows soundman Crockett comparing notes with actor Burt Lancaster about the differences between the guns used in films and those used on radio. One thing Lancaster learned was that on live radio, if the gun didn't work on air, you couldn't lay the sound in later like they did in Hollywood.

Before the development of audio tape, record companies tried to solve our gunshot problem by coming out with realistic shots on records. These recorded shots were fine as long as the director was aware of the limitations of these shots.

Single shots on records meant that the record had to be cued to a precise spot. If a second shot was needed, the record had to be cued again, or a second record used. There were records with multiple shots on one cut, but this meant that the actor was at the mercy of the shots' timing on the record. And rare are the actors or directors who want their timing dictated by a sound-effects record unless, of course, you worked on "The Lone Ranger."

While radio soundmen were still struggling with their gunshot problem, along came live television. Now, you would think if we could transmit pictures through the air, we could come up with better-sounding gunshots. We couldn't. In fact, one of NBC's early television dramas, *Petrified Forest*, starring Humphrey Bogart, was critically panned because of the horrible-sounding gunshot. The next day, June 6, 1955, the *Hollywood Mirror News* ran this headline: "The Shot Heard 'Round TV."

While NBC was having its headaches, the folks over at CBS were jumping in the air in jubilation. They felt they had finally solved, once and for all, the gunshot problems.

Don Foster, an excellent sound-effects artist and prolific inventor, had just perfected his shot machine, the "Foster Gun."

The Foster Gun, shown in Figure 8.12, could produce everything from a single shot to a machine gun, a ricochet to a dynamite explosion, and all at the flick of a switch to find the proper frequency for the sound we wanted to emulate.

So realistic were these sounds that the Marine Corps was interested in using the machine to accustom new recruits to the sounds they might encounter under battle conditions.

The gunshot problem was even more serious in television than it was in radio. In radio, we only had the sound of the shot to contend with. In television, it was both the sound of the shot and how realistic the shot looked. It must be understood that because a gun fired blanks didn't mean it wasn't dangerous. And I don't mean just deafening someone. Not only could the flame that came from the barrel cause serious burns, but the

Figure 8.12. The Foster Gun. Photo courtesy of Malachy Wienges.

paper waddings that held the powder in the casings could be shot from the gun like a fiery spit ball. Neither of these events appealed to the actor or actress being shot at. However, the only alternative to using blanks on the set was having the actor use an empty gun and letting sound effects make the gunshot sound.

This meant that the director had to cut his camera away from the actor doing the shooting or have the actor turn his back to the camera and "telegraph" (make a slight move with the shoulder) so the sound-effects artist would know when to fire the gun. The problem with these methods was the actors themselves, especially the few Hollywood actors who were testing the waters of live television. If the actors, in the excitement of the live telecast, didn't "hit their marks" (be in the proper position for the camera), the audience at home could plainly see that the guns were not doing the actual shooting, and the mood of the story was destroyed.

All these problems could be blamed on the film industry. As far back as the 1930s, movie-goers were accustomed to the shoot-'em-up thrills of the gangster films and hoss-opera westerns. However, unlike television, film directors spent hours, even days, critically lining up camera angles for the sake of realism and then spent weeks in post-production painstakingly making all those anemic gunshots sound like cannons. By contrast, television directors tried to accomplish the same results in a matter of minutes.

It was understandable, therefore, that Foster's electronic shot machine was looked upon as a step toward Hollywood's gunshot perfection. In addition, this ingenious little machine could be triggered by sound, much like today's sensored security lights that are turned on by sound.

That principal was applied to our gunshots. The sound-effects artist would first select the appropriate gunshot. If it was to be heard off-camera, the artist would trigger it manually. If the gun was to be seen on camera, the loudness of the blank in the gun used by the actor would trigger the shot machine.

The option of being able to adjust the shot machine to the loudness of the blank was important, because now a blank that was relatively harmless would have the same realistic fire-and-smoke-producing capabilities as the larger, more dangerous charges.

But, as we all know, nothing in this world is perfect. And as efficient as the electronic shot machine was, it couldn't discriminate between the sound of a gunshot and other sounds. *Any* other sounds. If they were of the same frequency as the sound predetermined for the gunshot, they would trigger the shot machine.

Because of this slight flaw, tuning these guns was extremely critical. They had to be sensitive enough to accept the signal from the blank, but reject sound levels that were below that threshold. This included incidental noises on the set. Unfortunately, nothing could be done about sounds of greater intensity. The only solution was to turn the machine off.

On CBS' prestigious and award-winning "Studio One," Arthur Strand used this shot machine with great success in a very dramatic scene involving two highly respected Hollywood leading men. As the four shots spewed realistic flame and smoke from the actor's pistols, the shot machine supplied four explosive shots in perfect synchronization. The scene faded out, with triumph for both man and machine, and Betty Furness, the spokeswoman for Westinghouse Refrigerators, began the in-studio live commercial.

As Betty smoothly extolled the virtues of the refrigerator, Strand was busy listening on his headset to the accolades about his great gunshots that were coming from the control room.

In the meantime, Miss Furness continued pointing out all the advantages that Westinghouse refrigerators had over the competition, not the least of which was their incredible quietness. By way of proving it, she gave the camera a warm, sincere smile and spoke the familiar promise of the sponsor: "You can be sure . . . if it's Westinghouse." And to prove how quiet the refrigerator door was, she did what she had done hundreds of times before on the program, she shut the refrigerator door. But this time, the closing of the quietest refrigerator on the market was accompanied by the loudest gunshot in the west. Strand had forgotten to shut off the shot machine!

Miss Furness, accustomed to hearing only a refrigerator door closing quietly, stopped smiling sweetly. And that night, viewers of "Studio One" across this great land of ours were treated to two unexpected events: the inaugural use of the Foster Gun Machine, and Miss Furness letting out a scream of fright that rivaled the loudness of that famous gunshot.

Later, when Arthur Strand related this story to George O'Donnell, his good friend and partner on the radio show "Let's Pretend," George, thinking of his own gunshot disaster, smiled supportingly and remarked, "Thank God she only screamed. She could have just as well farted!"

Not too long after Strand's misadventure, I had occasion to use the shot machine on "The Web." This program also originated from Studio One. When I arrived to begin setting up for my show, it was evident that Strand had used the shot machine again because taped all over the sound-effects area were graphic reminders written in large, bold letters: "Don't forget to turn off the Foster Gun, stupid!"

The story we were doing on "The Web" took place on the waterfront. The script called for 25 pages of water lapping against a dock, boat whistles, bell buoy sounds, and sea gulls. The final five pages took place at night, and meant adding a mournful fog horn (not the Lifebuoy one) and putting the seagulls to bed. On the final page of the script, the gunshot happened. So just to be sure, in addition to the reminders that Strand had put up,

I marked my script in big black letters with the warning, "It could happen to you."

The final action took place among the steel girders of the Brooklyn Bridge. Because the studio bridge was constructed of silver-painted wood, I had to synchronize my steps, done on a metal plate, with those of the actors, done on wood. And in addition to the four turntables of harbor sounds and the manual footsteps, I foolishly elected to add the recorded whine of a ricochet to the show-ending electronic gunshot.

When sounds have to run under entire scenes, a technique known as double-arming is employed (see Figure 8.9). This means that just before the record containing the water-lapping sounds runs out, the spare turntable arm is placed at the beginning of the record and the sound is crossfaded from the arm that is nearing the end of the record to the arm at the beginning of the record. This procedure could become confusing (as you are about to find out) when we had to do it with all four turntables and still monitor for other cues.

Although my idea of adding a ricochet sound to the gunshot was creatively inspired, in retrospect, it was a dumb idea.

The problem was, the ricochet sound that I had selected was on a record that contained 12 other ricochet sounds. Fortunately my ricochet was the first one of the twelve, so I didn't have a cueing problem. All I had to do is remember to close the mike I used for the Foster Gun.

During the day I must have reminded myself a hundred times to close that microphone. I even began humming it to the tune of, "Who's Afraid of the Big Bad Wolf."

On air, as the detective stealthily climbed through the maze of steel girders, accompanied by my background river sounds and distant harbor noises, I watched his feet like a hawk so that my footsteps were in perfect synchronization. Then, as he lifted the .45 caliber automatic for the fateful shot, I whipped my head around to make certain the mike was open . . . it was! Now for the moment of truth! As fire erupted from the .45, the Foster gun responded with a cannon-like explosion, followed immediately by my recording of the ricochet. My finger then dove for the microphone switch and closed it. I had pulled it off! The shot and ricochet had made a symphony of sounds! Whenever gunshot sounds were mentioned, this would be the one they were all compared to!

Heaving a mighty sigh of relief, I was suddenly stunned to hear another ricochet, followed almost immediately by another ricochet! In my exultation over closing the gunshot mike, I had forgotten to close the pot to the ricochet record! But which one was it? Pot number one? Number two? Three? Four? Five? In the meantime, two more ricochets whined through the Brooklyn Bridge. If I closed all the pots at once, all the sounds would go out suddenly. Another ricochet. If I killed each pot one after the other, it would take too long! Finally, my decision was made for me as the last two shots pinged their way into the night and Tony Mottola, the gifted guitarist, was plucking and strumming the closing theme over the shows credits.

Having privately suffered the embarrassment and humiliation of this horrendous screw up, I now had to face the combined wrath of Lela Swift, the director, and Herb Hirshman, the producer.

The sound-effects area at Studio One was located next to the lighting bridge high above the stage. To get there we had to climb a narrow metal ladder, which explains why the lighting man used to send a cardboard box down on a rope when he wanted coffee. Normally, the person doing sound effects had to scamper up and down that obstacle run dozens of times for script changes, conferences, or technical problems with the equipment. But this night, I wasn't moving. If Lela or Herb wanted me, they were going to have to come and get me! Finally, as the studio noises that accompanied the end of a show began to quiet down, I felt it might be safe to creep down from my crow's nest. I took one last look around the familiar sound-effects area, because even if I wasn't kicked off the show tonight, I would certainly hear about it tomorrow.

Halfway down the ladder, the quiet of the studio was shattered by Herb's voice bellowing, "Mott . . . over here!" As I made my way down the rest of the ladder, I came up with three excuses, none of which made any sense, even to me. So, with no other options, I figured, what the hell, you win some and you lose some.

By this time Herb had made his way over the Brooklyn Bridge and confronted me. "That was the damnedest effect I ever heard!" As I fumbled for something intelligent to say, he continued on. "A real stroke of genius! I could just see that single bullet ricocheting off all those steel girders. It made the show for me! Keep up the good work!"

Like I say, you win some . . . and when you do, cherish the moment, because times like that happen once in a lifetime.

Sound-effects artists weren't the only people having problems with guns. Actors had their share, as well. In an effort to compete with Hollywood films, early television shows were always striving for realism. On "Rocky Norton, Private Eye," shot in New York, the producer decided to add excitement to a script by having it done outside the Dumont studios on the fire escape high above the busy city streets.

To give the scene a look of realism and a sound of excitement, it was decided to use blanks with full loads, the loudest-sounding blanks made. They also were the most dangerous, but because the scene was being done outside and the two gun-fighting actors were far apart, it was considered safe.

On air, the scene began with the good guy climbing out a window onto the fire escape, hot on the trail of the bad guy. As loud gunshots began exploding back and forth between the two actors, the sound-effects artist in the studio dutifully supplied an occasional ricochet. Everyone in the control room was ecstatic over the realistic look and sound of the gunfight.

The camera was cutting back and forth between the two actors when, out of the corner of his eye, the bad guy saw police cars screeching to a halt down below in front of the studio. The police piled out of their cars and began aiming *real* guns at the startled and now thoroughly frightened actor!

Obviously, no one connected with the show had thought to inform New York's finest that the gunfight they were witnessing was all make-believe! The actor, after desperately trying to think how he could save the scene and still not get shot, decided the two weren't compatible and solved his dilemma by diving unceremoniously back through the window and into his dressing room. That left the cameras with nothing to shoot but an empty fire escape, and the viewing audience at home thinking what a dumb way to end a scene. Well, to many people, perhaps. But not to the actor, Ernest Borgnine. Not only was he smart enough to jump back through the window, he didn't do too bad later on in Hollywood, either. Hollywood, where they're smart enough to leave realistic looking and sounding gunshots up to the people in post-production.

But not exclusively. One night in 1946, Ray Kemper and Tom Hanley had just finished a heavy show on "Red Ryder" at KHJ on Melrose Avenue in the heart of Hollywood. The show's director had never stopped complaining about the sound of their gunshots.

After the show, Ray and Tom were in the washroom getting cleaned up when they heard two men suddenly start arguing in the room next door that served as an equipment room for the station's cleaning crews. The argument was over a gambling debt one was having difficulty collecting from the other. As Tom and Ray listened, the voices got louder and angrier.

Ray listened to the serious tones of the voices and commented, "Those guys are really getting ugly in there. I think we better go in there and stop them before they kill one another."

At that, Tom gave Ray a mischievous wink and, pulling one of the

.38-caliber pistols out of his coat pocket, began loading it with blanks. When he looked up, his eyes gleamed impishly.

"Follow my lead," he said, and then in a loud voice he snarled, "Don't give me that crap, you four-flushing bastard! I want my money now!!!"

Ray, caught up in his partner's drama, whined, "I told you I'd get the money as soon as I could...."

The voices in the other room suddenly became quiet.

Realizing he had the arguing voices' attention, Tom put even more angry emotion into his voice. "I told you, you bastard, what would happen to you if you didn't pay up!!!"

Not to be outdone, Ray raised his voice several octaves. "What the hell are you doing with that gun? Are you crazy?"

"Crazy, am I," echoed Tommy, "I'll show you what we do with people who welsh on bets in Chicago!!!"

Ray began whimpering in terror. "No ... no ... for God's sake ... give me a break!!! I've got a wife and kids!!!"

The three fast shots from the .38 sounded like cannons in the tiled men's room. Ray slammed his body against the wall and did an agonizingly slow body fall, complete with his fingernails making desperate scratching sounds against the wall as he slid to the floor.

The two conspirators then quickly opened the door and, while Ray watched, Tom slammed the door shut loudly and did the sound effects of a man running off down the hall. They both then hid around the corner to watch the results of their little impromptu drama.

For a full five minutes there was not a sound from the room the voices had come from. Finally, the door inched open a crack, and a pair of frightened eyes peered out nervously.

"See anything?" A voice in back of the eyes asked.

"Nope," the eyes answered.

"That don't mean that guy with the gun ain't still out there...."

To that possibility, the eyes replied, "You heard him running off just as much as I did."

The voice thought about that for a moment and then asked in a somewhat more fearful tone, "Do ya think he really killed that man with the wife and kids?"

This time the eyes took more time in answering.

"Them shots sure sounded like it." He then added, "So there ain't too much use of us staying here to get into trouble."

With that, the door opened wider and the eyes materialized into a head, arms, body, and legs, which were now running rapidly down the hall followed closely by the body of the voice.

📣 *VARIETY* 📣

CBS SHOOTS THE WORKS

Through the years, the sound of gun-shots has been one of radio's biggest bugaboos. Coming at crucial moments in westerns and mysteries, they can make or break the suspense and tenseness of a situation. And too often in the past, a gripping climax of a simulated .45 caliber pistol shot has sounded like a cap gun.

CBS Radio soundmen Ray Kemper and Tom Hanley six months ago, with permission from Cliff Thorness, head of CBS Radio's sound effects department, tackled this problem.

The pair assembled a small arsenal ranging from .22's to .405 Sharps rifles. Using all types of ammunition and changing the powder load, they spent weeks in CBS studios, firing guns, using echo chambers, boxes and empty drums until they discovered the studio, built for acoustics, either absorbed the sound or swirled it out of proportion.

Finally, with police permission, Kemper and Hanley spent two days near Mint Canyon firing every gun in their possession from every distance and angle with soundman Jack Sixsmith recording. Result was an authentic sound tape of gunshots.

For such CBS programs as "Gunsmoke" and "Yours Truly, Johnny Dollar," where guns play major roles, they tailor-make the shots. Working from the script, with split second timing, they take the exact shots needed from the master tape and dub them on the show tape.

Norm MacDonnell, "Gunsmoke" producer, stated, "This has finally brought to westerns, what they've lacked for years—absolute perfection in the sound of guns."

Jaime Del Valle, "Johnny Dollar" head man, opines, "It has always been a pet peeve of mine to build up a tense climax with fine acting, only to have it ruined with the pop of a cork substituting for what should have been a blasting gun. This is great."

Looking ahead, Thorness states the ultimate goal is a machine that might be called a "gun-shot piano," with 10 or 12 play-back heads loaded with gun-shot tapes and operated by a push button when a shot is needed. The tape would reroll automatically and be cued up for instant re-use.

Figure 8.13. Daily Variety *reports the Kemper-Hanley gunshot. The 1954 Daily Variety Ltd. Reprinted by permission.*

As Ray listened to the fading footsteps, he turned to Tom and asked, "Think we were too hard on them?"

Tommy shrugged his shoulders and smiled. "Maybe, but I think what we did was a helluva lot better than what they were about to do to each other." He then looked at his gun and added, "And we owe it all to these gunshots that the director thought were so damn unrealistic!"

Our gunshot dilemma continued for another five years. Then, in 1954, these two artists, Ray Kemper and Tom Hanley, created a series of gunshots for "Gunsmoke" that rivaled the gunshots in films. This breakthrough was heralded in the May 7, 1954, edition of *Daily Variety* (Figure 8.13).

Once these gunshots were heard on "Gunsmoke," they soon became the gunshot standard for the industry. Whenever a show needed a gunshot, the request invariably stated, "like the gunshots on 'Gunsmoke.'"

Figure 8.14. A MacKenzie cartridge. Photo courtesy of MacKenzie Laboratories.

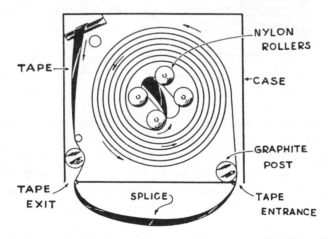

Figure 8.15. Schematic diagram of a sound effect cart. Photo courtesy of MacKenzie Laboratories.

In the beginning, the "Gunsmoke" shots were all on tape. It made no difference if a scene required one, two, or a dozen gunshots, the actors reacted to the sounds *the way they were on tape*. This was quite a departure from the norm: Now, instead of the sound-effects artists taking their cues from the actors, the actors were reacting to gunshots that were pre-recorded. Norm MacDonald, the show's producer, gave a high priority to

Figure 8.16. A MacKenzie cart machine. Photo courtesy of MacKenzie Laboratories.

his sound effects. His high standard of excellence was most dramatically noticeable with the gunshots, but it also extended right down to the sound effect of the beer Matt guzzled at the Long Branch (the sound of a shot of whiskey was just plain tap water, but because beer had a softer, bubbly sound, the only "beer" Miss Kitty served in shoot-'em-up Dodge City was ginger ale).

Reacting to the sounds of gunshots on tape was somewhat awkward and limiting for the actors. Therefore in 1955, when Louis MacKenzie introduced his cartridge machines to Disneyland for sound effects and instructional uses, he also convinced the networks of their practicality for sound effects in broadcasting. This, of course, delighted both the actors and the sound-effects artists: The machines gave cueing control back to the sound-effects people, while still producing excellent gunshot sounds.

MacKenzie's machine was a technological giant step forward, because it allowed much greater control over *any* recorded sound (not just gunshots!). The machine used cartridges loaded with quarter-inch audio tape. These cartridges quickly became known as "carts." The cart shown in Figure 8.14 contains the taped sound of a single engine airplane in continuous flight.

In the past, it had been necessary to double-arm records or rewind reel-to-reel tapes when the sound-sequence got to the end. But the MacKenzie carts would run for as long as we needed without any further attention.

Cueing these tapes to stop was also easy, requiring nothing more than a small piece of metallic foil placed on the tape just ahead of where we wanted the tape to stop. Figure 8.15 is a diagram of the innards of a cart. When a photoelectric cell picked up the illumination from a foil cue mark, it would trigger the solenoids to disengage and the tape would stop. We were thus able to produce the sound of a shot, or any other effect, almost instantaneously.

Figure 8.16 shows a MacKenzie cart machine. These machines came in banks of five units, and the five carts could be played separately or mixed together. For example, two of the cart channels might play different types of rifle shots, while two other channels might have shot-gun sounds with the fifth channel left open for a machine gun. And unlike using blanks in guns, we didn't have to load them, they didn't misfire, the sound of the shots never varied, they recued themselves automatically, and the shots were heard instantly at the flick of a finger. If we wanted more shots, we added another five units. If we wanted to do a war, we added another five units.

The convenience and technical superiority of audio tape and of equipment like the MacKenzie cart machine finally gave radio a gunshot sound that rivaled those used in films. It is, therefore, ironic that the development of equipment such as the MacKenzie machine, that so greatly improved the sound of dramatic radio, also sounded the death knell for live radio.

CHAPTER IX

THE SOAPS

SOAP OPERAS–YOU EITHER hate them or love them. But either way, where would the world of entertainment be without them? They are the wonderful world where women stay heavy with child anywhere from four months to three years. Where kindly old grandmothers pour oceans of lemonade and bake mountains of brownies while gramps is in the slammer facing a morals rap.

As hard as they've tried over the years, the detractors and critics of soaps have never been able to dent, let alone burst, their beautiful, rich, sudsy bubble of success. If anyone needs evidence of the staying powers of this venerable art form, here is a list of the soaps on the air in 1942.

1. Abie's Irish Rose
2. Against the Storm
3. Aunt Jenny
4. Bachelor's Children
5. Backstage Wife
6. Big Sister
7. The Brighter Day
8. David Harum
9. Dr. Kate
10. Doctors at Work
11. The Guiding Light
12. I'll Find My Way
13. John's Other Wife
14. The Johnson Family
15. Just Plain Bill
16. Life Can Be Beautiful
17. The Light of the World
18. Lorenzo Jones
19. Ma Perkins
20. The Man I Married
21. Myrt and Marge
22. Nobody's Children
23. One Man's Family
24. Our Gal Sunday
25. Pepper Young's Family
26. Portia Faces Life
27. The Right to Happiness
28. The Road of Life
29. The Romance of Helen Trent
30. Second Husband
31. The Second Mrs. Burton
32. Stella Dallas
33. This Is Nora Drake
34. When a Girl Marries
35. Young Doctor Malone

Nine years later, in 1951, the list of soaps on the air looked like this:

1. Aunt Jenny
2. Backstage Wife
3. Big Sister
4. The Brighter Day
5. The Guiding Light
6. Hilltop House
7. Just Plain Bill
8. King's Row
9. Life Can Be Beautiful
10. Lorenzo Jones
11. Ma Perkins
12. One Man's Family
13. Our Gal Sunday
14. Pepper Young's Family
15. Perry Mason
16. The Right to Happiness
17. The Road of Life
18. The Romance of Helen Trent
19. Rosemary
20. The Second Mrs. Burton
21. Stella Dallas
22. This Is Nora Drake
23. When a Girl Marries
24. Young Doctor Malone

Many of the shows that were on in 1942 were still dispensing their special brand of misery and woe in 1951. "Road of Life," for instance, began in 1937. It just goes to prove, you can't give people enough of what they want, no matter what it is.

It really makes no difference which soap was first. Whether it was "The Goldbergs," "The Smith Family," "Clara," "Lu and Em," "Painted Dreams," "Vic and Sade," "Amos 'n' Andy," "The Stolen Husband" or "Moonshine and Honeysuckle," the fact is, radio and the indomitable soaps grew up together. The love affair started in the mid–1920s and lasted until 1960 when the soaps said their bubbly goodbyes to radio and to an audience that had remained unflinchingly loyal through all their sufferings and heart-rending ordeals.

Everyone seemed to have a theory about why radio soaps were so popular and enduring. Some attributed it to nothing more than that the soaps were a habit. But probably the most informed opinion came from producers Frank and Anne Hummert, the undisputed king and queen of soapdom. Their loyal and obedient subjects included David Harum, Lorenzo Jones, Stella Dallas, Helen Trent . . . and on and on. Frank Hummert's explanation was: "We do successful stories about unsuccessful people. By unsuccessful, we mean they are not wealthy," and they went on to say that their stories were about the everyday doings of plain, everyday people. Anne Hummert's was more to the point: "I know what women want."

What they don't say is that on all of the soaps, no matter how plain or everyday these folks might be, it was the woman who was the problem solver. It made no difference how brilliant a brain surgeon the man might be, on the soaps, he still needed help from his wife to button his cardigan sweater.

Not that these good ladies of soaps didn't have their own share of grief, misfortunes, and dirty laundry to wash. They had more than their share. More than most listeners, anyway. But did these brave women complain? Never! Not Ma, not Helen, not Stella, and certainly not Nona from Nowhere. They just rolled up their sleeves, lifted their chins, and challenged the writers to come up with a problem they couldn't handle. And — surprise — the writers couldn't do it. Despite what pickles they got these resourceful women into, sooner or later, the ladies would triumph.

And what made listening to these programs so much fun was, they weren't *your* problems. The listener was just an innocent bystander, an eavesdropper. They made the listener's plight seem like a piece of cake. Little wonder that fans showed their gratitude to these wonderful matriarchs (and the actresses who played them) by showering them with birthday cards, Christmas cards, get-well cards, letters of advice, letters asking advice, and just plain adoring letters. Some of the more seriously involved (or maybe mentally incapacitated) listeners would actually call the radio station wanting to speak to their favorite character to warn them of an impending danger.

But if listeners hadn't cared and hadn't listened, then the good folks at Oxydol or Rinso or Tide wouldn't have sunk their money into these shows and there wouldn't have been such a thing as soaps. So whatever people like the Hummerts were doing, it must have been right. How else can you explain "Ma Perkins" going on the air in 1933 and staying there for 27 years?

So stay tuned and find out how you too can run away from your humdrum life and marry England's richest and most handsome Lord. Our Gal Sunday did. And look where she came from: some obscure mining town down in West Virginia. And if you don't find out Sunday's secret today, tune in again tomorrow, when once again, Oxydol will bring you … the stuff that dreams are made of.

The one problem producers of soaps had to contend with was guilt. Not theirs — the listener's. To avoid this, producers made certain that fans could remain faithful to the program and still get the housework done without missing a word. Well, that's not quite true. There would be a lot of missed words.

One way the producers of soaps dealt with that problem was to ensure that no matter how many words a listener missed, there was a typewriter full of others waiting to take their place. Nothing was ever said just once on soaps, it was said over and over and over and again and again and again. Even if a fan missed an entire program it was all right because the announcer would bring the story up to date the next day. Sometimes it seemed that between the announcer giving the commercials and reviewing for the audience what had happened the day before and what they could expect to hear today, it was almost time for the organist to start the closing theme. In fact, sometimes the only way to hear a show was to tune in the next day and let the announcer tell you what you had missed the day before.

Some of the staunchest supporters the soaps had in radio were the organists. Simply by dipping into their musical bag of "stings," they could make the most innocuous and inane words sound like poetry.

A sting was a high, single note used to signal the housewife to turn off the vacuum and come running, sort of like opening a can of yum-yums for your cat. These musical accents were used instead of words to make certain that even the newest, or busiest, listener didn't miss the importance and subtle shadings of certain plot lines:

MA: But if Nell Harris comes back to Summerspring that means...

MUSIC: *sting*

PA: Exactly.

MUSIC: *sting in and under*

PA: *(continuing)* ...but there's more...

MUSIC: *sting*

MA: More...?

MUSIC: *sting up and under*

PA: ...a darn sight more!

MUSIC: *sting up into big rip chord finish*

If you think the contributions that these organists made to the success of soaps is overstated, try making any sense out of that dialogue without those all-important musical crutches. They did more than supply openings, closings, and musical bridges; they actually supplied music for individual words.

These musicians were in such great demand that they often did three or four shows a day. Here are just a few of these talented people and some of their shows:

Charlie Paul: "The Road of Life," "This Is Nora Drake," "Young Dr. Malone," "The Shadow"

Paul Taubman: "Perry Mason," "Rosemary," "Thanks for Tomorrow"

Dick Leibert: "Big Sister," "The Life and Love of Dr. Susan," "The Second Mrs. Burton," "Stella Dallas"

Bill Meeder: "The Right to Happiness," "Pepper Young's Family," "The Brighter Day"

John Winters: "Myrt and Marge," "When a Girl Marries," "Young Widder Brown"

Rosa Rio: "Lorenzo Jones," "Myrt and Marge," "When a Girl Marries"

The radio soap organists have never been given the credit they deserve. In addition to the opening and closing themes, the musical bridges, the stings, pings, and rip chords, directors could always depend on them to hold notes and chords just a little longer to make the show end exactly on time. With all this to do, it seems incredible that they had time to do anything else. But they most certainly did, and the one area where they were most helpful was in sound effects.

When commercial recording companies began furnishing networks with some much-needed sounds on 78-RPM records, everyone in sound effects was ecstatic—at least for a while. It was soon discovered that these recordings, like anything else in life, were not the total answer to all our problems. For example, consider CBS' good old #209. This record had an excellent car crash. It had everything—a high frequency skid, followed by a metal-wrenching, glass-smashing impact that sent shivers up the spine of every soundman who heard it. And, naturally, every soundman wanted it for his or her show.

Even the writers wanted this excellent car crash, and so all the writers on all of the shows began beefing up the excitement at the end of their scenes by adding a screech of brakes, a scream from an actor, and that wonderful car crash with all its splintering glass.

The trouble was, good old reliable #209 became a little over-exposed. It was possible to listen to three successive shows and hear the same #209 car crash on all three programs! Obviously, something had to be done. And what was done didn't please the artists working the soaps.

A memo came out banning the use of records and manual effects "known to be of popular usage on prime-time programming." This, of course, included #209 as well as the rifle shot on "Red Ryder," the marching feet on "Gangbusters," the squeaking door on "Inner Sanctum," the train whistle on "Grand Central Station," and any wolf that just happened to howl like Brad Barker for the opening of "Renfrew of the Mounted."

In addition to these restrictions, there were others. All new recordings, of *any* sounds, were off limits to the lowly soaps. This meant that not only were the daytime soundmen forbidden to use the best sounds available on records, but the records they were allowed to use were often old, scarred, and scratchy.

When these soundmen did voice their objections, they were given this bit of rather curious reasoning. "They'll never hear it in Canarsie."

The rationale for this explanation was this: Canarsie, a section of Brooklyn, New York, was not very far from the CBS transmitter. Therefore, if the good people of Canarsie didn't hear anything scratchy about the rain on their favorite soap, no one else in America would hear it, either.

It was because of these restrictions, and the limited time given for rehearsals, that the sound-effects artists on the soaps needed all the help they could get. Enter the organists.

Each of these gifted musicians had a repertoire of stings, pings, chords, rip chords, "think music," "happy time music," bridges, glissandos, and whatever other type of music might be required to make a producer's heart sing. Having one of these gifted musicians available was a boon for any show. For example: If an actor wasn't conveying the proper amount of fear—play a sting; when a character whirls to see someone in the shadows—play a rip chord; while a character sips a scotch in a dingy bar and remembers better times—play a glissando. The list goes on and on. But no one on a soap appreciated the value of the organist more than the sound-effects artist.

There were union rules about musicians simulating sound effects, but there was nothing in the rule books about musicians accompanying sound effects. Therefore, on "Rosemary," when Monica wrestles the wheel of the car from Lonny, Rosemary's adopted son, and the car skids into a telephone pole, who was responsible for the sound of that crash? Was it #209? Or was it a very ordinary car-crash record accompanied by the artistry of Paul Taubman supplying a "skid-like sting" followed by a "crash-like rip chord"?

Even effects as ordinary as door knocks and footsteps took on a meaning all their own when the organist accompanied them. A simple tap on the door followed by a high-pitched sting portended danger. Ordinary footsteps climbing stairs could be made to sound mysterious or terrifying, simply by the notes the organist played in synchronization with the steps.

This addition of music to sounds was welcomed by most soundmen on the soaps because, with the exception of "Perry Mason," they had neither the time nor the inclination to make their sound effects anything more than just functional. If a writer requested that a blind girl "listen to the sound of sunlight," it would be done with a glissando of music, and not one minute of time would be spent searching for an appropriate sound effect. Interpretations for the "sound of sunlight" and other so-called artsy sound effects were left to the shows in prime time that had the luxury of budget and time to create them.

The sound-effects demands on a soap were for the most part uninspired and predictable. In addition to the phone bells, door buzzers, and bing-bong doorbells, we opened and closed a lot of doors, rang a lot of phones, opened and closed ice boxes, set off oven timers, poured coffee, whistled tea kettles, put ice cubes (really camera flash bulbs) into endless glasses of lemonade, clinked dishes and silverware, washed dishes and silverware . . . and so it went. However when you figure that pouring a cup of tea saved 10 precious words (20 with cream and sugar) you can understand why the soap writers never let sound effects out of the kitchen.

In those days, a soap only lasted 15 minutes, but it could be an awfully long time to fill up, considering the strict restrictions the writers were faced with. There could be no offensive language or violence, no religious beliefs or anything else of a controversial nature. This most certainly included sex. The sexiest thing they ever did on a soap was kiss but to make certain that the listener at home didn't get any funny ideas, the sound of a kiss on radio was silence. However, they did slip in a little spice by indicating that the longer the silence, the sexier the kiss.

Yes, the good folks in sound effects made car-loads of cookies and poured lakes of lemonade. As Figure 9.1 shows, we even did the laundry for these ladies of the soaps so they would have more time for problem-solving. That's Al Binnie and Vic Rubei (CBS, New York), doing a little gossiping as they go about their one of many soap opera chores.

This modest use of sound effects by soaps was not by accident, nor was it lack of imagination on the part of the writers. Most producers felt that their listening audience preferred their stories straight and on the rocks, without any help from sound effects. They felt very strongly that it was the spoken word that made soaps the darlings of housewives, and so it was the spoken word they were concerned with. Once a script was approved, it might just as well have been chipped in granite. There were to be no changes. And to make certain those words were always heard, the actors were forbidden to overlap their lines. Not surprisingly, producers certainly didn't want those precious words buried under "a bunch of meaningless sound effects!"

Perhaps these producers knew of what they spoke. On one soap, the regular soundman went on vacation and was replaced by a string of relief people. Unfortunately, it was during this time that the writers decided to conclude a very important story line they had been building for months involving the name of a monstrous blackmailer.

This important disclosure was to take place in an old warehouse near a railroad track. To give this rendezvous more atmosphere, the director

Figure 9.1. Al Binnie and Vic Rubei. Photo courtesy of Walter Pierson.

actually made a sound-effects request: He wanted the sound of a distant train whistle.

The director neglected to tell the relief soundman how long the listening audience had been waiting to hear the name of this nefarious blackmailer. Nor did he tell the relief soundman that the name of the blackmailer would only be said once. He also didn't specify exactly where he wanted that train whistle to occur. And he didn't explain that, it being Friday, if the audience didn't hear that name clearly and distinctly today, they wouldn't hear it again until Monday.

It should be pointed out that the soundmen who did relief work on soaps did not have the same knowledge of the show, or for that matter the same loyal interest, that the regular soundmen did. It should also be pointed out that no two soaps had exactly the same system for disseminating information to the cast and crew. Unfortunately, directors sometimes forgot these little facts of life.

Therefore when the director on this particular show added a few words to the script, just before the point when the blackmailer's name was disclosed, he assumed that the relief man was at his elbow, hanging on his every word just like the regular soundman always did. In fact, the relief soundman was out in the hall calling his wife to remind her he'd be home for lunch.

It therefore came to pass that, during the show, when the soundman decided to put the train whistle in just after the moment of disclosure, he wasn't aware of the addition of those three words. And in order to have a cue such as a train whistle time out correctly on those old 78 RPM records, you had to anticipate where the cue was to happen by several words. Which put his train whistle on a collision course with the name of the blackmailer.

Just as the actor began saying the new words, the artist played his lonesome train whistle. The two timed out perfectly. Both the whistle and the name of the blackmailer occurred at the exact same moment. Unfortunately, the listeners at home already knew what a train whistle sounded like, but on that fateful Friday, they never did hear who the blackmailer was.

I have always taken pains not to group "Perry Mason" with the rest of the soaps. Created by the famous author Erle Stanley Gardner, this show, was, for the soundman, a bitch. In fact, it was one of the most difficult shows I ever did in radio. The show opened with a sound-effects sequence that contained two words, "Yeah" and "Yeah," and lasted for three pages. It opened with a loud clap of thunder, followed by footsteps to the window and the window being closed. The thunder becomes softer but continues. Next is the sound of a chair scraping and the effort of a man sitting down (actor supplied the grunts). Then a cork is removed from a bottle and liquid is poured into a glass. The bottle goes back down onto a table and the cork is replaced. Some drinking noises and a slight coughing (by the actor) follow. The phone rings loudly and is taken off the hook.

LOUIE: Yeah...? *(nods)* Yeah....

The phone goes back on the cradle, the chair scrapes away from the table and Louie gets up, takes a violin case off the table and snaps it open and shut. He steps to the door, opens and closes it and locks it with a key. He walks down the stairs, opens the door (the thunder and rain get louder), closes the door (background traffic sounds), he steps onto the sidewalk, opens and closes a car door, starts the car and screeches off. Rain and thunder continue in the background, with windshield wipers predominating. Then the violin case opens, the car speeds up, and there's a sudden long burst of a machine gun.

And that was just the opening! Admittedly, "Perry Mason" was not your average soap and I'm reasonably sure this wasn't an average script, but the show had a reputation for using a great many sounds. Unfortunately, they didn't have a budget to go along with it. As a result, Jimmy

Lynch was often asked to do the work of two soundmen. He did it because he liked the show and he liked the people and he liked the schedule. For all I know he may also have been given a fee, and if he was, he most certainly deserved every penny of it.

But we had to be careful about fees. Networks were paid very well for our services, so if we did the work of two soundmen on a continuing basis, it deprived the networks of charging a show for the services of two artists and as a result we could be fired for collusion. That is why so many sound effects were not written into the script but "thought of" in the studio by the director. These were called "oh by the way" effects. As we rehearsed the script the director would say, "Oh by the way, on page 22 I have a little add for sound effects. We're cutting the first five speeches and adding the sound of an earthquake."

As a result of the "Perry Mason" show's love of sound effects, soundman Lynch devised a series of short cuts. For instance, he put all the bells, buzzers, and telephone noises (busy signals, clicks for a phone being picked up, and line rings) on one panel and clearly marked each in large black letters. But even with all these identifying markings, it could be very confusing if you weren't familiar with the marking system. Working a show as busy as Perry Mason, you needed all the help you could get.

On the "Yeah" episode, the script called for sound effects on nearly every page. Half were to be done with recordings and the other half had to be done manually. This kind of split made the job doubly difficult since, when we were cueing up a record, we couldn't be doing other things with our hands. And when we were ringing a telephone, we couldn't be cueing up a record.

One effect that kept turning up in a script that Lynch was doing was of a ladies' handbag being opened and closed. And in those days, many handbags were equipped with zippers. Therefore, the director insisted that Lynch use a zippered handbag. But the only zippered handbags available in the department were cumbersome, and their zippers were unreliable, one minute working smoothly and the next, becoming stuck. Not wanting to take any unnecessary chances, Lynch decided to substitute the handbag zipper with something more available. He unwisely chose the zipper on his fly.

The bogus pocketbook effect worked very smoothly up to air time. But then Lynch became a little overzealous about zipping the "pocketbook" open, and inadvertently managed to nip a bit of his Fruit of the Loom boxer shorts, along with what his Fruit of the Loom boxer shorts are worn to protect.

When the actress gave the cue to close her pocketbook again, she was puzzled when she didn't hear the effect. Turning to Lynch to see what was

Figure 9.2. Soundmen and friends. Photo courtesy of Walter Pierson.

the matter, she immediately knew. In fact, everyone in the studio knew. As Lynch delicately tried to extricate his boxers and, more importantly, what was in the boxers, the actress covered for the embarrassed Lynch by saying that the things were in her pocket rather than in her zippered purse. Of course, the words came out sounding muffled because of her hand over her mouth to keep from laughing.

Lynch, in the meantime, found out the true meaning of those show business words, "the show must go on!" Still snagged in the zipper, he tried to ease the pain by doing the rest of the effects in a hunched-over position. One actor said it was like having the sound effects done by the Hunchback of Notre Dame.

As for Lynch, no matter how busy "Perry Mason" got after that, he only used his zipper for what it was designed for. Even then, he was always, careful ... very, very careful.

Jimmy Lynch is in Figure 9.2. Actually, Figure 9.2 is a picture puzzle. Which of the three people in the photo actually do what they are doing in this picture and get paid for doing it? If you selected the second man from the left, George O'Donnell ("Let's Pretend"), the fourth man, Jerry Sullivan ("Rosemary"), and the hammer-wielding gentleman on the far right, Jimmy Lynch ("Perry Mason"), you had a perfect score. The pipe-smoking gentleman is Bernard Herrmann, musical conductor for Orson Welles, and the lady next to Lynch is Betsy Tuthill, production secretary. By the look on Lynch's face, it seems he hasn't forgotten his escapade with the errant zipper. Notice how carefully he's swinging that hammer.

I've probably given the impression that doing a soap schedule wasn't all that much fun. Well, it wasn't. At least not for the soundmen with a low threshold for boredom.

Each artist dealt with this problem differently. Some did crossword puzzles; some read books; one, Jim Rogan, wrote music; and Ray Kemper, Dave Light, and several others, wrote scripts. Gus Bayz both wrote scripts and did art work, and Figure 9.3 shows one of his watercolors of a Victorian house on Fulton Street in San Francisco.

Despite all the things that seemed to be wrong with doing soaps on a regular basis, many soundmen did them for years without complaining. They loved the regular hours, the weekends off, the camaraderie of the cast, and the fact that the sound effects on a soap were rarely difficult to do.

Although the soap schedule didn't pay extra money in the way of overtime, some of the shows had other ways of showing their appreciation for the unflinching loyalty of some of their noncast members. On "Helen Trent," for instance, the theme song, "Juanita," was played on a ukelele and hummed by Stan Davis, the show's assistant director. The fees for soundmen on soaps were neither as remunerative nor as frequent as on other types of shows. Their fees came in the form of small speaking parts or from vocals.

These vocals could be anything from the family cat or dog to baby cries. If producing these types of sounds was beyond the capabilities of the individual, that person would be given lines to say that required little experience, little training, and, to be honest, often only minuscule talent. But networks were strict about any payments to staff members other than the regular salary, and these so-called acting jobs were a way around this rule.

Most often these parts were never more complicated than a simple, "Did someone order a cab?" or "I have a telegram for...." And although these lines were hardly memorable even by soap standards, you received a whopping $19, and in early radio, that was approximately half a week's pay.

"Easy Aces" was a delightfully urbane, 15-minute domestic comedy that starred Goodman Ace and his wife, Jane. Despite the fact that it aired in the evening, it had all the qualifications of a genuine soap.

In addition to acting in the show, Goodman Ace also wrote it. On one particular show, Goodman had written his soundman the fee lines, "Flowers for Jane Ace" and "Thank you."

At the last minute, the regular soundman called in sick. His replacement

Fulton Street – San Francisco – A.D.   Geo. C. Bayz '72

Figure 9.3. Original watercolor painting by Gus Bayz. Reproduced by permission.

was a man known to Goodman Ace, because he had replaced the regular soundman on several other occasions. And although this new man was untried as an "actor," how could he screw up six words? So rather than cut the line, Goodman decided to give the substitute soundman a chance to make some extra money. This is what the script looked like:

> SOUND: *door knock*
>
> GOODMAN: *(calling)* I'll get it, Jane.
>
> SOUND: *door open*
>
> GOODMAN: Yes...?
>
> DELIVERY BOY: Flowers for Jane Ace.
>
> GOODMAN: Thank you. And here's something for your trouble.
>
> DELIVERY BOY: Thank you.
>
> SOUND: *door close*

Hardly a role for Dustin Hoffman, but still, when it has to be said into a microphone ... on radio ... live ... with millions of people listening....

That evening, on the air, that same pleasant little interlude played like this:

> SOUND: *door knock*
>
> GOODMAN: *(calling)* I'll get it, Jane.
>
> SOUND: *door open*
>
> GOODMAN: Yes...?

Not hearing the expected "Flowers for Jane Ace" line, Goodman peered over his script toward the sound-effects area. One look was all he needed. The substitute soundman was clenching his script with violently shaking hands, and displayed signs of worst case of mike fright Goodman Ace had ever seen. Hoping to help the poor man out of his catatonic state, Goodman began offering helpful feeder lines.

> GOODMAN: Do you have something for us...?

Still no response from the poor soundman.

> GOODMAN: Perhaps some flowers for Jane Ace...?

At this point Goodman would have settled for a simple "yes" or a "yeah" or even a "you bet your ass I do, Goody!" But instead he got one of the all-time great ad libs on live radio. The soundman responded by vigorously nodding his head up and down in mute agreement!

Goodman brought the brief monologue to a merciful close by saying, "I'll see that Mrs. Ace gets them." He then gave the glassy eyed soundman a good-natured smile and gentle reminder: "Don't forget to close the door." SOUND: *fast and much-relieved door slam.*

And yes, Goodman Ace did pay the soundman for his "acting" role. As he explained later, "Of course I paid him. Best damn bit of panto-miming radio ever heard!"

The real reason for the success of those early soaps was their ability to fill a radio station's schedule, a schedule that was long on time and short on money. Adopting the serial format that was used so successfully in silent films, the soaps' producers could turn out 15-minute programs, five days a week, 52 weeks a year, and do it inexpensively if not downright cheaply. By taking advantage of the fact that their audience couldn't see what was happening in the studio, a soap could get away with a small cast by having the performers play multiple roles. "Clara, Lu and Em," for instance, had a cast of only three people, while on "Painted Dreams," the cast consisted of two people, Irene Wicker and Irna Philips, who also wrote the show. And finally, in 1936, all roles on "The Johnson Family" were played by Jimmy Scribner.

Soaps have been ridiculed from the start, but they have outlasted many of their critics. "Ma Perkins," for example, was on the air for 27 years with a total of 7,065 broadcasts. What was their popularity? When asked why she didn't make her soaps less worrisome and more entertaining, the first lady of soaps, Anne Hummert, smiled knowingly and replied: "Worry, to women, *is* entertainment."

And so what started out as something "cheap to fill up time" became a love affair that is still going on. When the end of soaps on radio came, not all of them went quietly into the night. "Perry Mason," for instance, simply put on a thin disguise and went to television as "The Edge of Night." And with it went the "Perry Mason" soundman, Jimmy Lynch. Including his homemade, and infamous, bell and buzzer board.

From their inception, all the soaps had what can only be called a sound-effects fetish. It was quite common for directors of soaps to insist on their own special doorbells, but on one soap they even demanded their own door. When "Ma Perkins" was being done at NBC in Chicago, the only sound-effects door that the director, George Fogle, would accept in the studio was door #10, shown in Figure 9.4.

Figure 9.4. The "Ma Perkins" door, #10. Photo courtesy of Robert J. Graham.

While CBS in Chicago was caught up in a sort of musical chairs with doors, CBS in New York hired skilled cabinet makers to keep up with the increasing demand for more equipment. Figure 9.5 shows one of these carpenters, Peter Pedarson working on a house door that must not only have a nice appearance but must be sturdy enough to withstand the sound-effects world of slams and hard knocks.

With each soap director having his or her own idiosyncrasies about what sound effects were acceptable on their show, things could be extremely confusing to anyone who had to replace the regular sound-man.

On "The Edge of Night," for instance, Eric's house in the city used a melodic door chime, whereas his lake house used a door buzzer. Janet's house also used a door buzzer, but it wasn't the same as Eric's. On the sound-effects board, Janet's buzzer button was next to Eric's button, but it was slightly higher in pitch and was marked #2. The #3 buzzer button was for Hattie's apartment. Next to these buttons were the door chime buttons. Nell's house, the #4 button, was a simple bing-bong. Adele's chime was the same bing-bong button, but you had to close the mike so the audience wouldn't hear the beginning "bing" bit, just the ending "bong," because her bell went "Bong-Bing-Bong." God forbid you bing-bonged or bong-binged or, worse yet, *buzzed* her house.

Below these buttons were other buttons. One button, #5, was the phone bell, #6 was a dial tone, #7 was a busy signal, and #8 was a filter ring. Altogether, there were a total of 15 different buttons, each with a different role to perform. And whether we liked Lynch's communication system or not, we were obliged to use it. One thing we didn't do when we replaced a show's sick or vacationing regular soundman was try to change things. One interim soundman hated the phone bell the regular artist used and brought in one of his own. He hardly got one ring out when a voice over his headset sniffed indignantly, "That isn't *our* phone bell!"

Even lovable "Lum and Abner" were picky about having their own distinctive phone bell. Their special bell is shown in Figure 9.6. Figure 9.7 proves that "The Edge of Night" wasn't the only soap with its own set of buzzers. Fans of NBC's "Days of Our Lives" will recognize the names of these Salem house and apartment dwellers. All those buttons on the various soaps could be confusing under the best of conditions. Working with them when you had a busy show was downright frightening.

As if all this buttons and bells business wasn't enough, the directors on soaps would refer to the cast members by their real names, not by the characters they played in the show. Which means that Helen could play the part of Adele, and Adele could play the part of Helen.

This was bad enough in rehearsals, but on air, the director would continue calling the cast members by their real names, while the actors would naturally be calling each other by the character they played in the show.

On one memorable Friday, Jerry McCarty was sent up to the renovated

Figure 9.5. Peter Pedarson. Photo courtesy of Walter Pierson.

movie theater on 79th Street to replace the ailing Jimmy Lynch on "The Edge of Night." The show wasn't particularly busy, but one of the scenes required a doorbell sound. Simple enough? Sure, on almost any other show. But this wasn't just any show, this was "The Edge of Night," and the doorbell belonged to Adele, and the doorbell button was just over Adele's phone-bell button.

Figure 9.6. The "Lum and Abner" phone bell. Photo by author.

Figure 9.7. Door buzzer-board for "Days of Our Lives." Photo by author.

During all the rehearsals, everything went fine. However, late that afternoon during the live broadcast over the CBS Network, it was a far different story. This is the way Jerry explained it later that day over his second double gin martini in ColBeeS.

"When the cue came for the doorbell, I started to push the button marked #4 ... but suddenly I got confused and I couldn't make up my mind whether it was button #4 or button #5. To make matters worse, the director in the control room started screaming for the doorbell, but he didn't say *which* doorbell! Finally I said the hell with it and pushed #5 and the damn phone rang! The actress, Helen, the one who played Adele, had already started to take a step to the door in anticipation of the doorbell, but she stopped dead in her tracks when she heard the phone ring. What made it worse was that the doorbell cue came at the beginning of the scene and so, without that cue, she was all alone."

ADELE: *(unsure)* ...I wonder who can be calling at this time of day...?

"As I kept on ringing the phone," he went on, "I wondered why Adele just didn't pick it up and ad lib something like, "You have the wrong number," and then I would have rung the doorbell. That's the way we would have done it in radio. But this wasn't radio, it was television. And the thought suddenly occurred to me that the actress probably thought there had been a change in the script and she hadn't gotten it. Unlike radio, the actresses were busy from the time they got to the studio. First there was the wardrobe fittings, the hair to be made up, the makeup, rehearsing new lines in different dressing rooms with other actors, grabbing a quick sandwich, and God forbid you had to go to the bathroom. With all this going on, she probably thought all this was *her* fault! In the meantime I just kept ringing the damn phone."

ADELE: Whoever it is ... they're certainly insistent....

"By now," Jerry continued, "the whole studio was caught up in the drama. Even the control room became quiet and the director stopped cursing at me. All I could hear him say in a raspy voice was, '...what I wouldn't give for a drink....'

"Finally this Adele took a couple of slow steps towards the phone and I gave a half-ring to indicate the caller had hung up."

ADELE: *(on the verge of panic)* Well ... whoever it was ... hung up....

"And before the poor gal had a heart attack, I crossed my fingers and pushed the #4 button. This time the doorbell rang and Adele let out a yell of relief and fairly flew to the door."

ADELE: *Harriet!* My God, am I glad to see *you!*

With that Jerry drained his drink and stood up with a broad smile on his face. "There's a happy ending though. The office just told me I've been requested never to do 'Edge of Night' again!"

As I said, soaps, you either love them or you hate them.

CHAPTER X

TELEVISION – THE END
OF THE GOOD TIMES

LIVE DRAMATIC RADIO did not fold its tent and steal quietly into the night. There was an awful lot of hollering. And no one hollered louder or longer than those of us in sound effects. We simply refused to believe that something so exciting, vital, and important was dying. Today they call it denial. Back then it was something called television.

No matter how bleak the prognosis for radio became, we all knew that the listening public would never turn a deaf ear to such an old and trusted friend. After all, what busy housewife could afford the time to plop in a chair and stare at a flickering, snowy, 7-inch screen? How would the housework get done? The washing, ironing, sewing, cooking, feeding the baby? Besides, everybody knows there wasn't a housewife in America who could watch just *one!* Soaps on television – were they *crazy?*

All right. For the sake of argument, suppose they did put soaps on television. How could television, which was already losing money, afford to put on shows like "The Lone Ranger" or "Gangbusters"? How could television ever compete with the imagination of the radio listener? Television cameras were having difficulty enough trying to get acceptable pictures of something as uncomplicated as a cooking show. Where would they get the technical know-how and huge amounts of money to duplicate the scope, action, drama and excitement created by something as relatively inexpensive as the spoken word and sounds of radio?

With television you were limited as to what the directors wanted you to see. With radio, you were free to fantasize to your heart's content. To one listener the something-over-thirty-five lady, Helen Trent, might have blonde hair. To another it might be black. But if you wanted her brunette ... poof ... she's brunette. And what about the color of her skin? Try *that* magic on your seven-inch screen television! So much for wishing with your heart.

PHILCO RADIO TIME - STARRING BING CROSBY

Program #24B

INSTRUCTION AND CUE SHEET

This sheet will give your playback engineer and local announcer information about their part in the production of "PHILCO RADIO TIME" STARRING BING CROSBY - Program #24B in the 1948 - 49 series.

These recordings should be played at the Orthacoustic (or equivalent) setting on your playback equipment, and at a constant level. There should be no necessity to ride gain.

The program has been timed out to approximatedly 29:30. When the local announcer cuts into the program, the record should be cut out, but it should continue to play while the local announcer matches his reading time with recording, in accordance with cue list below.

It is not necessary for the local announcer to identify this program as "transcribed" since an opening and closing transcribed credit already is in the program.

CROSBY #24B

CUE FOR FIRST COMMERCIAL

1. At approximately 3:53, after the beginning of the program, Crosby and Rhythmaires conclude their opening song, "Busy Doing Nothin'". The following dialogue concludes at approximately 5:07: --

CARPENTER: "PARDON ME, BING, BUT BEFORE YOU AND PEGGY SING I THINK I SHOULD REMIND THE FOLKS THAT THERE ARE STILL BIG BARGAINS AT OUR PHILCO DEALERS."

CROSBY: "OH YES. IN CASE ANYONE DOESN'T KNOW ABOUT THOSE FINE PHILCO VALUES, LET THEM KNOW IMMEDIATELY KEN."

CARPENTER: "AH YOU'RE SO RIGHT, BING. AND OUR PHILCO DEALERS HAVE GOT JUST WHAT IT TAKES."

This is the cue for the first cut-in commercial.

2. First cut-in commercial as read by local announcer should run not longer than 56 seconds.

3. At approximately 6:03, cut back to the program with a very fast fade, picking up with the music that follows the commercial.

CUE FOR FIRST SWITCHOVER

4. At approximately 10:02, Phil Harris says: --

"YOU'RE GONNA LOSE YOUR SELF-RESPECT. IT'S ONLY GONNA HURT YOU."

This is the cue to switch over instantaneously to PART 2, PROGRAM #24B, picking up with Frankie Remley's line: "Don't worry about it, Curly, I can take it."

Figure 10.1. Cue sheet for "Philco Radio Time." Photo courtesy of author.

Figure 10.2. Fairchild turntable. Photo by author.

Ironically, as live radio prepared to do battle with television, it failed to recognize the equally serious problem coming from within radio itself. Live radio was slowly dying. Outside of the soaps, most of "live" radio was now being recorded on 16-inch discs. (See Figure 10.1.)

Figure 10.1 is a cue sheet for "Philco Radio Time" starring Bing Crosby. Although Bing was a veteran of live radio, he had a terrible time remembering the lyrics to a song. Therefore, when he had an opportunity to pre-record his show, he was one of the first to jump at the opportunity.

The recordings were made on 16-inch records like that shown in Figure 10.3. Playing back the recordings took two Fairchild turntables (Figure 10.2) and the equally important detailed instructions like the ones shown in Figure 10.1.

Once radio in general began pre-recording the programs, all the old rules of live radio went out the window. When the shows were live, everyone connected with the program gave it their best effort once the

Figure 10.3. Transcription recording. Photo by author.

ON AIR light went on. They knew there were no second chances to get things right. With the advent of transcriptions, no one knew for sure whether what they were doing was going to be accepted for the air show, or whether the show would have to be done over.

This uncertainty was especially frustrating to the seasoned radio actors accustomed to accepting roles on shows that were sometimes back-to-back with the one they were doing. When shows were live, the actors knew that, come hell or high water, they'd be off the air at a certain time, and sometimes even earlier. If their part was only in the beginning of the show, they could be out of the studio the minute the part was finished. If the show was being recorded, they had to wait until the director gave the all-clear signal. And that might not be until after they'd done two or three or even a dozen different "takes" (recordings).

For actors or sound-effects artists with a very difficult show, it didn't matter how well they did their part, they still had to sweat it out until the completion of the recording because the records couldn't be edited. One mistake, one cough, and the whole show had to be done over from the beginning. Even if the script was 30 pages long and the mistake occurred on page 29, the whole show had to be done over. Understandably, the person making the mistake on page 29 was not looked upon with affection by those anxious to be out of the studio. As a result, the wonderful camaraderie that had existed in live radio was eroded by a 16-inch blank record.

What was even worse, a show redo didn't have to be caused by a mistake or a cough. Directors with the luxury of safety, and haunted by uncertainty, agonized over whether they would accept a particular recording for broadcast. Shows that would be considered excellent by live standards were now being done over and over and over again. And by way of explanation, directors began setting everyone's teeth on edge with this new line of reasoning: "That was just great, everybody, but I think we can all do just a little better."

The one advantage that these transcribed shows had over live broadcast was that they eliminated the need to have us wait around for three hours to do the repeat broadcast for the time zone on the opposite coast. However, that was little solace for those of us accustomed to the excitement of live radio. As one actor so aptly stated, "Transcribed radio is depriving a lot of actors and directors from the opportunity of finding out how truly bad they really are."

Whatever hope the diehards had that live radio would rise again were smothered when the advocates of transcribed radio got help from an unexpected and unusual source—Adolph Hitler.

The vintage reel-to-reel tape machine shown in Figure 10.4 was discovered in a radio station in Germany at the end of World War II.

These tape machine made live radio a thing of the past. And just when we all resolved ourselves to that bitter pill, along came television.

At first, everyone in radio was fearful of what television would do to their beloved medium. But after actually seeing what television was offering on its 7-inch screen, we all smiled and relaxed.

So much for the people of radio as prognosticators of the future. It's ironic that while television was costing the networks huge sums of money, it was radio that was paying the bills. In just a few short years, television would show its gratitude by causing radio's demise. But in the meantime, radio shows such as "Suspense," were still employing huge casts as late as 1950, in a last-ditch effort for survival.

Pictured in Figure 10.5 are the show's cast (seated, left to right) Byron Kane, Joe Kearns, Rosemary DeCamp, Bill Conrad, Vic Dernn, Jack Kruschen, Lurene Tuttle, Bill Idelson, Sam Edwards, and two unidentified ladies. The staff (standing, left to right) are four unidentified people followed by: Bob Shue, assistant director; Bill Fromg, director; Bermard Hermann, musical director; Bill James, sound effects; Ray Kemper, sound effects; and Bob Chadwick, audio engineer.

Figure 10.4. German WWII tape machine. Photo by author.

Looking at this picture, it's hard to imagine that in just a short time, large casts such as this, and indeed, even dramatic radio itself, would come to an end, that the beloved theater of the mind would be forced to close its doors.

All the prestige and respect that sound effects enjoyed in radio suddenly went down the picture tube. This was a new medium with horrendous problems of its own without concerning itself with something called sound effects. All the old rules that we had played by in radio were thrown out. This was television . . . just like the movies . . . only better . . . in your own home . . . free . . . doo dah, doo dah.

Television studios started poking their ugly antennas against the skylines. Majestic old legitimate stage theaters and movie theaters were rapidly being converted to accommodate this fledging new picture medium.

Technical crews ignored the baroque splendor of these entertainment palaces, designed as a refuge from the Great Depression. Power lines, camera cables, microphone cables, lighting cables, and air conditioning cables crisscrossed and wrapped around each other under seats in a cobweb of confusion, each going in a different direction to a different destination. Control rooms were installed, klieg lights hung, microphones put in place, and cameras rolled down the aisles and up ramps and onto the stage.

Figure 10.5. Cast and crew of "Suspense." Photo courtesy of Ray Kemper.

The contrast between the gilded cherubs that adorned the proscenium arch and the electronic equipment that now commanded the stage was startling. Suddenly the words of Fred Allen, the brilliant radio comedian, had come true. Television was indeed "a triumph of equipment over people."

The television camera was a harsh and unforgiving god. Because of the bright lights they needed for good pictures, studios became suffocatingly hot. No one was spared from the overhead glaring lights that burned down. But if anyone got the brunt of it, it was the actors, who had to smile sweetly on camera while rivulets of sweat dampened the backs of their hair and made their faces glisten. Teams of makeup, hair, and wardrobe people hovered off-camera waiting for the actors to make hurried pit stops, so they could repair the damage from the relentless heat.

Doing an outdoor scene that was supposed to take place during the winter was asking for trouble. Despite the mounds of plastic snow and the gales of wind from sound effects, the poor actors had to submit to overcoats and gloves while tiny streams of perspiration trickled out from under their ear muffs.

Television even had restrictions on the color of the clothes you wore. Wearing anything white was harmful to the camera's picture tube. So was anything that glittered, so sequined dresses were out. And actresses couldn't even *think* of wearing a plunging neckline. Not because of the camera but because of the censors. And that was true for nipple-bulge, as well. If the camera saw it, they got covered with Johnson & Johnson Band-Aids.

Not even myopic actors were spared. No matter how essential eyeglasses were to an actor's vision, they couldn't be worn on camera because of the reflection. The actor could wear the frames, but they couldn't have lenses in them. What those poor actors in those days wouldn't have given for contact lenses!

It was the same for windows, mirrors, or the diamonds in the necklace around the star's neck. If it glared, it was either sprayed with a matting wax or simply eliminated. It is little wonder that sound effects were so far down the list of priorities.

Our understanding of the problems of this new medium didn't make it any easier on our egos. Having been so centrally important for so many years in radio, working in television was about as appealing as a warm martini.

The one saving grace for sound effects during those early years of television was that the calls were few and far between. Sponsors were still reluctant to take chances, so television shows that required the costly use of sound effects were rare. However, if the viewer wanted to watch old Hopalong Cassidy movies all day, or learn how to make a cheese souffle, or perhaps put another shelf in the bedroom, or watch people talking on a variety of subjects in a simulated living room—television was the answer.

The way television "simulated" a living room was quite simple and, of course, dirt cheap. All television studios had heavy curtains that hung from the ceiling to the floor. These were called cycloramas, or simply cycs. Because of their size and weight, these cycs were attached to wheels that traveled along a track around the perimeter of the studio. When a producer wanted an inexpensive set, she or he would have a black velour cyc stretched across the width of the background.

If the guests that day were going to have an intellectual discussion, the producer might attain a scholarly look by having several bookcases placed in the foreground. Of course, the bookcases contained only the backs of books, because real books were too heavy and cumbersome to move around.

If there was any bric-a-brac on the set, it was probably chipped or cracked or at best, bought in a second hand store. Producers (even to this day) never spent money on what the viewer at home couldn't see clearly on their television screen. If, however, the talk on that particular day required a homey atmosphere, all the producer needed was the black velour cyc and some pictures suspended from overhead with nylon fishing line.

Figure 10.6. Davidson Van Voorhees. Photo courtesy of Malachy Wienges.

This illusion, seen through the television camera, would give the impression to the viewer at home that the pictures were hung on a wall.

The problem was, several shows were often scheduled into one large studio, with a cooking show in one corner, a do-it-yourself show in another, and the talk show in another. So while one show was going off the air, another one was coming on, and the people leaving the studio had to be very quiet and careful. If a studio door was left open too long, the pictures on the "wall" suddenly began moving wildly about in the draft. More than once, viewers in California called the station in panic asking about the apparent "earthquake."

Figure 10.6 shows what a television studio set looked like in those early days. Little scientific thought was given to where the sound-effects area should be. As a result, it was any place that could accommodate an object the size of a sound-effects console. Figure 10.6 shows Davidson Van Voorhees, head of the CBS New York sound-effects department, doing his effects practically on camera.

With this type of programming being offered on a 7-inch screen, the American public felt little urgency about buying one of the mysterious electronic boxes. Not that there wasn't interest on the part of the public. They'd stand outside an appliance store in small groups and watch the programs shown on sets displayed in the store's window. But nothing they saw compelled them to go inside and plunk down their money. And so it went. No enticing shows, no viewers. No viewers, no sponsors to supply the networks with the money they needed to put on shows that would get the public off the street and up to the cash registers.

On the rare occasions when there was a need for sound effects on a television show, the person chosen was usually someone without a show or with the least seniority. And because no one was given any sort of indoctrination into this strange new medium, the person selected was given all the accord of an unlucky soldier about to go out on a mission behind the enemy lines.

Walking into one of those recently converted made-for-television theaters, the first thing anyone noticed was their shabbiness. Cracks in the huge golden columns on either side of the stage needed patching. The carpet down the center aisle was threadbare from countless excited moviegoers hurrying to their seats for the latest Clark Gable film or a Saturday Flash Gordon serial.

Overhead, the magnificent crystal chandelier was gray with dust and laced with cobwebs. Even the blue seats looked worn and stained from too many rubbings from buttery popcorn hands. As I stood there gazing about, I couldn't help thinking how wonderful radio was.

But this was not radio, this was television. And nothing about it was familiar. Not the equipment, not the scores of people who rushed up and down the aisles clutching scripts and yelling instructions to God knows who. And not the cursing, shirtless men perched high overhead on top of ladders, adjusting huge lights on orders from a man standing on the stage and consulting his light meter. "Open the barn door more on 231 . . . more stage right . . . back it off . . . hold it there . . . go to 233 . . . more upstage. . . ." As he continued shouting instructions, he continuously dodged scenery being dragged across the stage or cameras and boom microphones being wheeled into place. And in the middle of all this chaos stood a veteran of hundreds of radio shows who didn't know the first damn thing about which end of a camera took the picture!

In those days, sound effects for television wasn't so much planned as it was an afterthought. The first television show I did was a variety show called "The Real McKay" starring Jim McKay, who later moved to ABC and became host of "The Wide World of Sports." When I walked into the control room and introduced myself to the director, his response was, "Sound effects? What the hell do we need sound effects for? This is television, not radio!" When I explained that I was there to do some gunshots, he just shrugged and replied, "Well, don't let me stop you," and walked out of the control room.

My next encounter was with the technical director. When I explained my mission, he, too, shrugged and pointed to the audio booth. Relieved, I assumed I would at last deal with someone sympathetic and knowledgeable, but I was wrong. After explaining in detail what I needed, he told me abruptly what I was going to get. I ended up doing the gunshots backstage using the announcer's mike. That would have been all right, except that the audio man forgot to open the microphone and my gunshot was heard by an audience of two, the announcer and me.

As the popularity of television increased, television antennas began appearing on the rooftops of the people fortunate enough to be able to afford this electronic miracle. These antennas became so recognizable as status symbols, that even the people that didn't own a television set were putting up antennas!

Along with this increasing demand for more and better television programs was the need for sound effects. Unfortunately, the need wasn't always apparent to many producers. They understood that if the script called for a reenactment of World War II, they would need sound effects. If, however, the script had only a few door knocks, they would invariably try to save the cost of hiring a sound-effects artist by having the actor do his or her own door knocks, even though they knew that all off-camera sounds were considered sound effects by the union.

The biggest offender of this union infraction was "The Ed Sullivan Show." This show and "The Texaco Star Theater," starring Milton Berle, were two of the most popular shows in early television. Berle was a seasoned comedian with night club, stage, and film experience, while Sullivan had a syndicated newspaper column. Although much criticized for his awkwardness in front of the camera, Sullivan was an astute showman. In fact, Fred Allen had this to say about him: "Ed will be around as long as someone else has talent."

Doing sound effects on the Sullivan show was something else again. It was a variety show and so they had a large orchestra. Ironically, if an act needed a gunshot, door knock, or phone ring, instead of using a sound-effects artist, they would try to save money by having the drummer do the sound effects. Sound familiar?

This lack of regard for union rules and for the technical requirements of television came from Ed Sullivan himself. As popular as his show was, the man was a show business enigma. He didn't sing, he didn't dance, he didn't tell jokes, and some of his on-air mistakes are legendary—this was a man who wished America a happy new year in August.

And who can ever forget his introduction of the brilliant guitarist, Jose Feliciano? Unsure of how his audience would react to the young blind performer, Sullivan voiced concern to his producer about how the young guitarist would make his entrance onto the stage. Supposing he tripped, or fell? Shouldn't he have a seeing eye dog? Although assured and reassured that nothing would happen, Sullivan wasn't that assured. So to make sure that everyone at home understood the situation completely, this was the memorable introduction: "Now, ladies and gentlemen, on our stage, a gifted guitarist who is not only blind, but is also Puerto Rican!"

The uncertainty of whether there would or would not be sound effects on any particular Sullivan show meant that no one artist was scheduled to do the show. The one saving grace about the Sullivan show, once it was established who was going to do the sound effects, was that we at least knew where the sounds were going to be done. A section of the balcony had been set aside for our equipment although this separation from the control room, where the audio booth and production staff were, only further isolated the sound-effects artist.

On one particular Sunday, it was Orval White's turn in the barrel. Orval was the first and, to the best of my knowledge, the only black sound-effects artist in radio, television, or film. He had started at CBS as an equipment setup man. A setup man, as the name suggests, was responsible for carting and setting up all the equipment ordered by the sound-effects artists. By doing this, Orval had an opportunity to learn all the equipment. He also went to an electronics school and graduated with his first-class radio and telephone license. Unfortunately, however qualified Orval was, the year was 1952 and many Americans still associated blacks with menial work.

When Orval arrived at the Sullivan theater, the only information he had was that he was to do some automobile effects for the pianist-comedian, Victor Borge. After dutifully checking in with Tim Kiley, the Sullivan show director, Orval went up to the sound-effects area in the balcony.

After turning on his equipment and making sure that his head set was connected with the control room, Orval took out his copy of the Sunday

New York Times and waited for someone to bring him the latest revised copy of the Victor Borge sketch. Although he wasn't wearing his headset, he made sure it was close enough to him, and loud enough, so he could hear the talk in the control room.

Halfway through the crossword puzzle, Orval heard the director tell a production assistant to give the sound-effects man the new changes in the rehearsal rundown.

As Orval waited, he saw a young lady enter the balcony area, take one quick look around and, before Orval could stop her, disappear back down the stairs.

Orval was puzzled by her actions, and was close enough to the headset to hear the lady say, "But I just came from up there. I didn't see any sound effects man!" He then heard Kiley assuring her that there was indeed a sound-effects man up there, and she was instructed to try again.

This time when the lady came into the balcony, she shielded her eyes from the glaring lights from the stage and spent a long moment turning in a slow circle. When she had finished she once again disappeared down the stairs. Putting his ear to the headset, Orval heard her report in an exasperated and somewhat angry voice, "Not only isn't the sound-effects man there, the balcony is empty. There's only a colored man reading a newspaper."

This was too much even for the tolerant Orval White. Putting his paper aside, he left the balcony and walked into the control room. Before Tim Kiley had a chance to speak, Orval gave the puzzled young lady a smile and said, "Ah understands, ma'am, you got some changes for dis ole colored man."

That, I'm happy to say, was an isolated incident. But when Jackie Robinson became the first black ball-player in the major leagues, Orval felt some empathy toward him. It is therefore understandable that when the Dodgers, and Jackie Robinson, were scheduled to play their first game in Ebbetts Field, Orval was at the head of the line to buy two box tickets for himself and his wife.

When the big day finally arrived and the Brooklyn Dodgers took the field, Orval turned to his wife and said, "Well, honey, this is a great day for baseball." To which his wife nervously responded, "But you know I don't know anything about baseball. Which one is Jackie Robinson?"

The Mansfield Theater, at 47th Street and Eighth Avenue, was home to a new television entrant named Garry Moore. Moore had been a popular radio comedian on the "Camel Caravan Show" for five years but this was his first attempt at testing the quicksands of television. He enlisted the aid of such radio veterans as Herb Sanford, producer; Bill Demling, head writer; Ken Carson, a singer who'd been with the "Sons of

Fiture 10.7. The author during "The Garry Moore Show." Photo by the author.

the Pioneers"; and Durward Kirby, an announcer and brilliant comedic sidekick. Later a lovely singer named Denise Lor was added to the cast.

The show's informal format was in the vein of "The Dave Garroway Show," which came out of Chicago and was a forerunner of the "Tonight Show," which followed several years later.

"The Garry Moore Show" was on in the morning and included interviews, guest entertainers, songs, comedy sketches, and anything else Garry thought might amuse his audience. The show was on five days a week, 52 weeks a year, and that meant sometimes having fun with the commercials.

Figure 10.7 is a 1951 photo taken while I worked the show. The sound-effects area in the Mansfield Theater was located in a box seat overlooking the stage and the house audience. This was an excellent vantage point from which to see all the action on the stage, but a terribly cramped space to accommodate both me and my equipment.

My location was above a ramp that had been built specifically for the purpose of shooting live commercials. Tables were set up to enable the camera to move in for close-ups of the various products. Maggie Murphy was in charge of making these products look mouth-wateringly appealing. Helping her with this delicate job was something called an "electronic range." Today, we call it a microwave oven, but back in 1957, it was still being tested by people like Maggie and was not yet available to the general public.

Making products appealing was a difficult job in those days. Because of the heat given off by the lights, some substitutions had to be made—ice cream was really scoops of cream cheese for instance, and whipped cream was shaving cream. However, despite these little deceits, much of the food shown was genuine, and for this, the microwave was invaluable because if the commercial called for a cooked turkey, Maggie had to cook not just one, but three. One was the rehearsal turkey, one was the stand-by turkey, and the third was the on-the-air turkey.

One Thanksgiving Day, Garry Moore and the cast did a sketch about a couple of inept pilgrims trying to shoot their first turkey. The sketch required a number of live gunshots from me. And during the sketch, which was broadcast live, I suddenly started getting laughs from the studio audience each time I fired my gun. This was gratifying, of course, but also very puzzling. It got so crazy that once, when Moore told a joke that received no laughs, he looked up at me and shouted, "Quick Bob, fire your gun!" And of course I got howls of laughter.

Neither Moore nor I could figure out this strange phenomenon, that every gunshot produced gales of laughter, but Moore decided to investigate. Getting up from his desk on the stage, he had Clarence Schimmel, the director, follow him with a camera as he walked over to the commercial ramp.

As I watched this little drama unfold on my television monitor, I saw Maggie Murphy spread-eagled over her on-air turkey and her white-frosted layer cake, frantically waving her arms in the air! Her commercial was to follow the pilgrim sketch and everytime I fired my gun over the railing, black ashes from the blanks had showered down on her turkey and cake! Poor Maggie had to contort her body into a protective shield to save the appearance of her most important commercial props. From that day on, Maggie always had an umbrella handy. Months later, when a newcomer to the show once asked her why, she replied, "for unseasonable gunshots."

Another memorable commercial I would just as soon forget involved a line of Chun King Chinese food. To introduce it to the television audience, the advertising agency came up with a gimmick involving two little gongs, each about the size of a half-dollar. The gongs were suspended from either side of a T-shaped bracket. The gong on the left was tuned so that when it was struck, it would sound roughly like "Chun," and the gong on the right sounded somewhat like "King." The illusion was helped when they were struck in synchronization with Moore saying the words.

Everyone wanted to do a good job for this new sponsor, and more time was spent rehearsing the commercial than was normally scheduled. Synchronizing the gong sounds with Moore's words was a little tricky. But after several run-throughs, everything seemed ready for Chun King's inaugural presentation.

On air, I held the T-shaped gong contraption confidently in my left hand and the small mallet striker in my right hand and waited for Moore's two little words, "Chun King!"

As he spoke the words, I dutifully swung my tiny little mallet at the tiny little musical gongs, and missed it completely! To make it worse, both Moore and the members of his show orchestra, the Howard Smith band, knew I had once been a drummer. The absurdity of my missing that stupid little gong broke them up completely.

Moore, of course, loved it. Addressing the studio and home audience in overly distraught and serious tones, he apologized profusely for the mistake. He also said that it wasn't fair to the new sponsor to be treated so shabbily, that, after all, it wasn't King Chinese food, it was *Chun* King Chinese food, and therefore, they would do the commercial over!

By this time, the director, Clarence Schimmell, had positioned a camera so that in addition to the studio audience watching my every move, millions of viewers across this vast land of ours were also in on it. After all, how many people listening to the radio ever got to see a soundman make a horse's ass of himself?

As Moore approached the fateful gong cue, the lighting man focused a spotlight on me, while Eddie Shaugnessy, the drummer, started an ominous tympany roll. Then Garry said "Chun" and I obediently and accurately struck the "Chun" gong. And then he said "King" and I not only hit the "King" gong, I hit it right over the railing and into the lap of a lady from Ohio. Moore apologized profusely to the woman and invited her up on the stage. He then asked the woman if she would mind doing a big favor for him, the show, the sponsor, and the sound-effects man. He pointed out that one gong presented no problems, but the second one was something else again. Therefore, would she please help everyone concerned by ringing just the second gong? He then quickly added, "But please don't hit it so hard that it lands back in the sound-effects box, because already, this one minute commercial has lasted for more than half the show."

Chun King, and those stupid little damn gongs, stayed on the show for months. No one was as happy as I was to see a sponsor leave. It was replaced by a live Alka Seltzer commercial. Everytime Garry dropped a tablet in a glass of water, I had to make the fizzing sound. Not too early and not too late, not too loud and not too soft. In a week, I was longing for my old Oriental buddies, "Chun" and "King."

Durward Kirby, a veteran of the Ransom Sherman's "Club Matinee" radio show from Chicago, made the transition from radio to television look remarkably easy. He was cast as Moore's sidekick, and not only was that relationship the role model for the Ed McMahon–Johnny Carson relationship, but Kirby was a surprisingly talented comedic genius when it came to getting laughs both in the written sketches and in impromptu situations.

However, despite these enormous talents, the one thing the public at large couldn't know about Kirby was his keen business acumen. Like the time he went to purchase a new car. After selecting the Chrysler model he wanted, he approached the dealer with what at first may seem like an unusual request but really makes pretty good sense. After all, Kirby was basically in the advertising business where, if you wanted your product advertised, you paid for it. And if you wanted your product advertised by one of the celebrities on a very successful television program such as "The Garry Moore Show," you paid even more.

With these facts firmly in mind, Kirby entered the showroom for some serious rebate negotiations with Chrysler.

Durward felt that if Chrysler was going to have their name and logo on the car he was driving (or for that matter *any* car they sold), it constituted advertising and they should pay for that privilege. If not, they should remove all references to Chrysler from his car. The Chrysler people smiled that special corporate smile they reserve for the little people.

Predictably, although Kirby fought the good fight of the visionary, he lost. But looking back, I can't help wondering what life would have been like if our champion had won. No longer would only the rich and famous profit from endorsements. Not only would we be able to negotiate as to whether or not we wanted the name of the automotive manufacturer riveted on our cars, but jeans giants such as Jordache and Calvin Klein would have to pay you for the privilege of emblazoning their names across our butts.

But alas, all that came to an end when the mighty Chrysler Corporation prevailed.

During the eight years that I worked on Garry Moore's daytime show—live, five days a week, 52 weeks a year, all holidays included—I never regretted a moment of it. In addition to being one of the true pioneers of early television, Moore helped launch the careers of such stars as Don Knotts, George Gobel, Don Adams, Jonathan Winters, and, of course, Carol Burnett.

It was this unselfishness in sharing the spotlight, and his innate talent for being able to reach his audience, that made Garry Moore such a joy to work with.

CHAPTER XI

CAPTAIN KANGAROO

TEN OF THE MOST imaginative, challenging, and frustrating years that I ever spent in television were with the "kindly old Captain," a gentleman known to millions of children as "Captain Kangaroo." Before that, he was "Clarabel," the clown on "Howdy Doody." But before any of these colorful sobriquets, he was Robert Keeshan.

Bob started his broadcasting career the way many successful people in radio and television did, as a page for NBC in New York. His assignment was the hugely successful children's show, "Howdy Doody."

That show was done live from 30 Rockefeller Center with a studio filled with screaming, restless, adorable children. Now, even if you haven't had any experience with young and adorable children, at one time you were certainly one yourself. And whether you were a boy or a girl, you know that sooner or later, despite your adorableness, you had to do what you had to do. And it was Keeshan's job to see that in all the excitement they did it where they were supposed to do it.

Anxious viewers began writing in to the show asking, "Who is that man in uniform taking children from the audience? Is he a law officer? A security guard? What crime could these young children possibly commit?

Even after numerous explanations that Bob was an innocent NBC page assisting little tykes to the proper potty, interest in this strange uniformed man only became more intense.

It was finally decided that the uniform was too ominous-looking. Something more appropriate for a children's show as impromptu as Howdy Doody was needed. *Voila*—Clarabel the Clown was born. And Bob Keeshan, flushed with success (so to speak), began his show business career.

The "Captain Kangaroo Show," was a one-hour program shown on the CBS Network six days a week, Monday through Saturday, 52 weeks a year. That's an awful lot to say, let alone do. But by taping two shows a day, five days a week, we not only managed to keep up, we would actually get ahead of ourselves with a surplus of shows.

Although the show was taped, it was "live-on-tape," a technique also used on the "Tonight Show," for which the show was done exactly as if it were live and nothing short of the most horrendous mistake, would cause the cameras to stop recording. Even then, only Keeshan himself had the authority to give that order.

When the show got far enough ahead with future shows, the cast would take a hiatus. Everyone, that is, except Keeshan. He would utilize this time away from the cameras to go out into the hinterlands doing concerts, personal appearances, and promotional work. If there is any doubt as to why the show remained on CBS for over 25 years, the credit belongs to the indefatigable Bob Keeshan. His energy, dedication, and belief in the show never wavered.

Trying to do two one-hour shows a day was extremely difficult for everyone concerned. And although he had a staff of writers, they functioned more in the capacity of supplying Keeshan with ideas rather than with completed scripts.

One of these "scripts" is shown in Figure 11.1. As you can see, they were simply outlines to give Keeshan direction. It was up to the cast and the crew to expand on these ideas.

Please note the spelling of FIBBER MAGEE CRASH. Although the writers were all too young to have heard "The Fibber McGee and Molly Show" when it was being broadcast on radio, they all were aware of its famous crash.

Rehearsals for the show consisted of Bob and the cast having coffee around a table with the director, Peter Birch. And unless there was some special production number or a difficult sketch involving costume and makeup changes, the only rehearsals with cameras were reserved for the commercials.

This loose and easy format was fine for the regulars. Trying to do two one-hour shows with firm, detailed scripts would have been humanly impossible.

Even doing two ad lib shows daily depended on the cooperation and anticipation of everyone in the studio. It also meant understanding some of Keeshan's little idiosyncrasies (no one understood all of Keeshan's little idiosyncrasies).

The problem with working on this type of show was that you didn't learn it overnight. Nobody understood this better than CBS, but even though there were backup people who were familiar with the show, sometimes emergencies arose, such as presidential elections, when every

	(continued)
7.	Dancing Bear watches his toy soldier march for the mousehole. As the toy gets close to the mousehole door, the door opens and the toy marches in. The door closes and after a beat it opens. Toy marches out. Again toy turns and marches towards mousehole. Door again opens. After a beat, toy marches out. Toy marches in wide circle and back to the door. But this time the door doesn't open.... SOUND EFFECTS: FIBBER MAGEE CLOSET Dancing Bear gets dustpan and sweeps up the remains of his toy-SE: TIN CANS. Bob holds the toy box open and Dancing Bear dumps the imaginary contents of the imaginary toy soldier into toy box. SE: PIECES GOING INTO BOX. Bob is about to throw away the empty shoe box when the Dancing Bear stops him. DB shakes box-SE:PIECES SHAKING. Finally, opens top and pours the invisiible pieces into his paw. Then he winds his " toy " up. SE: WINDING IN SYNC WITH ACTION. He then puts " toy " on floor. SE: TOY WHIRRING SOUND FADING. Dancing Bear " watches " it leave. Mister Greenjeans comes down the stairs and they all decide to go out into the Garden.
8.	COMMERCIAL:

Figure 11.1. An example of a "Captain Kangaroo" script. Photo by author.

available camera person was needed on other assignments. When this happened, or when someone called in sick on the Kangaroo show, CBS scheduling had to send whoever was available. And one time they sent Casey Coy to replace Allan Scott on the important #3 camera.

Casey's regular camera assignment was the "Jackie Gleason Show." Although this should have taken up only two days of Casey's time, his other, perhaps more serious, duty was as Jackie Gleason's favorite drinking companion. CBS didn't approve of the "Great One" monopolizing Casey's time, but no one wanted to suggest this to him.

In addition to his prowess as a cameraman and drinker *par excellence*,

Casey was an ex–New York Giants tackle and part-time professional wrestler. (This was prior to the days when wrestlers began wearing funny hats.)

It wasn't bad enough that Casey had never worked the Kangaroo show before. Most likely, he had never even seen the show before, because, thanks to Gleason, it is doubtful whether he had gotten up that early in a very long time. We therefore marveled that Casey had arrived at the studio on time, until someone suggested he probably hadn't been to bed yet.

On air, Casey was doing fine despite all odds, until the Captain decided to tell the story of "Goldilocks and the Four Bears." Now, any experienced "Captain Kangaroo" cameraman, upon hearing this fairy tale faux pas (if you've forgotten, it's three bears), would have followed the show policy and dutifully wagged the camera from side to side in a negative manner to indicate a "no" response from the children in the home audience. Casey was unaware of this added responsibility, however, and besides, he was having more than his hands full simply keeping the Captain in focus.

The Captain, still waiting for the familiar camera-wagging response, repeated his question to the "audience."

"That's right, isn't it, boys and girls? It is Goldilocks and the *six* bears?"

Casey continued watching the Captain, and the Captain continued watching Casey.

In the control room the director, Peter Birch, suddenly realized that Casey wasn't aware of how this little game was played, and instructed him to "say" no.

This was a serious mistake on Birch's part. He assumed that Casey was aware of how cameras said "no." He didn't realize that only on the Kangaroo show did the cameras represent the views of the boys and girls in the home audience. Therefore, when Birch asked Casey to "say no," he meant for Casey to move the camera from side to side, as if the children were shaking their heads.

Still the Captain persisted.

"Perhaps it's Goldilocks and the twelve bears? Two bears? No bears at all?"

Even if the Captain had said "Chicago Bears," Casey wouldn't have known what Keeshan was talking about. If Birch had said *throw* the camera at Keeshan, an increasingly annoyed Casey would have gladly complied. But it wasn't throw, it was "say no" with his camera.

Totally confused, frustrated, perhaps a little hung over from his encounter with Gleason the night before, and definitely fed up with both the director and the Captain, Casey pulled his head out of the viewfinder, leaned around the side of the camera and, in answer to Keeshan's latest question, "Was it Goldilocks and the twenty bears?" bellowed in a loud and clear voice, "No, goddamnit!"

That incident as you might expect, caused one of the rare tape stop-pages.

When a show is largely unscripted and unrehearsed and must depend on an ad-lib format for its success, there must be a tremendous amount of mutual respect and trust among everyone connected with the show. Ad libs can't be done for personal gratification or the show would soon become an undisciplined competition of egos. And although ad libs are, by their very nature, unpredictable, it is essential that careful albeit instantaneous thought must be given to their appropriateness for the audience at home and to the other performers.

To illustrate what it was like working a show that was often made up as it went along, here are some of the more memorable moments from the "Captain Kangaroo Show."

When CBS built their Broadcast Center on 57th Street and Tenth Avenue in New York City, they didn't quite build it from scratch. Instead, they gutted much of the original building and adapted what remained to the demands of broadcasting.

It's important to know that the previous tenant at the site had been a dairy company. In fact, an area that had once contained stalls for milking purposes was now the Broadcast Center's audio-effects room for producing echoes.

In addition to supplying us with milk, cows also attract flies. Although I can't say there was any connection between the former dairy tenant and the present fly problem, I can say that when the milk company left the building in search of greener pastures, a number of flies decided to come into the studio and take a shot at show business.

At first they just made the rounds of the different offices. But when word got buzzed around that the Captain Kangaroo was going to be doing his show in the building, the flies all made the equivalent of a bee-line for his studio. Or, to be more specific, for his Hostess Twinkie commercials.

What was incredible was their uncanny timing. It was as if they all had stop watches in their antennas, because at the precise moment that the Captain would begin the Twinkie commercial, in would buzz one of the flies, and the show would have to stop taping.

Naturally, CBS was not happy about this time-consuming and costly pest. The studio was ordered to spray, fumigate, and even keep a prop man, out of camera range, riding shotgun with a fly swatter during the commercials. It was all to no avail. The problem only seemed to get worse.

In the meantime, the Captain joined forces with CBS and attacked the fly problem by offering a bounty of 25 cents per fly, dead or alive. This generous reward however, had to be withdrawn, when one of the more enterprising stagehands was suspected of submitting for payment a jar of outsiders he had gunned down at the diner down the street.

The solution to this sticky (and hairy) problem came about quite by accident in the form of an ad lib. One of the musical numbers that day required the sound of a bumblebee buzzing. The effect I used was not Barney Beck's razzberry but a small and more reliable door buzzer. By manipulating the tiny spark gap on the buzzer, I could create a very convincing bee sound.

When the musical number was over, I began putting the buzzer away while Keeshan began the Twinkie commercial. Over my head set, I heard one of the camera operators warning the director that a fly had been spotted getting ready to make his appearance on camera and pig out on one of the Twinkies.

Knowing how bugged the Captain got over these insect intrusions, I picked up my bee-buzz effect, and decided to try a desperation ad lib. I realized the chance of it working was practically zero, but I had to try it.

I should point out that *any* ad lib is a brief interlude of madness that is compulsory in nature and must be done with great speed before the moment is gone. An ad lib also must be free-spirited. Put too much pressure or restriction on it and it becomes self-conscious and contrived. Put too little thought into your actions and it can become embarrassing or in poor taste.

Keeshan was halfway through the commercial when the fly made a low-flying pass at the Twinkie. In equal parts disgust and sarcasm, and more for the benefit of the crew than the home audience, Bob announced, "Well, well, here he comes . . . our old friend the fly."

At that point we would normally have stopped the tape, gotten rid of the fly, and reshot the commercial. This time, however, I decided to give my idea a try.

Opening my microphone, I gave a few short bursts of buzzes. Without a moment's hesitation, Keeshan reacted to my sounds by responding, "Good morning Raymond. How are you this morning?"

I did a few more conversational buzzes and then Bob ended the fly's intrusion into the commercial by saying, "You go outside, Raymond. A house is no place for a fly." With that he walked over and opened the door of his Treasure House set and I buzzed Raymond out.

This story is perhaps the best example I can give of the merits of an ad lib. Without that little exchange between Bob and the fly sounds, those tape stoppages would have continued indefinitely. And even though Raymond was a pesky house fly, we probably received less objecting mail than Walt Disney did when he took a large eared, long tailed rodent and gave him the name Mickey.

The cast of the "Captain Kangaroo Show" consisted of Keeshan, Lumpy Brannum, and Gus Allegrhetti. Lumpy was a fine musician who, prior to becoming "Mister Greenjeans," had played with Fred Waring and his Pennsylvanians. Gus Allegrhetti, who did all the art work as well as the animation and voices of Grandfather Clock, the Dancing Bear, Mister Moose, and Bunny Rabbit, had been a serious art student. Although each had a talent that would have allowed him to be successful individually, it was their work as a team that made the Kangaroo show the dominant children's show for such a long period of time.

When a show had no script, it was essential that each cast member stay in a constant state of alertness in order to make contributions. This included sound effects. As an example, one of the running routines on the show was the Bunny Rabbit's ability to trick the Captain out of his carrots. Although the ruses were many, the ending was always the same: As the Captain leaned on the Treasure House desk bemoaning his losses, the juicy sound of carrots being crunched would waft up from the Bunny Rabbit's hutch. We must have done a thousand variations on this carrot-eating ploy, but it's dangerous to take anything for granted.

On one show, the Bunny Rabbit had once again duped the Captain out of his precious carrots. As the clever Bunny Rabbit quickly scooped up the carrots (*wind whistle*) and ducked down behind the desk (*slide whistle*), the familiar sound of carrots being chomped filled the Treasure House (*a bunch of ice cream-bar sticks being rapidly squeezed together in chewing fashion*).

Preoccupied with producing these crunching sounds, I glanced up at my monitor and was startled to see the Captain, Mister Moose, Mister Greenjeans, and, most importantly, Bunny Rabbit all staring down behind the desk in a very perplexed manner, wondering what was making that strange crunching sound.

Even though my sound-effects area was located behind one of the Treasure House walls, they had somehow known that I wasn't paying attention and they had decided to teach me a lesson. And so the game was on. While I tried to think my way out of this, I of course had to keep crunching—and suffer their little digging remarks.

The Captain wanted to know if the Bunny Rabbit had invited another Bunny over to share his carrots. In response, the Bunny gave the Captain a long, withering, incredulous stare, as if to say, "Are you crazy!" More crunching sounds.

Mister Greenjeans volunteered that they had a mystery on their hands. The crunching continued.

Mister Moose, in Allegrhetti's falsetto voice, suggested that maybe it wasn't a carrot being eaten. "Sounds more to me, Bunny, like a bunch of ice cream sticks being rubbed together."

They all had a good laugh at that little inside joke. In the meantime, I kept on making carrots-being-consumed noises with my handful of ice cream sticks. And the more I crunched, the more desperate I became for a way out of my embarrassing dilemma. And then suddenly it came to me.

As the three continued their jokes, I added a new sound to the carrot crunches—the familiar buzzes of Raymond the Fly.

The reaction of Bunny Rabbit to the sound of this interloper in his carrot horde was immediate and decisive. As Bunny Rabbit stiffened his body in shocked surprise, the Captain brought the segment to an end by announcing that perhaps Raymond had gotten over his "sweet tooth" (a reference to Twinkies) and become a vegetarian.

When the show returned after the commercial break, the crunching and buzzing had stopped and the Captain and Mister Greenjeans had left the desk area. On the desk, however, and marching in determined military fashion was Bunny Rabbit holding his beloved carrots in one paw, while, on his shoulder, his other paw held a very ominous-looking fly swatter.

The trick to doing sound effects on Captain Kangaroo was very simple. The first rule was to have the following effects available at all times: bulb horn (Beepo the clown's nose), Deagon chimes (the Treasure House doorbell), police whistle, postman's whistle, fire gong, train whistle (hat tree game), small buzzer (Raymond the Fly), ice cream sticks (Bunny Rabbit's carrots), and a special recording of crazy clock ticks (Captain Kangaroo watch). In addition, a special library of 100 often-asked-for sounds (birds, dogs, cows, horses, sheep, rain, thunder, etc.) and dozens of often-used manual effects. All of these effects had to be within easy reach because you never knew when the kindly old Captain was going to turn on you.

As I've said, Bob never rehearsed. Therefore, when he had time to fill you never knew what to expect. He might read a story, do a playtime, or if you were really unlucky, he'd go out into the Treasure House Garden. This meant you had to be prepared to come up with any record or manual effect the Captain called for. To give you an idea of how nerve-racking this could be for sound effects, I've scripted one of these little pastoral strolls. Please note that all the lines italicized are directed to SFX (sound effects) . . . me. (Everything after SFX in parentheses describes my thoughts and actions.)

> CAPTAIN: Ummm, smell that good fresh air. *Usually you can hear Mister Harkin's dog barkin'.* . . .

Figure 11.2. The author trying to outguess the Captain. Photo by author.

SFX: (PUT DOG RECORD ON TURNTABLE. BUT JUST BEFORE YOU OPEN THE POT, YOU HEAR HIM CONTINUE ON TO SAY)

CAPTAIN: ...*but I understand he's not feeling well and is at the veterinarian.* Mister Harkin's dog ... not Mister Harkin.

SFX: (TAKE DOG RECORD OFF TURNTABLE)

CAPTAIN: ...what a beautiful day ... *I wonder where the birds are?*

SFX: (DIG THROUGH THE PILE OF RECORDS AND GET BIRD SOUNDS)

CAPTAIN: *With each passing year they seem to get later and later.* Oh look, there's a *horse* over there....

SFX: (AFTER A QUICK SEARCH, I FIND HORSE RECORD, NEXT

TO IT IS A COW RECORD, I TAKE IT JUST IN CASE. CUE UP HORSE WHINNY AND PLAY IT)

CAPTAIN: . . . and a COW. . .

SFX: (I WAS RIGHT. PLAY COW MOOING. EVEN THE CAPTAIN IS SURPRISED HOW FAST THE COW SOUND COMES. BUT THIS IS HIS ONLY RESPONSE)

CAPTAIN: I hope there's nothing seriously wrong with poor Mrs. Clearie's cow . . . *its moo sure sounds scratchy!*

SFX: (AN OBVIOUS REFERENCE TO SOME SURFACE NOISE ON THE RECORD)

And so it went. With this little insight of what it was like to be on the receiving end of the Captain's playfulness, you will perhaps appreciate better the time I had my revenge.

One summer, Keeshan decided to give the show a different look, and instead of the action taking place in the Treasure House, he had a set built that resembled an old-fashioned river boat.

On the very first show, the script called for the Captain to discuss the most improbable subject that I could imagine: He was to give a demonstration of radio sound effects.

What was unusual was that the feature writer who had come up with this idea didn't discuss it with me. Instead, she had gone directly to the CBS sound-effects department and borrowed a number of manual effects for Bob to use in the demonstration. There were even coconut shells, for doing horses hooves. It seemed to me that this whole thing was getting curiouser and curiouser.

CAPTAIN: Boys and girls, now I'd like to do a demonstration on sound effects. In the *old* days of radio, they used to put on little dramatic shows. And to help the people understand the stories better, they used sound effects like these. *(indicates props)* If they wanted to indicate that someone was at the door, they rang a doorbell. *(rings bell)* Or to ring a telephone they just pushed a button. *(rings phone)* And that's what sound effects *were.*

Already I could tell by his sarcasm that Bob was looking for trouble.

CAPTAIN: But that was in the old days. The old, old, *old* days, that maybe your grandparents remember.

For a man who had impeccable taste and timing, the kindly old Captain was digging himself a deep hole with a few too many sarcastic "olds."

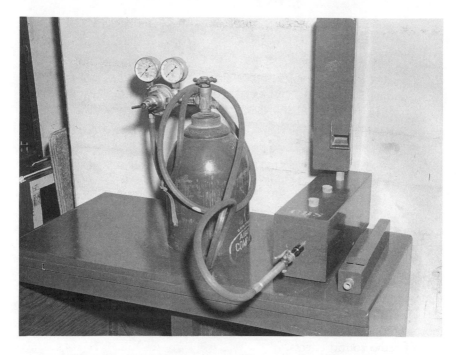

Figure 11.3. Outwitting the Captain. Photo courtesy of Walter Pierson.

CAPTAIN: But here on our boat, we only use things that are real. Everything here makes its own noises. Sound effects, boys and girls, went out with radio.

I had no idea what Bob was going for but I did know it was unusual for him to deceive the children into thinking this was a real boat. Something warned me I was in for some trouble.

One of the first things I learned when I started doing sound effects was to try to anticipate problems. For this reason, I had inspected the set for possible trouble spots when the show decided to use a boat setting for the summer. And the major problem I found involved the boat's steam whistle.

Keeshan loved to play with sound effects. He'd squeeze Beepo's nose (Beepo was a clown face that was part of the set) and I'd beep a bulb horn. He'd go to the hat tree and ask the children to identify various occupations according to the hats he'd put on, and what sound effects went with each hat: a policeman's hat-whistle, a train engineer's hat-train whistle, and so on. The trouble was, you never had any warning.

On one occasion, as we were coming out of a commercial, I looked at my studio monitor and saw Keeshan's hand on Beepo's nose. Lunging for the horn, and nearly chipping two front teeth, I blew a horn sound. But this wasn't good enough for the Captain. He kept his hand on Beepo's nose until I nearly had a hernia trying to sustain the horn sounds for as long as Keeshan held Beepo's nose. So when I found that a steam whistle was going to be part of the set, I rigged a hose from the large, wooden, manual boat whistle to a large tank of pressurized air.

Figure 11.3 shows the setup I used to foil the kindly old Captain. Incidentally, those two "boat whistles" in the picture were originally part of a pipe organ that was salvaged from an old vaudeville theater near Coney Island in Brooklyn.

With this arrangement I could control the flow of air with the regulator at the end of the hose, once the air-tank valve was open. Now I was prepared to give Keeshan anything from a short toot to a full-blown boat whistle that lasted for 15 minutes. And the best part of it all was, he thought I still had to blow the boat whistle with my mouth.

> CAPTAIN: . . . and so, boys and girls, when I want to signal to another boat or it's very foggy out and I want to warn another boat that we're in the area, all I do is pull this lanyard . . . which is a rope connected to a whistle that operates on steam from the engine room.

In all my many years in show business, never was I presented with more of a setup. In fact, it was too good to be true. I was totally confused about what was expected of me. I could understand the sarcastic little digs about the "old, old, old days of sound effects," but it was completely out of the Captain's character to purposely mislead his audience about the legitimacy of the "real" boat whistle. As the Captain moved toward the lanyard, my mind began to race. Had they indeed rigged a real boat whistle for the Captain to play with? Why else would he be treating sound effects in such a cavalier manner?

As the Captain took hold of the lanyard, even the staff in the control room fell silent, and in the studio, all eyes (and most assuredly mine) were on the rope, in the Captain's hands.

Finally, he gave the rope a mighty yank, and the studio was filled with sweet and glorious silence. Not complete silence, however, for from the far end of the studio came the unmistakable sound of a suppressed snicker.

Suddenly, the control room exploded into a frenzy of conflicting instructions directed at me. Half the voices believed the Captain was going for an undisclosed comedy routine, while the other half of the brain trust was screaming for me to blow the "goddamn boat whistle!"

Again he pulled the lanyard. And again he was greeted with silence.

Suddenly I realized that this wasn't a trick at all. He really needed me to blow the whistle! Sound effects unimportant, huh! You want the old, old, *old* days of radio, do you! I'll give you a taste of old days, me bucko!

The Captain began stomping his foot on the "deck" of the boat and calling out in a loud voice, "Mister Greenjeans, Mister Greenjeans, can you hear me in the engine room?"

Lumpy Brannum, who had gone behind the set to have a quick cigarette, blew out a lungful of smoke and answered, "Yes Captain?"

"I need more steam for the boat whistle!"

Lumpy could be heard deliberately bumping into things as he made his way behind the narrow space that separated the studio wall and the set. He did this so that his voice would indeed sound like it was coming from the engine room instead of from somewhere off in the middle of the river.

"I'll tend to that right away, Captain. . . ."

The control room, on safe ground now that they realized that Keeshan really did need the sound effect of the whistle, all began yelling at once. "Blow the whistle, blow the whistle!"

With everyone screaming in my ears, we mercifully went to a commercial.

During this two-minute break, I was certain that Keeshan would come over and demand that I give him the sound of the boat whistle. But that wouldn't be part of the game. That would be admitting defeat. As I peered around the corner of the set, I could see the kindly old Captain deep in thought. Which didn't bother me in the least, because I had control of the all-important boat whistle.

When we came back from commercial, Keeshan addressed the camera. "Well, boys and girls, Mister Greenjeans found the small problem and fixed it. Now, when I pull the rope, I guarantee you will hear the sound of a boat whistle."

As Keeshan walked slowly towards the rope, the whole situation took on the drama of a western shootout: Captain Kangaroo versus the sound-man at high noon. Even though I had put on my head phones again, there wasn't a sound to be heard other than some nervous coughs.

As the Captain slowly raised his hand towards the lanyard, even the coughing in the control room stopped. And as he gripped the rope and gave a mighty pull, the studio was filled with the sound of the familiar steam-boat whistle. He continued to hold the rope down, and a crooked smile of revenge creased his mouth under his mustache.

After 10 seconds of holding the rope down, it was evident why he had been so deep in thought during the commercial.

After 20 seconds, his smile was replaced by a flickering look of puzzlement. After 25 seconds, he began frowning perceptively. At 30 seconds, he realized that there was more to the show than just trying to get even with the sound-effects man, so he reluctantly gave up his little game and released the rope. But now it was my turn.

Instead of the steam whistle stopping, it continued to blow. The Captain, unprepared for this turn of events, began jerking at the rope and stomping his feet and shouting to Mister Greenjeans, all at the same time. "Lessen the steam, Mister Greenjeans. Lessen the steam!"

And suddenly, as quickly as the boat whistle had started, it stopped. He walked slowly and with an air of some bewilderment away from the lanyard. Little did he suspect I was saving my best until last!

He then told the children how good it was to be floating down the river with a good, "seaworthy ship under you." And for emphasis, he stamped his foot—perhaps a trifle too hard, giving me the excuse I was looking for to start blowing the whistle again.

As the closing theme began, Keeshan started moving around the set hitting various items in hopes of striking something that would shut off the capricious whistle. Shouting to be heard over the din, he apologized to the children for the behavior of the boat whistle but promised to have it "fixed by tomorrow," and looking in my direction, added, "or we'll get a new one."

Of course he did neither. The boat whistle became a part of the fun, along with the Treasure House doorbell, Beepo's nose, the Hat Tree sounds, Raymond the Fly, Mister Bainter's backfiring truck, and all the other wonderful sounds that helped make a show that was so short on scripted material but so long on imagination, such a joy and challenge to do.

CHAPTER XII

THE ARTISTS AND THEIR CREDITS

PERHAPS ONE OF THE strangest love triangles during the live days of broadcasting was the one that involved sound-effects artists, producers, and network vice-presidents. Both the producers and network executives loved the new dimension that sound effects gave to their programs, but looked the other way when it came to giving credit to the artists who created them. This included credit both on the air and in the printed media.

The producers and the networks each felt that the public was better off knowing as little about a program's dependence on sound effects as possible. As one producer put it, "Telling the listeners that the Lone Ranger's horse is nothing but two coconut shells drummed in a tray of dirt would be like telling kids there's no Santa Claus."

Perhaps they were right. Anyway, it's too late to argue now. But it isn't too late to right some wrongs that have been going on since the 1930s.

Keene Crockett, an outstanding artist at both ABC and NBC in New York, recalls the time a magazine asked NBC for a picture of one of their sound-effects artists, to be used in an advertisement. When Keene learned that he was the artist selected, he was delighted—until he saw his picture in the magazine. Instead of his name under the picture, he saw the name "Jack Gibson."

Now it's one thing to have a magazine misspell your name. But it's quite another to see someone else's name under your picture. When Keene called the magazine to find out why they made such a blatant mistake, the magazine responded by saying that was the name given to them by NBC.

Keene soon learned that it was the network's policy not to give out the real names of its sound-effects artists to the media. Supposedly, it was a way of "protecting" them from too much publicity. And if all that wasn't bad enough, in addition to not being given credit for the picture, he didn't get paid for its use, either. Perhaps "Jack Gibson" got the money.

Although this problem of receiving recognition seems like a singular problem only affecting the sound-effect artists, comedy writers of the 1930's were subjected to this same type of "sheltering." Only in their cases, it was felt that revealing the mundane fact that the comedy stars needed help in creating all those wonderful jokes week after week, would be disillusioning to the audience.

It wasn't until Jack Benny decided that this foolishness had gone on long enough when he shocked America by announcing that he did indeed employ writers. And to prove it, the names of Ed Beloin and Bill Morrow were the first comedy writers to be given writing credits over network radio. Although it isn't known who the first sound-effect artists were to be given name credit, with our luck it was probably good ole Jack Gibson.

But after 35 years went by, conditions in live radio changed. The photo in Figure 12.1 was shot during a live show produced for the benefit of UNICEF. To the right is Tom Buchanan, ready to step in if opening a door proves too much for the author (center). The television camera crew was supplied by KABC-TV, for the program, "Hollywood Close-Up."

And now it's time to right a wrong that has been done over the years to all those creative sound effects artists who contributed so meaningfully to the success of live radio.

Although a number of the stories in this book involve live television, they are included only because the artists that worked them were also from live radio. And that is the focus of this book, sound effects during the live days of broadcasting. And although many artists have labored long and hard in films and taped television, that is a book for someone else to write.

One cautionary bit of explanation involves the amount of credits each artist received. Some very competent artists are given credit for one show and others have twenty. This often meant that the artists with a limited number of credits, worked on shows that occurred five days a week and were on the air for years. But more on that in a moment.

Also if I didn't (or couldn't) receive verification on what artists worked in live radio, rather than possibly misinform the reader, I omitted them. The same is true in regards to show credits.

A number of the artists listed below have several network call letters following their names, in particular NBC/ABC. This does not necessarily meant that sound-effects artists couldn't hold a job. Instead, it reflects a bit of sound-effects history.

In 1926, the National Broadcasting Company (NBC) was formed jointly by General Electric, Westinghouse, and RCA, under the guidance

Figure 12.1. The author and Tom Buchanan. Photo by Cinda Y. Mott.

of David Sarnoff. From that time until 1943, NBC owned two networks, called the Red Network and the Blue Network.

When the Federal Communication Commission began its investigation into broadcast monopolies, NBC sold the Blue Network to Edward Noble, owner of the LifeSaver Candy Company. This network of stations became the American Broadcasting Company (ABC).

Although the two networks were separate and distinct, NBC in Hollywood continued to supply sound effects and artists to ABC on a leasing arrangement. This practice continued until the popular soap, "General Hospital," went on the air in 1961. It wasn't until then that ABC decided to have its own sound-effects department. This explains why so many artists who worked for NBC in Hollywood were given credit for shows that were actually heard on ABC.

As I began gathering information for this book, it soon became evident that, paradoxically, the longer I spent acquiring information, the less information was available.

The networks, plagued by storage problems, had destroyed, or had simply lost, the personnel records and the few pictures they had from those early days of sound effects. The tragedy of all this is the fact that so little is known about the artists of sound effects to begin with.

As a result, what you find in this book is unique. All the information was graciously given to me by people that were personally involved during those golden years of live broadcasting. A period of time that happened more than a half a century ago.

Retrieving facts that happened that long ago was particularly difficult when it came to giving show credits to the various artists. In particular the women. It always seemed curious to me why more women didn't stay in sound effects inasmuch as sound effects as a career was started by a woman.

It would seem that inasmuch as Ora was doing the recruiting for this new field, that sound effects would be more appealing to women. But this was not the case. In fact, it took a war to get these ladies to take off their high heels and "walk like a man."

With the outbreak of World War II, the networks began hiring women to take the place of the men that entered the service. When the war was over and the servicemen returned, the women were let go. This was not ingratitude on the part of the networks, this was the law. Men that served their country were guaranteed their old jobs back. This was true of sound effects: this was true of all jobs filled by women during the war years.

Even during those war years, there never was more than a dozen women in all of sound effects, from one coast to the other. Part of the reason for this could be blamed on the relatively low wages that sound effects paid. After all, if a woman wanted to do a job that often required a lot of dirty work and sweating, she could get a high paying job in the defense industry . . . or perhaps, forego the money and just get married.

Another reason why so few women stayed in sound effects was the relatively few jobs available. If you added up all the sound-effects artists at the networks and freelance, you would come up with a number well under 100. And if you waited around for one of those jobs to open up, you could grow old and poor in a hurry.

My final guess and explanation is that the scarcity of women in sound effects, can be blamed on the networks themselves. How can you prepare and apply for a career that the network publicity department always avowed never existed?

I truly believe it was this final reason that made it so difficult for not only the women, but men as well to get into sound effects. Sound effects at the time, was a better kept secret than when and where the allies were going to invade Europe.

But now it's time to give credit to all those artists. You will notice that some names only received a few credits, or worse still, no show credits at all. This has no reflection on those artists' qualifications or ability. It only needs a little explanation.

If you did "Ma Perkins," you started in 1933 and didn't get finished until 1960. This meant you only did one show but you did it 5 days a week, 52 weeks a year for 27 years! That's a lot of sound effects over the years just for one credit.

In the case of those few artists not receiving any credits at all, this was the most difficult decision for me to make. However I decided that giving credits just for the sake of giving credits, would compromise the credibility of the other artists and make this category meaningless. Therefore if there was no verifiable live radio credit information available, no credits were given.

As far as credits for live television shows is concerned, many of the artists I have mentioned who did live radio made the transition into television. But that was not our medium, live radio was.

Therefore, to the ladies and gentlemen who labored long or briefly in the art of sound effects, I offer my apologies for any credits I might have missed. Please believe me, it wasn't because I didn't try.

Amati, Ralph (NBC, Hollywood): One Man's Family, I Love a Mystery

Amrhein, Jack (CBS, New York): Mr. Keene, Tracer of Lost Persons (1937), The Mysterious Traveler (1943), Mr. Chameleon, The Fred Allen Show, Inner Sanctum, The Robert Q. Lewis Show

Anderson, Jack: Brighter Day, The Light of the World

April, Al (WOR, New York): Under Arrest (1949), The Shadow (1948), The Mysterious Traveler

Bailey, Ed (NBC, Chicago): Backstage Wife, Bachelor's Children, Vic and Sade, Lights Out

Bayz, Guz (CBS, Hollywood): Yours Truly, Johnny Dollar, Suspense, Fanny Brice, Dr. Christian, The Fire Chief, Studio One, Amos 'n' Andy

Beck, Barney (Mutual, New York): Beatrice Kay, Comic Weekly Man, The Shadow (1936), Bobby Benson's Adventures, Bob and Ray, Tom Mix, Sea Hound, I Love a Mystery, Real Stories from Real Life, True Detective Mysteries (Murray Burnet, one of the writers of "True Detective Mysteries," wrote the story that the film *Casablanca* was based on.)

Binnie, Al (CBS, New York: 1939–68): Mr. and Mrs. North, Columbia Workshop, Howie Wing, Wilderness Road, Cimarron Tavern (1945), Crime Doctor, Superman

Blainey, Ed (NBC, ABC, New York): The Fat Man (1945), Hop Harrigan (1942), Grand Central Station, Gangbusters, The FBI in Peace and War (1944)

Blatter, Frank (NBC, Chicago): Backstage Wife, Ma Perkins, Gangbusters, Vic and Sade, Mary Marlin

Boyle, Betty (NBC, Hollywood) (WWII replacement): Lum and Abner

Brachhausen, Maurice (NBC, ABC, New York): When the NBC network split in 1943, he became head of the ABC sound-effects department. In addition, he wrote

Figure 12.2. Bill Brown. Bill (CBS, New York) had an outstanding career as an artist before becoming head of the sound-effects department when Malachy Wienges, the former manager, moved up the corporate ladder. And if you think Bill's list of credits is long, they only cover the radio portion of his 50-year career. Photo by author.

for such shows as "Captain Video," and "Dick Tracy."

Brinkmeyer, Bill (NBC, Hollywood): The Aldrich Family

Brown, Bill (CBS, New York: 1936–87): Big Sister, Our Gal Sunday, Brighter Day, Let's Pretend, David Harum, Campbell Playhouse (formerly Mercury Theater), Lights Out, Kitty Foyle, Cavalcade of America, Life Can Be Beautiful, Dr. Christian, The Human Adventure, Strange Romance of Evelyn Winters, Studio One, The Perfect Crime, Lone Journey, Strange as It Seems, Pretty Kitty Kelly (1937)

Brownell, William (NBC, Hollywood)

Bubeck, Harry (NBC, Chicago): Lights Out, Captain Midnight, Jack Armstrong, The All-American Boy, Gangbusters

Buchanan, Tom (Freelance/CBS, New York/Hollywood): Radio Free Europe, Voice of America, So Proudly We Hail, The Romance of Helen Trent

Cabbibo, Joe (CBS, ABC, New York): Tennessee Jed, Counterspy, Yours Truly, Johnny Dollar, Bob and Ray, This Is Your FBI

Caminito, Tony (WXYZ, Detroit): The Lone Ranger, The Green Hornet

Casey, Clark (CBS, Hollywood) (Co-organized sound effects at KNX): Adventures of Philip Marlowe, The Red Skelton Show (1941), Dr. Christian (1937), My Favorite Husband (1948), Calling All Cars, Gary Breckner Baseball

Figure 12.3 shows the staff of the CBS Hollywood sound-effects department in 1945. In the front row from the left are: Jim Murphy, Clark Casey, Cliff Thorsness, Gus Bayz, Berne Surrey, Dave Light, Jack Dick and Al Span. Feeding the birthday boy is Billy Gould. In the rear from the left are: Ralph Cummings, Gene Twombly and Bob Wendell, a maintenance technician. Cutting the cake is Al Span's secretary, Lee Randolph. Photo courtesy of Clark Casey.

Game Recreations, The Baby Snooks Show, Pursuit (1949)

Caton, Floyd (NBC, Hollywood): One Man's Family, The Jack Benny Show, Abbott and Costello, The Great Gildersleeve, Six Shooter

Cole, Dewey (WXYZ, Detroit): The Lone Ranger, The Green Hornet, Sgt. Preston of the Yukon

Cole, Fred (NBC, Hollywood): When a Girl Marries, One Man's Family, The Red Skelton Show, Kool Cigarette Commercial (sound of the Penguin)

Conant, Wes (CBS, New York): Portia Faces Life (1940), Ma

Perkins, Theater Guild on the Air (1943)

Conlan, Bob (NBC, Hollywood): Roy Rogers, The Screen Director's Playhouse (1951)

Cooney, George (Mutual, WOR): I Love a Mystery

Cornel, Parker (NBC, Hollywood): The Spike Jones Show, Blondie, The Bob Hope Show

Creekmore, Lloyd (NBC, Hollywood: 1930s): Truth or Consequences, Joe Penner, Reunion of the States

Crockett, Keene (see page 248)

Cummings, Ralph (CBS, Hollywood): General Electric House Party

Cuomo, John (CBS, New York): Campbell Playhouse

Curtiss, Ralph (CBS, New York; freelance): Rosemary, The Romance of Helen Trent, Man Behind the Gun

Dick, Jack (Mutual, CBS, Hollywood): Life with Luigi (1948 CBS), Hollywood Star Showcase, The Cisco Kid (1943), Tell It Again, Stars Over Hollywood (1941)

Dwan, Jimmy (CBS, New York: 1939): Aunt Jenny, The Second Mrs. Burton (1945), Ma Perkins, Let's Pretend, Crime Doctor

Eisenmenger, Michael (NBC, Chicago): Mary Marlin, Captain Midnight, Don Winslow of the Navy, Backstage Wife

Erlenborn, Ray (see page 254)

Essman, Harry (CBS, Hollywood): The Bing Crosby Show, Lum and Abner, Screen Guild Theater

Fenton, Ed (CBS, New York): The March of Time

Finelli, Al (ABC, New York): Dick Tracy, Terry and the Pirates

Fitzgerald, Roland (CBS, New York): The Perfect Crime, Philip Morris Playhouse, The March of Time, (Invented the recirculating sink and many other sound-effects props.)

Fletcher, Jimmy (WXYZ, Detroit): The Lone Ranger, The Green Hornet, Sgt. Preston of the Yukon

Flowerday, Fred (WXYZ, Detroit): The Lone Ranger (later directed the show), Sgt. Preston of the Yukon, The Green Hornet

Flynn, James (ABC, New York): Dick Tracy, Tennessee Jed, This Is Your FBI, My True Story, Whispering Streets, Gangbusters

Foster, Don (WLW, Cincinnati; WOR/CBS, New York): Famous Jury Trials, Stoopnagle and Bud, True Detective Mysteries, (Invented the electronic gun; Became department head at CBS in 1957)

Fraser, Monty (see page 257)

Fry, Fred (WXYZ, Detroit): The Lone Ranger, The Green Hornet, Sgt. Preston of the Yukon

Gainor, Russ (CBS, New York): Road of Life, Ma Perkins

Gauthier, Henry (CBS, New York): Mercury Theater on the Air, Aunt Jenny, Joyce Jordan—Girl Intern

Gideon, Mary Ann (CBS Hollywood) (WWII replacement): Mayor of the Town

Glennon, John (NBC/Mutual, New York): Superman, Pick and Pat, Elsie—The Borden Show, Stella Dallas, The Edgar Bergen and Charlie McCarthy Show, Mary Small Show, The Pat Barnes Show, It Pays to Be Ignorant

Goode, Jim (Mutual, New York): True Detective Mysteries, The Mysterious Traveler

Gould, Bill (CBS, Hollywood): Our Miss Brooks (1948), Escape, Camel Caravan, My Favorite Husband, Joan Davis Show, The Eddie Bracken Show (1946), Maisie

Graham, Robert J. (see page 269)

Grapperhaus, Bob (NBC, Hollywood): One Man's Family, The Fitch Bandwagon, The Screen Director's Playhouse

Grey, Elliot (ABC, New York) (created and built effects)

Gustafson, Walt (ABC/Mutual, New York): Counterspy (1942), Terry and the Pirates, The Shadow, Superman, Boston

Figure 12.4. This may look like a party, but these CBS-New York sound-effects artists are really working. On the left, kneeling with the hammers, is James Rogan. Standing behind him is Walt Pierson, head of the sound-effects department. The two men standing next to Pierson are unidentified. Al Binnie is in the center, playing records. Jack Amrhein, behind Binnie, is also playing records. Vic Rubei is on the right, near the drum.

Blackie, Bulldog Drummond, Philo Vance, The Jack Pearl Show, The Witch's Tale, (head of sound department at ABC)

Hanley, Tom (CBS, Hollywood): Gunsmoke, Straight Arrow, Have Gun Will Travel

Harper, Ron (Mutual, New York): Official Detective, The Mysterious Traveler

Haus, Leona (NBC, Hollywood) (WWII replacement for the duration.)

Hengsterbeck, Bill (WXYZ, Detroit): The Lone Ranger, The Green Hornet, Sgt. Preston of the Yukon

Hill, Chet (NBC, New York): Backstage Wife, Colgate Sports Newsreel starring Bill Stern

Hoffman, Bill (NBC/Mutual, New York): Mark Trail, Sherlock Holmes (1930), True Detective Mysteries, Mystery Is My Hobby, The House of Mystery

Hogan, Al (CBS, New York): FBI in Peace and War, Mr. and Mrs. North, Crime Doctor

Holmes, Robert (NBC, Hollywood): A Date with Judy

Horan, Tom (NBC, Chicago): Ma Perkin, Backstage Wife, (Became the head of the sound department.)

Horine, Agnew (CBS/NBC/Mutual, New York): The Fred Allen Show, Stella Dallas (1937), Archie Andrews, Dimension X

James, Dick (CBS, Hollywood): Columbia Workshop, The Cisco Kid, Red Ryder, Voyage of the Scarlet Queen

Johnson, Harold, Jr. (ABC, New York): Grand Central Station, Inner Sanctum

Johnson, Urban (CBS, Chicago): First Nighter

Joyce, Ed (NBC, Chicago): Captain Midnight, Jack Armstrong, the All-American Boy, Lights Out, Vic and Sade

Katulik, John (NBC, Chicago): Mary Marlin, Backstage Wife, Ma Perkins

Keane, Jack (Mutual, New York): The House of Mystery (1944), Superman, Martin Kane, Private Eye, Mark Trail

Keating, Joe (Mutual, New York): Crime Fighters, Magazine Theater

Kemper, Ray (CBS, Hollywood): Gunsmoke, Straight Arrow, Have Gun Will Travel, Suspense, Voyage of the Scarlet Queen, (In addition to writing for "Gunsmoke," "Have Gun Will Travel," and "Count of Monte Cristo," Ray was associate producer on "Straight Arrow.")

Kenworthy, Wayne (NBC, Hollywood): Dragnet, The Man Called X

Kremer, Ray (NBC, Chicago; CBS, New York): Don Winslow of the Navy, Gangbusters, The Fred Allen Show, Mercury Theater *(War of the Worlds)*

Lamb, Tiny (CBS, Hollywood): The Red Skelton Show (1941)

Langley, Dorothy (Mutual, New York) (WWII replacement): Murder Is My Hobby

Lehman, George (CBS, New York): Columbia Workshop

Light, David (see page 271)

Livoti, Vic (CBS, Hollywood): Beulah

Loughran, Frank (NBC, New York): The Right to Happiness (1939), Lorenzo Jones

Ludes, Ed (NBC, Hollywood): First

Nighter, Ozzie and Harriet, The Jack Benny Show, The Bob Hope Show, The Groucho Marx Show

Lynch, James (CBS, New York: 1936–71): The Goldbergs, The Romance of Helen Trent, Perry Mason, The Joe DiMaggio Show

McCarty, Jerry (CBS, New York): Columbia Workshop, County Fair (One of the first audience participation shows; 1945), Gangbusters, Arch Oboler Presents, Lights Out, Young Dr. Malone, The Texaco Star Theater, Crime Doctor, You Are There, Casey, Crime Photographer, The Adventures of Mister Meek, Road of Life, The American School of the Air, Gay Nineties Revue (1940), Cabin B-13 (one of the first shows to be taped), Armstrong Theater of Today, Gene Autry's Melody Ranch

McClintock, Bill (Mutual, New York): Theater Guild on the Air (1943), Listening Post, Dick Tracy, The Sheriff of Canyon County, Quiet Please

McCloskey, John (CBS, New York): Our Gal Sunday, Hilltop House, Young Doctor Malone

McDonough, Walt (CBS/ABC/WOR, New York): The Mysterious Traveler, Terry and the Pirates, Coast-to-Coast on a Bus, Dick Tracy, Big Sister

McGee, Jerry (NBC, New York): Radio City Playhouse (1940s)

McQuade, Stuart (NBC, New York) (Invented dozens of ingenious sound effects, including the thunder screen, rain machine, and wagon wheels with speed controls.)

Martindale, Ross (NBC/Mutual, New York): Front Page Farrell

(Mutual, 1941), This Is Nora Drake (1947), Young Widder Brown, Pepper Young's Family (NBC, 1936)

Mautner, Bob (CBS, New York): Columbia Workshop

Mellow, Frank (CBS, New York: 1940–60): Grand Central Station, Columbia Workshop

Mihan, Donald (NBC, Chicago): Fibber McGee and Molly

Mitchel, Curt (NBC, Chicago): Jack Armstrong, the All-American Boy, Sky King, Silver Eagle

Monroe, Sam (NBC, New York): Dimension X (later called X Minus One), Mr. and Mrs. North

Morse, Lloyd (CBS, New York): Armstrong Theater of Today, (primarily maintenance tech.)

Mott, Robert (CBS, New York; NBC, Hollywood)

Mowry, Paul (CBS, New York) (WWII replacement): Man Behind the Gun

Murphy, James (CBS, Hollywood): The Jack Benny Show, My Friend Irma, The Cisco Kid, Life with Luigi

Murray, Ross (CBS, Hollywood): The Whistler, The Cisco Kid, Pursuit

Nelson, Harry (ABC, New York; CBS, Hollywood): Terry and the Pirates (1937, NBC), Gangbusters, Counterspy

Nichols, Arthur (CBS, New York: 1929–31) (He and his wife, Ora, introduced sound effects to radio.)

Nichols, Ora (CBS, New York: 1929–   ) (First lady of sound effects.): The March of Time, Mercury Theater, Roses and Drums (1932), 45 Minutes in Hollywood,

Buck Rogers in the Twenty-Fifth Century, Stoopnagle and Bud

Nugent, Bill (NBC, Hollywood) (Mostly maintenance and some vacation relief work on shows.)

O'Donnell, George (CBS, New York: 1931–59): Let's Pretend, Young Doctor Malone, The March of Time

O'Hara, Hamilton (CBS, New York: 1946–72): Young Doctor Malone, The Guiding Light, Wendy Warren and the News, Hilltop House

Otto, Walter (CBS, New York): The American School of the Air, Young Dr. Malone (1939), Let's Pretend

Owens, Lavern (WMCA/CBS, New York) (WWII replacement who stayed on to become a technical-scheduling supervisor): Big Sister

Penner, Adrian (Mutual, New York): Nick Carter, Affairs of Peter Salem, The Falcon (1945), Mystery Is My Hobby, 2000 Plus, Bulldog Drummond, John Steele Adventurer

Pierson, Walter (CBS, New York: 1933–47): Lux Radio Theater, March of Times. (Took over from Ora Nichols in 1933 to become department head of the CBS sound-effects department; was responsible for modernizing the departments both in New York and Hollywood.)

Pittman, Frank (NBC, Hollywood): Fibber McGee and Molly (later directed the show)

Powers, John (CBS, Hollywood): Mr. District Attorney (1939), Big Town (1937), Radio City Playhouse

Prescott, Bob (ABC/NBC/CBS, New York): Gangbusters, Death Valley Days (1930s), The Goldbergs

Quantro, Romeo (CBS, New York): The Romance of Helen Trent, (transferred into audio-mixing department)

Range, Charles (CBS, Chicago/New York): Grand Central Station, Gay Nineties Revue, Columbia Workshop, Crime Doctor

Reimer, Virgil (NBC, Hollywood): This Is Your FBI (1945), Sherlock Holmes, First Nighter, Duffy's Tavern, Nero Wolf, Olsen and Johnson, The Eddie Cantor Show, The Jack Benny Show, Richard Diamond, Hollywood Playhouse, Burns and Allen, Walter Winchell, The Bob Hope Show, The Buster Brown Gang, The Great Gildersleeve (Left sound effects to direct this show.)

Rinaldi, James (CBS, New York): Wendy Warren and the News (1947), Armstrong Theater of Today, The March of Time

Robertson, Ken (WXYZ, Detroit): The Lone Ranger, The Green Hornet, Sgt. Preston of the Yukon

Robinson, Jack (CBS/NBC, Hollywood): The Amazing Mr. Malone, The Red Skelton Show (1941), Dragnet (Became a writer, director for this series.)

Rogan, James (CBS, New York: 1936–73): Grand Central Station, You Are There (1947), Gangbusters, Man Behind the Gun, Casey, Crime Photographer, Mercury Theater (War of the Worlds)

Ross, Terry (ABC, New York): Greatest Story Ever Told

Rubei, Vic (CBS, New York: 1933–), The Phil Baker Show, The Kate Smith Hour, Walter O'Keefe, Report to the Nation

Saz, Harry (NBC, Hollywood)

Schaffer, Al (CBS/WOR, New York): The Shadow, Quiet Please, The Doctor Fights, The Mysterious Traveler, Voice of America, Radio Free Europe, Report to the Nation

Scott, Al (NBC/CBS, Hollywood): The Big Story, Cavalcade of America

Segal, Manny (NBC/CBS, New York): Front Page Farrell, The Right to Happiness, Road of Life (1937), Lorenzo Jones

Shaver, Walt (Mutual, New York): Exploring the Unknown, Bulldog Drummond (1941)

Siletti, Mario (Mutual, New York): Nick Carter, Master Detective, House of Mystery, Murder by Experts, Incredible But True

Sixsmith, Jack (CBS, Hollywood)

Sorrance, Art The Case Book of Gregory Hood

Span, Al (CBS, Hollywood): I Love a Mystery, Burns and Allen, (Started the sound-effects department in Hollywood, 1936.)

Strand, Art (CBS, New York: 1940–74): Let's Pretend, Casey, Crime Photographer

Street, Fritz (Mutual, New York): The Shadow, Witch's Tales, (Head of the sound-effects department at NBC, New York.)

Sullivan, Jerry (CBS, New York): Rosemary (1947), This Is Nora Drake, Cimmaron Tavern, Winner Take All

Surrey, Berne (CBS, Hollywood): The Whistler (1945), Adventures of Sam Spade, Suspense, Pursuit (1949)

Sutton, Rod (NBC, Hollywood): You Can't Take It with You (1951), Night Beat (1951)

Thorsness, Cliff (CBS, Hollywood (Co-organized KNX sound department): Adventures of Philip Marlowe, The Eddie Cantor Show, Escape, Fanny Brice, The Jack Benny Show

Tollefson, Bud (NBC, Hollywood): Dragnet, The Buster Brown Gang (did dog barks for Tige), The Man Called X

Troy, Sarah Jane (Mutual, New York) Mystery Is My Hobby (WWII replacement for the duration.)

Turnbull, Bob (Mutual, New York): Red Ryder

Twombly, Gene (CBS, Hollywood): Gene Autry's Melody Ranch, The Jack Benny Show, The Whistler (1945), The Hallmark Playhouse

Uhlig, Max (CBS, New York: 1935–42): The March of Time, Lux Radio Theater, The Stebbins Boys of Bucksport Point Maine, (Department head 1935–42.)

Van Brackels, Al (CBS, New York): March of Time

Vojtal, Ed (CBS/WGN, Chicago): First Nighter

Voorhees, Davidson (CBS, New York: 1946–52) (Department head 1946–52; promoted to CBS vice-presidency.)

Wauknitz, Dotty (NBC, Hollywood) (WWII replacement for the duration.)

Westbrook, JoLine (CBS, Hollywood) (WWII replacement for the duration.)

White, Orval (CBS, New York: 1949–71): Gangbusters

Wienges, Malachy (CBS, New York) (Head of CBS, New York, sound-effects department.)

Wingett, Byron (CBS, New York):

Figure 12.5. When those wagon trains on radio got rolling, this is what kept them going. Berne Surrey (left) is doing the recorded whinny, and Clark Casey (far right) keeps the wheels a-turning. Gene Twombly and an unidentified artist do the horse's (or oxen's) hoof beats. Although Berne was an excellent artist, shortly after this picture was taken, he decided to become a psychiatrist. I suppose doing horse whinnies for a living could do that to you. Photo courtesy of Clark Casey.

We the People (1936), Gangbusters, The FBI in Peace and War, Mr. Chameleon

Wormser, Jack (NBC, Hollywood): The Jack Benny Show, Fibber McGee and Molly

Now that you have become acquainted with the names of the artists and the shows they worked on during the live days of radio, I thought you'd like to meet a few of them close up. Although there were many artists equally deserving of these short profiles, my reason for selecting the artists I did was more influenced by the amount of information available on them than for any individual superior achievements.

As you read their stories, perhaps you'll come away with a better understanding of not just sound effects but, more importantly, what it was like to live and work during the live days of radio.

Today we romantically refer to those days as "the Golden Age of Radio." But live radio also encompassed some lesser golden times called

Figure 12.6. Keene Crockett goes over a script with Bob Hope and Jerry Calonna. Photo courtesy of Keene Crockett.

the Great Depression and World War II. Perhaps now, as you read further into the lives of some of these artists, you will have a little clearer idea of what those times were like.

Keene Crockett (NBC/ABC, New York: 1935–62)

Death Valley Days	Modern Romances
Theater Guild on the Air	The Bob Hope Show
When a Girl Marries	The Rudy Vallee Hour
The March of Time	Land of the Lost (1944)
This Is War	Dick Tracy
Men at Sea	Arch Oboler Presents
Superman	Charlie Chan
Cafe Istanbul	Topper
Chandu the Magician	Tom Corbett, Space Cadet
Inner Sanctum	True Story Theater
Deadline Dramas	Day of Reckoning

As you look at his list of credits, you will see that Keene Crockett was one of those rare artists who was equally at home both on comedy and on dramatic shows.

Figure 12.7. Keene Crockett and Marlene Dietrich. Photo courtesy of Keene Crockett.

Keene Crockett was born in 1909 and raised on a large farm in Moline, Illinois. After graduating from Knox College with a B.A. in English and psychology and a minor in theater, Keene took off for Boothbay Harbor, Maine, for a summer at the Theater in the Woods. As a member of the Harbor Players, he was given the job of stage manager plus. Although it had a lofty sound, the "plus" meant he did any other job that needed doing, and all for the sum of one dollar a week and room and board. Even for the 1930's, it was terrible pay.

It was, therefore, with absolutely no regret that when the Maine foliage began signaling that summer was over, Keene left for New York City and never looked back. When he arrived, it seemed that every actor from every summer stock company across the United States was getting off the same train. This situation was complicated by the Great Depression and it all made the dollar a week he had earned in Boothbay Harbor look good.

After months of desperate job hunting, Keene's perseverance (and college education) paid off. He was offered a job at NBC as a page, with a starting salary of $65 a month. Although that doesn't seem like a great deal of money to pay a college graduate, everyone who applied for the job was a college graduate. Those were difficult times. Besides, considering that a room at the Wellington Hotel was only $7 a week, the money was considered good.

The network had such stiff job requirements because they never expected anyone to remain at that level. The job of page was NBC's way of familiarizing new employees with all the intricacies of a large broadcasting company. And one of the intricacies that Keene discovered was something called sound effects.

After a suitable length of time as an apprentice, Keene was allowed to do a show as an assistant to the regular soundman. The show was "Bamby," a half-hour romantic comedy starring Helen Hayes.

The effect that Keene was required to do was that of a horse-drawn carriage riding through Central Park. Miss Hayes was so impressed with Keene's adroitness with the coconut shells that many years later, when she was starring in *Harriet* on Broadway, she sent for Keene to help her daughter with the sound effects for her school play.

Although these warm relationships between the sound-effects artists and the actors were discouraged by the networks, they existed in spite of the restrictions.

For instance, while doing "Cafe Istanbul," Keene and Marlene Dietrich developed a close relationship that included the film star's disclosure to Keene of something that even Hedda Hopper didn't know: Marlene's favorite recipe for stuffed cabbage. Now that's getting about as close as you can get.

For all you stuffed cabbage lovers, here is Marlene's recipe:

> 10–12 cabbage leaves
> ⅓ pound chopped beef, pork, veal, or leftovers
> 1 egg
> 3 slices of bread torn into small pieces
> sauteed chopped onions (optional)
> can of tomato soup
> salt and pepper to taste

> Braise meats in frying pan until cooked. Boil cabbage leaves for 5 minutes. Mix meats, bread pieces, egg, and other ingredients together.

Figure 12.8. Keene Crockett as the district attorney in Dream Girl. *Seated in the witness chair is Betty Fields, while Bill Lee plays the judge. Photo courtesy of Keene Crockett.*

Spoon 2 tablespoons of mixture onto each leaf. Close and fasten the leaves with toothpicks. Place leaves in a Dutch oven on a cooking rack or on pieces of leftover cabbage. Spoon the undiluted tomato soup onto leaves. Fill the soup can with water and pour the water into the Dutch oven. Close lid and cook over low heat for 1¾ hours.

In 1942, Keene left NBC for a part in Elmer Rice's comedy *Dream Girl*, starring Betty Fields. It ran for 14 months, with Keene playing the role of the district attorney.

With the success of this show, other plays came Keene's way, including *O'Daniel* for the Theater Guild and *Joan of Lorraine* with Diana Barrymore. During this last show, Maurice Brachausen, then head of the newly formed ABC sound-effects department, persuaded Keene to return to sound effects and do the effects on the "Theater Guild on the Air" for U.S. Steel.

When Keene returned to sound effects, he found the atmosphere at ABC less restrictive than at NBC. Among other things, he was allowed to accept acting roles while still on staff as a soundman.

Many artists did vocals or were given small under-five-lines roles, more

Figure 12.9. Keene Crockett running a scene in Lady in the Dark, *with Gertrude Lawrence. Photo courtesy of Keene Crockett.*

Figure 12.10. Keene Crockett and MacDonald Carey. After a successful radio and film career, MacDonald Carey went on to star in the long-running NBC television soap, "Days of Our Lives." Photo courtesy of Keene Crockett.

Figure 12.11. Keene Crockett and Jimmy Stewart during a rehearsal break of "Screen Guild Theater." The difference between this picture and the others is that Keene is back to his familiar role of doing sound effects. If Figure 12.11 could talk, we'd probably hear: JIMMY: "Gosh, Keene, this sure is a real swell phone you have here . . . aaaaaaah, real swell . . . real swell . . . indeed. Aaaaaaah, when the hell are they going to take the picture, Keene?" KEENE: "Maybe they're waiting for you to put the phone to your ear, Jimmy." JIMMY: ". . . Aaaaaaah . . . wouldn't that look sorta dumb with me listening to a sound effects phone, Keene?" KEENE: "No dumber than what we're doing now, Jimmy." Photo courtesy of Keene Crockett.

for a fee than for their acting ability, but Keene was an honest-to-goodness actor. Therefore, in addition to doing the sound effects for the "Theater Guild on the Air," Keene also accepted acting roles in *Dream Girl* and with Joan Bennett in *Light Up the Sky*. He also performed with Gertrude Lawrence in *Lady in the Dark*, playing the part of Russell, which was originated on Broadway by Danny Kaye. Of this last, *Daily Variety* wrote, "Keene Crockett, the photographer, was another plus among the performers."

In 1961, Keene resigned from ABC and returned to Moline, Illinois. Although he continued to do freelance sound-effects work for industrial shows in the auto industry, his interests were channeled into film work.

In 1963, he produced a film for which he played two acting roles and won the prestigious Fairchild Award. In 1964, he won the Bolex-Palliard award for a Bolex television commercial he filmed in Illinois. The narrative was done by his old friend Bret Morrison, better known for his radio role of The Shadow.

Today, Keene is still as active as ever. Although he lives in Iowa, a

Figure 12.12. Keene Crockett chats with an admiring neighbor during a break in the movie Bix. *Photo courtesy of Keene Crockett.*

Rome-based Italian film company, Due-a-Film, selected Keene to play the part of the minister in *Bix* which should prove to aspiring actors that you don't have to live in Hollywood. This film was of such high artistic merit that it was chosen to be shown at the Cannes Film Festival.

Ray Erlenborn (CBS, Hollywood)

Al Pearce and His Gang	The Joe E. Brown Show
Big Town	Blondie
Calling All Cars	The Joe Penner Show
The Texaco Star Theater	Gene Autry's Melody Ranch
Dr. Christian	Scattergood Baines
The Bickersons	

Ray Erlenborn was born in 1916 in Los Angeles, California. By the time he reached the ripe old age of 12, Ray was already a veteran of vaudeville and had a starring role in a silent film comedy serial entitled "Winnie Winkle." See figure 12.14.

These silent films were so much in demand that a new comedy was shot each week for more than two years. Today in television, some child

Figure 12.13. Many talented sound-effects artists in radio found it difficult facing a live studio audience of 500 people, but Ray Erlenborn, on the right, seems quite at home doing a comedy sound-effects routine seen by millions. Assisting Ray is Art Linkletter, star of the popular television show "House Party." Photo from the file of Ray Erlenborn.

stars make as much as $35,000 a week. Ray earned $25 a week, period. No wonder Ray went into radio.

In 1933, he began writing and directing, and was the master of ceremonies of the "Marco Dog and Cat Food Juvenile Revue." The show featured new and talented youngsters from around the country and stayed on the air for almost five years.

In 1937, Charles Vanda, program director at KNX in Hollywood, offered Ray a job doing sound effects. Although Ray was without experience, Vanda felt that his many years in film and radio as a comedian and actor provided him with the necessary timing to do the job. Vanda also felt reasonably certain that the "mike fright" bugaboo wouldn't affect someone as used to performing as Ray.

One of the first shows that Ray was assigned to was "Scattergood Baines." Figure 12.15 is a photo of some of the show's cast and crew. Billed as "Our Sound Effects Man," Ray stayed with the show from 1938 until 1943.

As Figure 12.16 demonstrates, Ray was also good at creating sound-effects props. But that was all part of the job in those early days. A writer

Figure 12.14. Ah, that old gang of mine. This picture, taken in 1927, shows the Rinkeydink Gang in action during a filming. Standing in the middle is Junior Johnson, who played Perry Winkle. The members of the Rinkeydink Gang are Albert Schaeffer as Spud, in the derby hat; Billy Bassett as Chink, sitting in front; and to the far right our star, Ray Erlenborn, as Spike. Photo from the Ray Erlenborn file.

would come up with a sound-effects gag and, more often than not, the effect had to be built. The problem was, once it was built, nobody wanted to throw it away for fear that someday it might come in handy. As a result, the shelves in the sound-effects rooms contained more one-of-a-kind gadgets than the Smithsonian Institution.

Throughout Ray's career, the valuable experience he received in films and as a performer on radio helped him become one of the top sound-effects artists in Hollywood. And, as if all these accomplishments weren't enough, he was also in demand as an excellent vocal-effects artist. On "Blondie," he was the bark of Daisy the dog, and on "The Red Skelton Show," he hopped from Daisy the dog to Finelli the Flea.

In 1977, Ray retired from CBS. However, this was only a milestone, not the end of his career. Today, Ray is not only busy doing sound effects for old-time radio recreations presented by SPERDVAC (Society for the Preservation of Early Radio Drama, Variety, and Comedy) and for the Pacific Pioneer Broadcasters, he also has a busy schedule with a community light opera company.

Figure 12.15. "Scattergood Baines" cast and crew. Clockwise from the left are director Dave Owen, actresses Jane Morgan and Jean Vanderpyle, actor Dink Trout (at mike), an unidentified actor at the rear, child actor Tommy Cook, announcer Maurie Webster, an unidentified actress, and Scattergood himself, Jeff Pugh. In the center foreground is Ray Erlenborn. Photo from the Ray Erlenborn file.

Monty Fraser (NBC, Hollywood)

Fibber McGee and Molly (1942–52)	The Jack Benny Show
Red Ryder (1942–45)	Lum and Abner (1944)
This Is Your FBI (1945–50)	Maxwell House Coffee Time (1945–48)
The Life of Riley (1944–47)	
Tales of the Texas Rangers	The Joan Davis Show (1945)
The Red Skelton Show (1943–50)	Unlimited Horizons (1942–44)
Kay Kyser	Ozzie and Harriet (1940s)
The Great Gildersleeve (1944–55)	The Bob Hope Show

Monty (Carol) Fraser was born in 1913 in Globe, Arizona. By 1934, his love for music, especially the trombone, led him to the University of Arizona, where he began his studies as a music major. While there, his talents as a fine trombone player soon got him not only a place on the school band but also jobs with the local dance bands.

After two years of school, Monty decided it was time to do two things that were more important than staying in college: marry his childhood

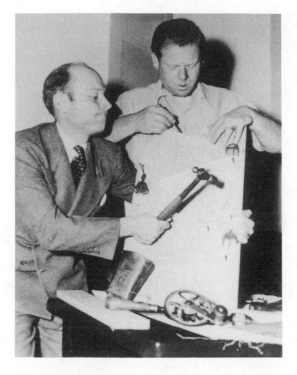

Figure 12.16. Ray Erlenborn and Al Pearce put the finishing touches on a comedy sound-effects prop for the "Al Pearce Show." An unusual picture: Where else but in radio could you get someone to hold a nail for you who also happens to be the star of the show? Photo from the file of Ray Erlenborn.

sweetheart, Opal, and travel to California for the musical opportunities he kept hearing about out in Hollywood.

What Monty and his wife hadn't taken into consideration was that even the mystical Hollywood wasn't immune from the Depression that was paralyzing the country. Although he managed to find an occasional band job, the money he was paid just about lasted until his next job.

Therefore, when Monty heard that NBC wanted to hire someone for their sound-effects department, he didn't hesitate to apply for the job. Later, he admitted that he had no idea what something called "sound effects" was.

Unlike many of the other applicants applying for the job, Monty didn't have the required college degree, but luckily, NBC felt that his extensive musical training was just the background a successful sound-effects artist needed. And so in 1938, Monty was hired by NBC to start his apprenticeship program.

Figure 12.17. Years after his retirement, Ray Erlenborn continues to combine his acting and sound-effects talents for the dual role of Professor Marvel and the Wizard in the theatrical production of The Wizard of Oz. *Photo from the file of Ray Erlenborn.*

In those days, it could take up to three years before an apprentice had the knowledge and experience to be able to work a show alone.

That training period might seem excessive for some shows, especially some of the soaps that required only the more basic effects, but in reality it wasn't. Even on shows that normally required only door knocks and phone bells, a script could come along that was exceedingly busy. If the sound-effects artist lacked the ability to handle these situations, he or she would most likely be replaced. And once an artist was replaced, it was rare to be accepted back on that show or any other show with the same director or sponsor.

The rehearsal time allotted for most shows was designed for economy, not artistic perfection. Therefore, an artist assigned to a show that had a short rehearsal time had to know how to handle any and all situations involving sound effects. In order to get this knowledge, artists had to spend

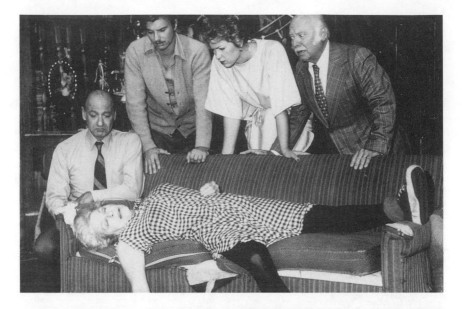

Figure 12.18. Ray Erlenborn (right) as the horrified doctor in the stage play The Trouble with Opal. *Sprawled on the couch in disarray is the seeming source of Ray's horror, Opal herself, former screen star Martha Raye. In spite of the Opal's unfashionable black cotton stockings and sneakers, at one time Martha Raye rivaled Betty Grable as owner of the best-looking legs in Hollywood. Photo from the file of Ray Erlenborn.*

their free time learning the functions and care of the technical equipment, experimenting with the hundreds of manual effects, and trying to find new ways to make different sounds. And then there was the huge record library to learn. It was extremely important, in a business measured in terms of seconds, that the artist could quickly find a particular sound from the more than 7,000 recorded sounds we had in our library.

Once all this information was learned, the artist had to put it into practice by working on shows as a "second" or "third" man (or woman). Although the sound-effects duties given to these trainees were usually never more involved than such basic effects as phone bells, gunshots and opening and closing doors, it was a crucial part of the training. In addition to gaining practical on-air experience, the apprentice became a familiar face to the directors and until a director got to know the artist personally and professionally, even if it was only opening and closing doors, the chances of working their shows were slim.

In 1942, during World War II, many people in the entertainment industry volunteered their services to local hospitals to help wounded veterans deal with their difficult physical or emotional recuperations.

Figure 12.19. Ray Erlenborn appearing in the role of Captain Andy in the musical Show Boat. *Playing the part of his granddaughter is Holly McDonald. Photo from the file of Ray Erlenborn.*

Figure 12.21 shows Monty Fraser helping two servicemen learn the art of sound effects for their weekly in-hospital radio dramatic show, and perhaps find a career in radio after they were discharged.

To help the veterans gain an understanding of the workings of sound effects, Monty wrote a little study guide. Here are some of his observations:

> There are two basic requirements asked of anyone hoping to make a career in sound effects. First you must understand the meaning of sound effects. Sound effects are those controlled noises which create an illusion, paint an aural picture or carry an impression to the brain of the listener which causes them to associate the sound with a mental image. For that you need imagination, a good touch and timing.
>
> The second requirement is the ability to take orders. There is only one boss on a program — the producer. He or she is in the driver's seat. What

Figure 12.20. Monty Fraser (center) shows a young and appreciatively smiling Marilyn Monroe how to make the sound of a creaky Old West wagon train. Judging by the admiring look Floyd Caton (left) is giving Marilyn, he's heard the story before. Photo courtesy of Opal Fraser.

they say goes. Of course there are times when a producer can be wrong. But even at those times, the soundman must be a diplomat and take the producer aside to point out the error. It is very bad psychology to call attention to the mistake in front of the cast. Not only can this lead to a breaking down of cordial relations between the soundman and the producer, it can be very embarrassing to both parties. . . .

As you can see, a soundman is called on to fulfill a great many more duties than is generally supposed. He must be alert to mistakes in writing, must be a diplomat, and above all, must never lose sight of the ultimate goal – the best radio entertainment possible.

This last bit of advice was extremely important, because no matter how competent, a sound-effects artist had to know how to handle the often

Figure 12.21. Monty Fraser (center) with unidentified wounded WWII servicemen. Photo courtesy of Opal Fraser.

delicate situations with the production staff. And this took experience, not so much in doing any one particular effect, but experience in the knowledge of which effects could actually be done at all.

For instance, if a director asked for the sound of snowflakes falling on snow or a nude woman sitting down on a marble bench (as they did, almost weekly), an artist might assume that the director had been down in the ColBeeS bar too long. But an experienced artist would know how to handle the situation.

The first requirement was to keep a straight face. After all, if the writer had requested the sound of snowflakes, then as far as some directors were concerned, perhaps they did make a sound. It was at times like this that the artist had to be extremely diplomatic.

Besides, hadn't one director asked for, and gotten, the sound of sunlight? And are rays of sunlight any noisier than snowflakes? It was times like this that experience paid off. Was this sound of snowflakes a perceived sound, as in the case of the sunlight? A fantasy sound? A comedy sound? Or was the director just trying to break the monotony of a run-through rehearsal by seeing what sound-effects could come up with?

Doing sound-effects jokes in rehearsals could be a very dangerous practice, especially if someone in the cast was new. At the request of the direc-

Figure 12.22. Monty Fraser selecting props for Fibber McGee's closet. Photo courtesy of Opal Fraser.

tor on one early radio show, Monty had ad-libbed the sound of a toilet flushing as a joke during rehearsal. On-air, the new actress failed to deliver her line on cue and spoiled the timing of the scene. After the show, the director demanded to know why she took so long to say her line. The actress simply shrugged and said, "I was waiting for the toilet to flush."

Gaining this amount of knowledge and experience all took time. A lot of time, even by conservative network calculations. From the time an apprentice was hired until he or she was capable of doing a show alone was a minimum of three years.

This element of time was one of the major factors that worked against the women who worked in sound effects during World War II. When the soundmen returned from the service, all companies were required by law to give the returning veterans their jobs back. As a result, during the war, the women worked as assistants to the more experienced people in the department, and there just wasn't enough time to gain the experience to move from assisting to working alone.

It is interesting to note that although many of these women had the potential to become fine sound-effects artists, they all pursued other careers at the end of the war, with the notable exception of LaVerne

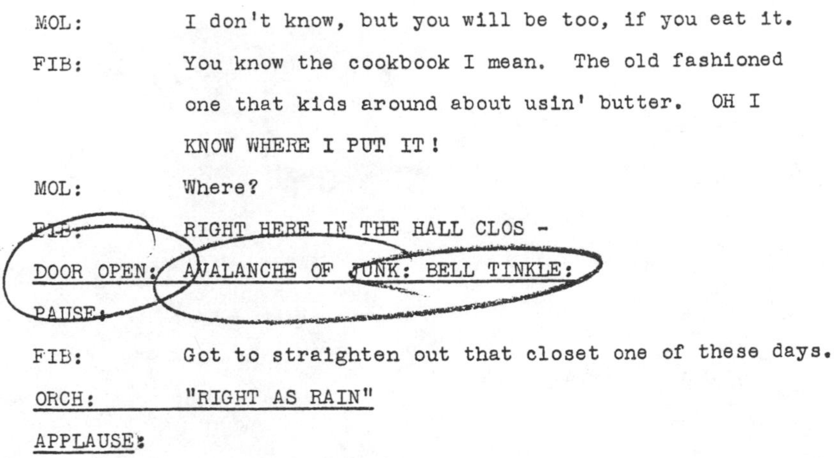

```
MOL:        I don't know, but you will be too, if you eat it.

FIB:        You know the cookbook I mean.  The old fashioned

            one that kids around about usin' butter.  OH I

            KNOW WHERE I PUT IT !

MOL:        Where?

FIB:        RIGHT HERE IN THE HALL CLOS -

DOOR OPEN:  AVALANCHE OF JUNK: BELL TINKLE:

PAUSE:

FIB:        Got to straighten out that closet one of these days.

ORCH:       "RIGHT AS RAIN"

APPLAUSE:
```

Figure 12.23. The all-important cue for the Fibber McGee closet crash. Photo courtesy of Opal Fraser.

Owens at CBS. Today that has all changed. Some of the finest sound-effects artists in the film industry are women (and just possibly, the children and grandchildren of those patriotic World War II women).

Perhaps the most famous sound-effects crash Monty Fraser ever did in radio occurred on Tuesday night at 79 Wistful Vista, the home of Fibber McGee and Molly. What started out as an ordinary "junk" crash became one of the most listened-for sounds in all of radio. The situation never varied. Fibber McGee would need to get something out of his hall closet, and when he opened the door, "an accumulation of junk would fall out." That was the original concept dreamed up by Don Quinn, the producer and writer of the show. However, sound-effects artists such as Monty Fraser had other ideas. They envisioned it as an opportunity to create a crash to end all sound-effects crashes. Although it lasted only a matter of seconds and took hours and hours of preparation, what a glorious crash it was while it lasted!

Fraser began the Fibber McGee closet crash by trying to select just the right sounds from the hundreds of props stored on the shelves of the NBC sound-effects room in Hollywood. That could be a very time-consuming process. Even though it was for radio, the importance of the studio audience's reactions on a comedy show could never be ignored. Not only did the effects Fraser selected have to sound funny to the radio listeners at home, they had to sound and *look* funny to the people in the studio audience. A very delicate balance indeed.

Next came the job of placing all those props in just the right positions

Figure 12.24. Ready. Get Set . . .

Figure 12.25. Go . . .

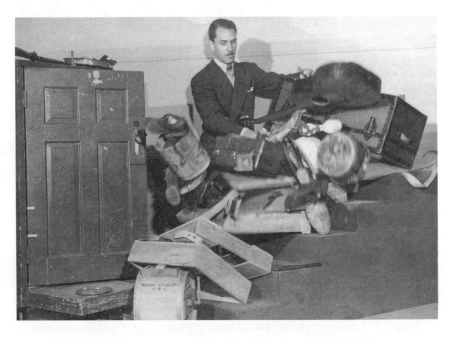

Figure 12.26. . . . and go . . . and go. . . . Photos courtesy of Opal Fraser.

Figure 12.27. Monty Fraser adds the final touch. Photo courtesy of Opal Fraser.

with watch-maker's precision. Everything had to be balanced just so because, like dominoes, when one prop fell, they all fell (see Figures 12.24, 12.25, 12.26, and 12.27). That was what we wanted when the cue came. What we didn't want was for the crash to occur before the cue. Virgil Reimer, another Fibber sound artist, use to pray that if Los Angeles did have an earthquake, it wouldn't happen on Tuesday night between nine and nine-thirty.

All the hours of painstaking preparation come down to this—the Fibber McGee script (Figure 12.23) giving the cue that all America eagerly listened for each week.

The avalanche starts!

Now comes the tricky part: Timing out the crash to get the most laughs.

The crash continues and continues and continues . . . with the sound-effects artist always mindful of the amount and intensity of the laughs from the audience. Stopping it too soon was called killing the joke. Dragging it out too long was called milking. Somewhere sandwiched between these two extremes was that devoutly-to-be-wished-for thing called comedy timing.

Out of the dust and rubble comes the coup de grace, the one comedy effect that, more than any other, separated the stars from the pack—the plucky, precocious, little tinkly bell. An artist who knew when to ring this bell at the conclusion of the crash would guarantee a whole new outburst of laughs. Ringing it a moment too soon, or a fraction too late, would get nothing but silence and a one-way ticket off the show.

In sound effects, there were no secrets. And no matter how much pride we took in creating new sound effects, once they were used on a show they had to be shared with other members of the department. And that included the Fibber McGee closet crash. This sharing was only fair to the show because, even during illnesses or vacations, there always had to be someone who could take the regular artist's place.

Figure 12.28 shows Monty demonstrating the fine art of creating the Fibber McGee crash to other artists.

In 1975, Monty retired after a career that spanned 37 years as an artist and a department head. But before he left the hallowed halls of NBC, he took care of two very important matters. First, he took a trombone refresher course from one of the trombonists with the "Tonight Show" band. And second, he rejoined the musicians' union.

With these important details taken care of, Monty put his trombone in the car and, with his wife, Opal, headed for Palm Springs to look up an old flame, his music, and see if she'd still have him back after all these years.

Figure 12.28. Monty Fraser (center) demonstrates the fine art of creating the Fibber McGee crash to (from the left) Floyd Caton, Dorothy Wauknitz, an unidentified man, and Betty Boyle. Photo courtesy of Opal Fraser.

Bob Graham (NBC, Chigaco)

Mary Marlin
US Steel Hour
Ma Perkins
Captain Midnight
Don Winslow of the Navy

Jack Armstrong, the All-American
    Boy
Fibber McGee and Molly
Backstage Wife
Lights Out

Bob Graham was born in 1916 in Iowa City, Iowa. He attended the University of Iowa and graduated in 1937 with a major in theater arts. Part of the requirements of his broadcasting classes was to work at the school's radio station. While there, Graham was asked to help out with supplying sound effects for various school programs, of which one was a dramatized version of the weekly news similar to "The March of Time."

After graduation, Graham found out what most graduates were learning during the Great Depression—jobs were difficult to find, and especially so for graduates without work experience. Finally, after months of trying unsuccessfully to locate work in and around Iowa, Graham went to Chicago where he was interviewed by Tom Horan for a job at NBC.

Although Graham got the job, he was surprised to learn that it was

Figure 12.29. Although they are supposed to be on a five minute rest break, Bob Graham (seated in the center) listens to director Homer Hech give some critical notes, while Curtis Mitchell is at the console checking and rechecking his records for the 14-record opening sequence of "Don Winslow of the Navy." The man in the control room is unidentified. Photo courtesy of Robert J. Graham.

his air-time experience at school, rather than his degree in broadcasting, that most impressed Horan.

Graham's starting salary as a soundman, in 1938, was $37.50 a week. Although this was supposed to be for 40 hours of work, he discovered he could be asked to work Saturday mornings at no extra pay. Furthermore, although Graham had been hired to do sound effects, he was soon to learn that the job also included setting up folding chairs if the show had a studio audience, and seeing to other studio janitorial responsibilities.

These and other poor working conditions led Graham to become instrumental in the sound-effects department becoming unionized. And the union they elected to have as their bargaining agent with NBC was the American Federation of Radio Artists (AFRA).

In 1944, Graham's career at NBC was interrupted by World War II. After serving his time in the OSS (Office of Strategic Services, which became CIA) and with Armed Forces Radio, Graham was discharged in 1946. Instead of going back with NBC, Graham spent the next 10 years working in the theater. Later he was to use this experience in a teaching career that lasted more than 30 years at the San Francisco State University.

Figure 12.30. When Bob Graham did sound effects for "Don Winslow of the Navy," it took 14 records and all these turntables, as well as a pair of quick and steady hands, to do the opening. Photo courtesy of Robert J. Graham.

Although Bob Graham's sound-effects career was relatively short, he was an important member of the sound-effects community. This included both his staff work at NBC Chicago and for the contributions he made for sound effects with AFRA on a national basis.

One of Bob's hobbies during his days at NBC was photography, and as Figures 12.31, 12.32, and 12.33 show, he did it well. Naturally, all the pictures deal with sound effects.

David Light (CBS Hollywood)

The Man Called X
Hopalong Cassidy
Lum and Abner
Ozzie and Harriet
The Line-Up
Silver Theater
Gene Autry's Melody Ranch (1940)
Mayor of the Town

Yours Truly, Johnny Dollar
The Judy Canova Show
The Adventures of Champion
Sweeney and March
Escape
Amos 'n' Andy
The Frank Sinatra Show
Burns and Allen

Figure 12.31. Closeup of a pickup arm's needle being placed on the chalk mark of the sound of an explosion called for in a script. The ability to "spot" such cue marks on dozens of different records during a live show was a talent not shared by everyone. Photo courtesy of Robert J. Graham.

Broadway Is My Beat   Gunsmoke
The Baby Snooks Show   Lux Radio Theater
The Jimmy Durante Show

Dave Light, born in 1920, grew up on a farm in Patterson, California. In 1937, at the age of 16, he went to Los Angeles and got a job with C. P. MacGregor Studios at 729 South Western Avenue. The work entailed packing and shipping 16-inch recordings of in-house radio shows produced and owned by MacGregor. These shows included "Eb and Zeb" starring Al Pearce and Will Wright, "House of Peter MacGregor" starring Norman Field, and "Lady Courageous" starring Bea Benaderet and Hanley Stanford.

Other actors and actresses who got their start at MacGregor's included Gale Gordon, Hans Conreid, Lurene Tuttle, Joe Kearns, and Pat Mc-Geehan. The pay? For each 15-minute recording, they received the magnificent sum of five dollars.

One day Dave was readying another stack of records for shipping

Figure 12.32 is a montage of bells and horns that became a photo mural for the sound-effects department at NBC in Chicago. Photo courtesy of Robert J. Graham.

when Victor Quan, the head (and only) soundman working at Mac-Gregor's, suddenly needed help on one of the shows.

The sound effect Dave was asked to do was nothing more complicated than a car door being opened and closed. However, Quan was so impressed with Dave's timing and the self-assurance Dave had doing the cue that he made Dave his assistant. The pay was $50 a month.

Although it was difficult for Dave to tear himself away from such a

Figure 12.33. And finally . . . this picture is simply called SUSPENDERS AT WORK. Working these RCA sound "trucks" are Michael Eisenmenger (top), department head Tom Horan (left), Curt Mitchell (right), and Bob Graham (bottom). Photo courtesy of Robert J. Graham.

Figure 12.34. Dave Light with Joan Crawford. Photo courtesy of David Light.

well-paying job, he went on staff at CBS in 1942. It was there that Dave made his experience of growing up around cows, horses, ducks, dogs, and chickens pay off. In a short time, his reputation as an animal imitator was earning him more for one dog bark and cat meow on "Mayor of the Town" than he earned in a month at MacGregor's.

So proficient was Dave at doing vocals that whenever Judy Garland did the *Wizard of Oz* on radio, Dave was requested to do the dog barks for Toto. The same was true with Gene Autry. The only person he'd trust with the snorts and whinnies for his horse, Champion, was Dave. And if all these accomplishments weren't enough to crow about, Dave had acting roles on "Meet Corliss Archer" and "Lum and Abner," and wrote scripts for "Suspense"!

One big difference between film and radio involved the amount of contact a sound-effects artist had with the stars. In radio, such contact was casual and constant. But in film, where sound effects were done in the post-production department under the supervision of the director, contact was unheard of. Therefore, when film stars were involved with busy sound-effects shows on radio, they were delighted to have the opportunity to talk over their sound-effects cues.

Figure 12.35. Some cast members of "Meet Corliss Archer" meeting their fans at a Los Angeles high school during the 1940s. The cast are David Light (center, in the suit) doing hoofbeats; "Corliss" herself, Janet Waldo, on David's left; Louise Erickson, on Janet's right, doing the sound of milking a cow by squirting seltzer into a pot; and David Blees, "Dexter," kneeling in front with a microphone at his ear. Notice the latest style craze—loafers and bobby sox and little flowered hats.

If ever the sound-effects artist had to "be" the effects he was doing, it was on "Sorry, Wrong Number" (Figure 12.36). The show starred Agnes Moorehead, and the motivation for all of her terror was focused on what most listeners considered their most useful and reliable means of communication in time of distress, the telephone. But after listening to "Suspense" that night, they wondered. This was a telephone caller's nightmare, and every sound of it was true. Every delay, every annoyance, every bureaucratic frustration that any subscriber to Ma Bell had ever experienced was exploited with hand-sweating accuracy. No wonder that, at the completion of the show, Agnes Moorehead and David gave each other a mutual squeeze of admiration . . . and relief (Figure 12.37).

One of the most difficult sound-effects shows that Dave ever did was with film legend Bette Davis on "Silver Theater."

The script called for Davis to play the part of a mother raising her children while her husband was serving overseas during World War II.

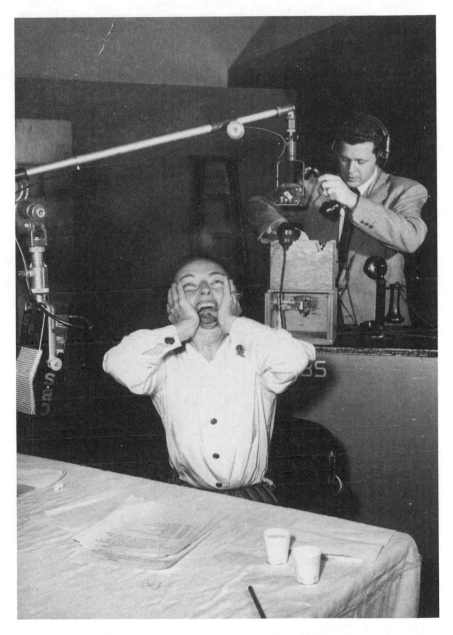

Figure 12.36. David Light and Agnes Moorehead. David is ringing the all-important telephone during the "Suspense" broadcast of "Sorry, Wrong Number." Those who imagine that the actors in live radio did nothing more strenuous than stand around a microphone and read from scripts might like to know that after Agnes Moorehead completed this demanding show, she collapsed against the table from nervous exhaustion.

Figure 12.37. Dave Light and Agnes Moorehead after completing "Sorry, Wrong Number."
Photo courtesy of David Light.

Although it lacked the intensity of "Sorry, Wrong Number," the sheer number of effects associated with a large family going about the normal business of living was tremendous.

Children running upstairs and downstairs, singularly, in pairs, and in groups was just part of it. There was also the doors: Both screen doors and wood doors heralded each child's run upstairs, downstairs. All of the

Figure 12.38. Bette Davis autographed this picture to David Light, her "co-star" for his fine job on "Silver Theater." Photo courtesy of David Light.

Figure 12.39. Fiesta by David Light. Photo courtesy of David Light.

effects required different microphone perspectives (sounds that seemed to be near or far away), and perfect timing, and it was done by Dave, without the benefit of a second man or woman.

Figure 12.38 expresses how Miss Davis felt about the sound effect job Dave did.

In 1952, Dave resigned from CBS and moved to Tuscon, Arizona, where he went into a business unrelated to sound effects. Although the venture proved to be extremely successful, he was sorely missed as one of the top sound-effects artists at CBS.

When he retired from business, Dave decided, like many retired folk, to while away his golden years with a paintbrush in his hand. But Dave has a considerable amount of talent, and his work is in demand, which has made his golden years as active as all those non-golden years.

Today, Dave still lives in Tucson, where his skills as a painter have earned him a "Grandpa Moses" reputation. Not only are his paintings in demand at art gallerys, but reproductions of his works are published in card form as well. Figure 12.39 and 12.40 show examples of his work.

Opposite: *Figure 12.40.* The Garden of Eden *by David Light. Photo courtesy of David Light.*

A FEW FINAL WORDS

AND THERE YOU HAVE IT. My tribute to the men and women who made the serious business of radio and television so much fun. Today it isn't like that. Today the stories I've written about could never have happened . . . nor will they ever happen again. It seems Fred Allen was right: The technical equipment has taken over the business.

In closing, I just want to say that although I have checked and rechecked the accuracy of all the information in this book, I have tried wherever possible not to let the facts ruin the fun.

INDEX

To assist the reader in putting the radio programs in the proper time frame, the network and year of first broadcast are noted. When a program switched networks this is also noted, and whenever possible the year of the change is given.

285